A.T. Thomson

The Queens of Society

Vol. 1

A.T. Thomson

The Queens of Society
Vol. 1

ISBN/EAN: 9783337323769

Printed in Europe, USA, Canada, Australia, Japan

Cover: Foto ©ninafisch / pixelio.de

More available books at **www.hansebooks.com**

THE

QUEENS OF SOCIETY

BY

GRACE AND PHILIP WHARTON

NEW EDITION WITH A PREFACE

BY

JUSTIN HUNTLY McCARTHY, M.P.

Original illustrations by C. A. Doyle

TWO VOLS.—VOL. I.

New York
FREDERICK A. STOKES COMPANY
PUBLISHERS

DEDICATION.

DEAR MR. AUGUSTIN DALY,

May I write your name on the dedication page of this new edition of an old and pleasant book in token of our common interest in the people and the periods of which it treats, and as a small proof of our friendship?

Sincerely yours,
JUSTIN HUNTLY M'CARTHY.

LONDON, *July*, 1890.

CONTENTS.

Preface to the Present Edition . . p. ix
Preface to the Second Edition . . p. xxv
Preface to the First Edition . . . p. xxix

SARAH DUCHESS OF MARLBOROUGH.

Queen Sarah's Birthplace.—La Belle Jennings.—'The Queen of Tears.'—The Handsome Englishman.—Marlborough in Love.—Privately Married.—Queen Anne upon Dress.—Yearns for Equality.—An Afternoon in the Seventeenth Century.—'Est-il Possible?'—Anne Flies from Court.—Colley Cibber as Footman.—Colley's Enthusiasm.—Mary of Orange.—The Model Queen.—The Cockpit.—Sidney Godolphin.—Sarah the Object of Calumny. —Marlborough to his Wife.—King 'Caliban.'—Marlborough Disgraced. —The Court in Full Dress.—The Royal Sisters.—Lady Marlborough Tabooed. — Royal Spite. — Cold Receptions. — The Little Whig. — The Churchills.— The 'Dictatress's' Insolence. — The Shorn Tresses. — Mrs. Oldfield, the Actress.—Whig and Tory.—Poor Relatives.—A 'Back-stairs' Conspiracy.— Queen Sarah Dethroned.—Takes Leave of Queen Anne.—The Building of Blenheim. — The Duchess's Economy.—Her Wonderful Shrewdness.—Death of Marlborough.—A Suitor for the Richest Peeress in England.—The 'Proud Duke.'—Anecdote of the Duchess of Buckingham.—The Duchess of Marlborough's Pet Aversion.—The Duchess as Portia.—'A kind of Author.'—'Old Marlborough' Dead.—'Old Marlborough' Buried. . . . . . . p. 1

MADAME ROLAND.

The Studious Child.—Her First Catechism.—Early Education.—In a Convent. —Religious impressions.—Poor Ste. Agathe.—Grandmamma.—Religious Doubts.—A Lazy Confessor.—Atheism.—The Spirit of the Age.—'A Bas les Aristocrats.'—Manon's Portrait.—Her many Suitors.—Phlippon's Idea of a Match.—Matchmaking.—Death of Madame Phlippon.—Manon writes a Sermon.—A New Suitor.—Roland's History.—Phlippon Refuses.—A Marriage of Reason.—Madame Roland as Nurse.—Brissot and the Girondins.—Brissot's Story.—Young Buzot.—The Meetings at Madame Roland's.—The King of Blood.—Robespierre's Ingratitude.—Dumouriez in Love.—Madame Roland the Centre of the Girondins.—Ministers, no Ministers.—Madame Roland's Famous Letter.—At the Head of Parisian Society.—Anarchy Reigns.—The 20th of June.—The Inauguration of the Republic.—Madame Roland at the Bar of the Assembly.—Conspiracies Rife.—Roland Arrested.—Roland Escapes.—Madame Roland Arrested.—Prison Life.—Madame Roland writes to Robespierre.—Prepares to commit Suicide.— Her Letter to Her Child.—Her Trial.—Sentenced to Death—Before the Guillotine.—Reflections on these Deaths.—Let them Go. p 45

Contents.

LADY MARY WORTLEY MONTAGU.

Her first Début.—The Kit-Kat Club.—Early years.—A Female Scholar.—Anecdote of young Burnet.—Lady Mary's Verses.—Dolly Walpole's Troubles.—Mistress Anne Wortley.—A Country Gentleman of the Seventeenth Century. Lady Mary on 'the World.'—Classical Flirtation.—Mr. Wortley.—A Doubtful Lover.—Love-letters.—Unsettled Settlements.—Lady Mary Elopes.—Her Appreciation of Scenery.—The Curate's 'Nightgown.'—Lady Mary's Beauty.—A Disgraceful Court.—'The Schulenberg. —The King's Creatures.—Introduced at Court.—The Town Eclogues.—Anecdote of Lady Mary and Craggs.—Her Letters from the East.—Pope's Love for Her.—Travels to the East.—Arrives at Adrianopol.—The Beautiful Fatima.—Rambles about Constantinople.—Introduces Inoculation.—A Cooing Couple.—Lady Mary's Turkish Costume.—Quarrels with Mrs. Murray.—All about a Ballad.—The Twickenham Set.—The Quarrel with Pope.—Lord Fanny and Sappho.—Reply to the Imitator of Horace.—Odious Verses.—Lady Mary's Society.—Walpole's Description of Her.—Lady Mary at Louvere.—Her Disreputable Son.—In the Harpsichord House.—Death of Lady Mary.—Satirists.—Lady Mary's Character.—Her Portrait. . . . . . . p. 91

GEORGIANA DUCHESS OF DEVONSHIRE.

Her Parents.—The Duchess when a Girl.—The Duke and the Lustres.—Devonshire House.—Prince Charles Stuart.—An Atrocious Nobleman.—Sheridan. —The 'Maid of Bath.'—Fox.—The Gambler and Herodotus.—The Ladies' Canvass.—The Duchess and the Butcher.—Fox Elected.—Mrs. Crewe.— The True Blue.—The Smile that Won.—Scandal about the Duchess.— George the Third goes Mad.—'The Weird Sisters.'—Burke and Fox.— Death of Fox.—Lines on his Bust.—Death of the Duchess.—Lady Elizabeth Foster.—Report relative to her. . . . p 137

LETITIA ELIZABETH LANDON (L. E. L.).

Brompton of Yore.—The Landons.—At Hans Place.—Mrs. Rowden's Dayschool.—Giving out the Prizes.—Genius against Education.—Reads Walter Scott.—Mrs. Landon.—First Poem.—Bulwer on L. E. L.—Self-Independence. —Goes into Society.—'Sally Siddons.'—'The Improvisatrice.'—Never in Love.—More Imputations.—Deaths.—Miss Landon Defends Herself.—Return to Hans Place.—Her Life there.—Two Hundred Offers. —Her Society.—Literary Pursuits.—Visit to Paris.—More Calumny.—Engagement with Mr. Forster.—Broken Off.—Letter on the Subject.—Morbid Despair.—Meets Mr. Maclean.—Mr. Maclean.—His Mysterious Conduct. —Marriage.—Last Days in England.—Sails from England.—Voyage out.— Life at Cape Coast Castle.—Her Mysterious Death.—Investigations.—The Mystery Unsolved.—Suspicions.—The Widower's Tribute.—Mrs. Landon. —Remarks on L. E. L.'s Death.—Her Last Letter.—Past and Future. p. 160

MADAME DE SÉVIGNÉ.

At the Age of Fifteen.—The Saint—Her Grandmother.—Her Marriage.—The Cardinal de Retz.—Society under Louis XIV.—The Hotel de Rambouillet. —The Précieuses Ridicules.—Madame de Sévigné among them.—The Reward of Virtue.—Temp. Louis XIV.—Madame de Sévigné in Love.—The Outbreak of the 'Fronde.'—Ninon de l'Enclos.—De Sévigné Killed in a Duel.—The Court of Louis XIV.—Anecdote of Racine.—The Arnaulds.— Religion of the Day.—The Bandits of La Trappe.—The Ascetics of PortRoyal.—Madame de Sévigné's Idolatry.—Anecdote of Boileau.—Anecdote of Fénelon.—The Knox of the French Court.—La Rochefoucauld.—Fouquet the Swindler.—Madame de Sévigné at Paris.—Madame de Sévigné Introduced.—A French Marriage.—Madame de Grignan.—Classics and Vice.—An Indulgent Mother.—Young de Sévigné.—Madame de Sévigné's Letters.—Madame de Sévigné's Affection —Letter-writing.—Death.—Death of Madame de Grignan. . . . . . p. 202

SYDNEY LADY MORGAN.

Lady Morgan of What ?—Her Ladyship's Eyes.—The Old Irish Girl.—The Pet of the Green-room.—Her First Literary Attempts.—Attacked by Croker.—Party Lies.—Lady Morgan as an Irish Apostle.—Family Ties.—Sir Charles. —Lady Morgan's Religious Opinions.—Sets Out for Italy.—At Paris.—The False Miladi Morgan.—Arrives at La Grange.—La Fayette.—At La Grange. —Society in Paris.—The City of Calvin.—Meets Lord Byron.—Byron's Miniature.—Lady Cork and the Watches.—Lady Charleville in her Chair. —Pink and Blue Nights.—Lady Morgan's Drawing-room.—The Princess. —Winnows her Society.—Last Years and Death.—Her Geniality and Benevolence. . . . . . p. 236

JANE DUCHESS OF GORDON.

Jane Maxwell's Portrait.—A Haughty Beauty.—The Court of George III.—The Beautiful Duchess of Rutland.—The Splendid Duke.—The Duchess as Whipper-in.—Lord George the Rioter.—No-Popery Riots.—Fire and Destruction.—The Agreeable Dinner Party.—Lord George in the House.—From Protestant to Jew.—Beattie's Absurd Adulation.—Anecdote of Hume. —Beattie at Gordon Castle.—Eccentric Lords.—The Duchess's Sons.—A Pit for Pitt.—Pitt Outwitted.—True Nobility.—Paris in 1802.—Waiting for the First Consul.—Enter Bonaparte.—Eugène Beauharnais.—' Had I Known.'—The Father of Lord John Russell.—The Prince of Wales.—A Public Lie.—Death of the Duchess. . . p. 262

SUBJECTS OF THE ILLUSTRATIONS.

VOLUME I.

	PAGE
THE BEAUTIFUL DUCHESS OF DEVONSHIRE—A KISS FOR A VOTE	*(Frontispiece)*
THE DUCHESS OF MARLBOROUGH PLEADING HER OWN CAUSE	41
THE INAUGURATION OF THE REPUBLIC	78
LADY MARY, POPE, AND KNELLER—THE PORTRAIT SCENE	121
THE POET'S EXILE—L. E. L. AT CAPE COAST CASTLE	200
THE HOTEL DE RAMBOUILLET	207
THE COUNTERFEIT LADY MORGAN	249

PREFACE.

IN that enchanting harlequinade which we call Paris in the last century a great lady desired and devised a new amusement. Weary of the routine pleasures of the mode, weary of the eternal confluence of men and women in their Danse Macabre of folly, the Countess of Custine sought and found a novelty. It was an age of suppers, Parabère suppers, Pompadour suppers, Du Barry suppers, Polignac suppers. Madame de Custine found that the pleasure in supping began to pall, that the lights seemed to burn dimly, that the flowers had lost their perfume, the viands their savour, the wines their warmth, the wit its brilliancy. The Piquette of pleasure was in need of new grapes. Madame de Luxembourg, conscious of the growing ennui, proposed to meet the difficulty by giving supper parties composed entirely of men. Madame de Custine, more original, retaliated by giving supper parties composed only of women. The idea amused, pleased, took the popular fancy. For a season women's supper parties became the rage, and great ladies derived, or affected to derive, infinite satisfaction from sitting at social boards with only their own sex for company. We are told that many of these banquets were very delightful, that my lady Lysistrata and her Athenians in powder and brocade were much diverted by their own audacity and independence, that the talk was very witty, the humour very varied, in those nights and suppers of the Goddesses. It may well have been so; the student of the last century in France, as he reads, wishes with all his heart that he could leap back some hundred years and more, and slip unperceived, a periwigged Clodius, through the folding-doors of Madame de Custine's supper-room.

Yet it is permitted to us to feel something of a kindred sensation in reading the "Queens of Society" of Grace and Philip Wharton. For here in these pages we meet with a charming company—and all, like Madame de Custine's guests, are women. Indeed, we are exceptionally fortunate, for, while the guests of the great French lady were limited to her contemporaries— to a charming de Louvois, a charming de Crenay, a charming d'Harville, a charming de Vaubecourt—we can move in a society invited from many times, and can, in fancy, feel that we look in the same hour upon the faces of fair and witty women, sundered in fact by generations. Indeed, we might perhaps be tempted to wish that an even wider range had been taken: that more Ladies of Old Time had been bidden to the feast; that Queens of Society who reigned before the spacious Elizabethan days might have been included. But this were unmannerly; this were to quarrel with our host and hostess. Madame de Custine's supper parties could not entertain all her friends. It is our part to accept with gratitude the company our hosts have been pleased to choose for us.

Indeed, there is cause for gratitude. The eighteen women whom the Whartons chose as representative Queens of Society are almost all exceedingly fascinating, exceedingly delightful. If they reigned in their day royally, the empire of many of them still endures, even in some instances exercises a more extended sway. As these sweet shadows rise up before us, one by one.

E paion sì al vento esser leggieri,

we see a face here and there that attracts us, as Dante was attracted by the face of Francesca, and specially we bid them stay and tell their story.

To a student of the French Revolution, glancing down the list of names, the name of Madame Roland naturally appeals. No character in that absorbing time is more attractive, not Lucile Desmoulins, nor the brown-locked Theroigne, nor the girl from Caen who struck down the friend of the people. Most of the great characters of the revolutionary drama have been misunderstood and misrepresented, over-praised by their admirers, over-blamed by their enemies. Madame Roland has suffered like the rest, from friends and from foes. It must be admitted that the Whartons hardly rise to the gravity of the situation in their study of Madame Roland. They are more at home with lighter themes; the French Revolution is a little too much for them. They consider it and its figures with a thin conventionality, their criticism is not suggestive, their historical appreciation neither wide nor deep. To apply in any sense the term "demons" to Madame Roland and her husband is but to provoke a smile; to call Roland a coward because he died in the high Roman fashion, is but to shuffle with words. We might wish that Roland had not died by his own hand, that Condorcet had not taken poison, that Valazé had waited for the common fate of his brother Girondins, that Romme had not thrust the knife into his breast on that fatal day. But in considering all these cases we should consider also the conditions of the time. We should remember how deeply the exalted spirits of the age were imbued with the neo-classic spirit which justified self-slaughter. We should remember how subtly and ingeniously Rousseau, the ruling mind of the time, had defended suicide in the pages of the "Nouvelle Heloise". We should remember the tremendous influence which the "Sorrows of Werther" had for nearly twenty years exercised upon imaginative minds. However excellent our own morality may be, it is well in passing historical judgment upon others to take into account the moral atmosphere of the age we are considering, and at least allow those who have had the misfortune to be less virtuous than ourselves the benefit of any doubt that can be extended to them. Naturally enough, the kind of criticism which converts the Rolands into demons and cowards is scarcely more discriminating in its treatment of the other revolutionary figures, who are incidental to the article on Madame Roland. It is a kind of criticism which is especially obnoxious to the serious student of history— the "Fiend-in-human-shape" school of criticism. Robespierre of course is the favoured victim of this kind of criticism, but to baptise him as "king of blood," and "apostle of hate," is not to offer any serious aid towards the study of one of the strangest characters within the range of history. Robespierre has found his defenders, who are as injudicious as his denunciators; the mean is still to seek. But when we remember the words of Gouverneur Morris, one of the shrewdest of the contemporary observers of the French Revolution, we are forced to believe that a mean must be found. "Robespierre has been the most consistent, if not the only consistent. He is one of those of whom Shakespeare's Cæsar speaks to his frolicsome companion 'he loves no plays as thou dost, Anthony'. There is no imputation against him for corruption, he is far from rich and still further from appearing so. It is said that his idol is ambition but I think that the establishment of the Republic would (all things considered) be most suited to him."

But after all it is not for serious study or judicious speculation upon the French Revolution that we turn to the bright pages of the Whartons. We want to be amused, interested, entertained, and their pages afford amusement and interest. We may—indeed we must—object to the study of Madame Recamier as a further proof of the incapacity of our authors to appreciate the revolutionary epoch; we must find fault with much that is childish in the chapter on Madame de Stael—and yet it is in one sense the very childishness of all these essays that is their chief charm. They have no claim to deep knowledge, to profound judgment; they reel off as readily as tales told by a fire, and they have in them much of the amiable prolixity and the genial inconsistency which is the attribute of a nursery tale. This airy gossiping diffuseness is seen to best advantage in the essays which treat of Englishwomen. The writers understood their own countrywomen very much better than they understood the daughters of France, and the result of their better acquaintance with their subjects is a more decided entertainment to the reader. In the pages devoted to Mary, Countess of Pembroke for example, our authors show at their best. They are in warm sympathy with the stately sister of Philip Sidney, whom Osborn praised so highly and —since no good work is done without sympathy—

the picture they paint of "Sidney's sister, Pembroke's mother," is one of the best in the gallery.

In the picture of Madame Piozzi, best known to the world as Mrs. Thrale, the authors are successful in telling over again with skilful abbreviation the main features of Mrs. Thrale's life, and of the life of her most famous friend, Dr. Johnson. There is a time which always attracts; there are people who can never fail to be interesting. To see Johnson's name on a printed page is to call up at once the whole of that enchanting epoch of English literature—an epoch as splendid as that of Anne or of Elizabeth, the epoch of Burke, of Sheridan, of Goldsmith, of Garrick. The epoch lives for us, sempiternally young, brilliant, inspiring, in the pages of Boswell's marvellous biography—the biography which more than any other book in the world, more even than Eckermann's Conversations with Goethe, has made a man of the past a living reality to the children of the present. Boswell had his faults and Boswell had his follies, but the world has heard too much of them—has heard too little of the merits of the Laird of Auchinlech. What if he did go about absurdly with Corsica Boswell written on his cap; what if he did allow himself to be deluded by the Ireland forgeries; what if he was a little vain, a little affected. He had every excuse for vanity. He was the intimate friend, the chosen companion of one of the greatest men of a great day; he lived to see the book in which he recorded, and admirably recorded, that famous friendship take its place among the classics of English literature.

We may perhaps admit that the Whartons are scarcely just to Mrs. Thrale. That delightful woman who fascinated so many in her day, who still fascinates so many, has failed to fascinate the writers of these essays, and they deal her out scant justice. They object to her marriage with Piozzi almost as strongly as Dr. Johnson himself or Dr. Beattie. They appear to be amazed at the fact that Mrs. Thrale showed no very enduring sense of sorrow for the husband she had lost when Thrale died. It would we fancy surprise most persons more if Mrs. Thrale had felt any abiding regrets for Thrale's memory. Thrale was not an amiable husband. Johnson, it is true, had a great regard for Thrale, but his regard was largely for qualities which could hardly be supposed to appeal very strongly to a wife like Mrs. Thrale. Thrale did not include fidelity among his virtues; he was the cause of much and most undeserved unhappiness to Mrs. Thrale while he lived. It is curiously unjust to blame her who was always an exemplary wife if after the death of a man who was more a master than a husband she sought for happiness in her own way. We can all see as clearly as Beattie, as clearly as Johnson, as clearly as the Whartons the many objections that could be raised from a social point of view to the marriage of Mrs. Thrale with Piozzi the singer. In an age which with all its admiration for art had a covert scorn for artists, in an age when Chesterfield could write to his son imploring him above all things not to be a fiddler, in such an age the marriage of a woman of wealth, of position, and of influence with an Italian singer would seem inevitably to be a degradation and an offence against good manners. But after all if Mrs. Thrale chose to sacrifice that slight and fragile thing, the good opinion of society, in seeking for her own personal happiness she is not much to blame. She had a bright, lovable, slightly shallow nature; she had known much unhappiness; she had a right to please herself; and the grumbling even of the great Johnson always seems in this regard a little unmanly. She was a wonderful woman; she lived to be eighty and to write some foolish, gushing, kindly letters to Conway the actor which have been much misinterpreted. Horace Walpole was very bitter against her, but Horace Walpole was given to bitterness and his wit did not spare women. There is another one of these Queens of Society to whom his pen was even crueller than it was to Mrs. Thrale, and that was Lady Mary Wortley Montagu. It would be difficult for any one who had once read it to forget the picture Walpole drew of her when she was in Florence in 1740. The picture is so repulsive, so mercilessly brutal, that it rivals the terrible attacks of Pope and arouses inevitable pity for the luckless woman who had the misfortune to find two such enemies as Pope and Walpole. The daughters of Lycambes, who hanged themselves because Archilochus lampooned them had scarcely more justification for their acts of folly than Lady Mary. But Lady Mary went her way through the world, always ready to give as good as she got, erratic, audacious, independent; it would take more than the stings of Pope or the sneers of Walpole—which must, we should imagine, have reached her ears—to crush her spirit.

The essay on Lady Mary Wortley Montagu is one of the best of the series. The sympathy which its authors refuse to mete out to poor Mrs. Thrale they extend, cordially and without stint, to Lady Mary. While we condemn the want of sympathy in the one case we heartily welcome the abundance of sympathy in the other. Indeed it would be difficult not to feel sympathetic with Lady Mary. Her famous letters are among the brightest things in literature; they can be read again and again as agreeably as Horace Walpole's and they do not leave the same bitter taste behind them that so many of Walpole's leave. Every episode in her long career is interesting. The fair-haired child of eight who took so readily to the toasts of the gentlemen of the Kit-Kat club, the studious maiden of nineteen who taught herself latin and translated the "Enchiridion" of Epictetus from a latin translation, the gallant champion of Dolly Walpole, the lover of Edward Wortley Montagu, the star of the evil court which could not make her evil, the satirist of the "Town Eclogues," the Ambassadress to Turkey, the champion of inoculation, the friend of Hervey, the enemy of Pope, the Continental traveller, the mother of a scapegrace son, whose adventurous wanderings have furnished food for romance, in all these characters Lady Mary shines, ever interesting, ever witty, ever on the whole good. The lover of the East, the student of Oriental things owes her a very deep debt for the keenness and the accuracy of her observations of Eastern life during her residence in Stamboul, observations which bring the interior of Eastern life home to the student in a way that few other books have ever succeeded in doing. It is curious to note that Orientalists are indebted too, to another bearer of the name, to the Wortley Montagu whose manuscript of the Arabian Nights in the Bodleian museum at Oxford has lately been carefully studied and translated by Sir Richard Burton.

No subject in all this interesting series of sketches is more interesting than that of the beautiful Georgina Duchess of Devonshire. The very mention of the name acts like a charm. It has the power of calling up one of the most fascinating periods of English history, that period when a "Prince's Party" reigned at Carlton house, and when the Westminster Election marked an epoch. The beautiful Duchess is famous for her beauty, the beauty that lives to us a measure in the portraits of the time; she is famous for her wit, for the exquisite manners which made the Prince Regent declare that she was the best bred woman of her day; she is famous most of all for her friends, and for one friendship in especial. One of the greatest names in English History is inseparably associated with that of the Duchess of Devonshire—the name of Charles James Fox. The Whartons feel in duty bound to pass their censure upon the misdemeanours of Fox's early youth. We in the present day can afford to dwell longer upon the genius, the patriotism, the magnificent gifts of the man, and to pay less heed to the fact that in a drinking age he drank, that in a gambling age he gambled, that in a dissolute age he was not austere. Of few men can the often quoted saying of Bolingbroke about Marlborough be more pertinently applied. Fox was a great man, and we can very well afford to forget the faults—faults which were as much a part of the age in which he lived as the mode of powdering the hair. To read of Fox in however short a record is to rekindle an old enthusiasm, to awaken an old regret. The enthusiasm is for that brilliant fragment of historical biography, Sir George Trevelyan's "Early life of Charles James Fox," one of the most valuable and one of the most fascinating contributions yet made to the ever fascinating history of the Eighteenth Century. The regret—and it is a keen regret—is for the determination which Sir George Trevelyan has taken never to finish his story of the great statesman's career, to leave what might be the most attractive biography in the language only a fragment—a brilliant fragment indeed—but still a fragment. "The unfinished window in Aladdin's Tower unfinished must remain."

Of course Sheridan comes into any sketch which deals with the days of the glories of Carlton House and Devonshire House. The Whartons paint a grim picture of the degradation into which Sheridan drifted after such great and such varied successes, and they express a due and deserved sympathy for the beautiful wife whose portrait as Saint Cecilia is one of the most haunting of last century ghosts. But they do not tell—perhaps they did not know—the curious legend which has been linked with the name of Mrs. Sheridan. It is said that Lord Edward Fitzgerald, the "gallant and seditious Geraldine," who was a great friend of Sheridan's, became deeply enamoured of his friend's wife. It is said that the charm of the young nobleman affected Mrs. Sheridan so profoundly as actually to hasten her death, and that when Lord Edward Fitzgerald married, as he afterwards did, the fair Pamela, daughter of Madame de Genlis and Philippe Egalité, he only did so because of the surprising resemblance which she bore to the beautiful wife of Sheridan. It is a curious, a pathetic story; it may be true.

There is a certain note of melancholy over the stories of all the Queens of Society. This note is most strongly found in the sketch which follows immediately upon that of the Duchess of Devonshire, the sketch of Letitia Elizabeth Landon, the once so famous L. E. L. The fame of L. E. L. and of her poetry has considerably diminished; other and greater stars have swum into the horizon since the days when she wooed her tender, gentle muse, and since she glittered for a while, the butterfly heroine of certain circles, the butterfly victim of so many calumnies. The story of her life is pathetic enough, with its little cheap triumphs, its imitation laurels; the story of her death is, and must no doubt remain, a mystery. After life's fitful fever, she sleeps well by those seas of "silvery purple," which she describes in the last letter she ever wrote—the letter the ink on which was scarcely dry when she was found in a dying condition with that empty prussic acid bottle in her hand, the possession of which has never been satisfactorily accounted for. "I like the perpetual dash upon the rocks; one wave comes up after another and is for ever dashed in pieces like human hopes that only swell to be disappointed." These words are in that same last letter; they are very characteristic in their graceful pathetic platitude of poor L. E. L.'s melancholy life.

Perhaps the pleasantest essay in the book, because it deals with the pleasantest person, is the sketch of Madame de Sevigné. Madame de Sevigné occupies something of the same place among women that Montaigne holds among men; she exercises the same subtle personal charm; she attracts her readers with the charm of a personal friendship; those delightful letters might have been written to oneself, they are so fresh, so vital, so exquisitely, so fallibly human. Ah, if only one's post hour in the morning brought such epistles to the breakfast table! If only anyone anywhere now-a-days in this bustling world, this fin de siècle, had time to write such letters to friends, and friends with time to read them! The Penny Post is a blessing and so is the electric telegraph and the telephone, but between them they have annihilated correspondence. Could we hope for a Pliny the Younger under the scientific conditions of modern life; could we hope for a Horace Walpole, could we hope for a Madame de Sevigné? Alas, life is too much of a rush; when we take up our pens to-day we have indeed to write quickly. The writing, and even more, the reading of long letters—of real letters such as Sevigné wrote, imply great margins of leisure, ample spaces of smooth tranquillity such as few can find to-day. An exception there is of course now and then; a Fitzgerald in some quiet nook of Sussex, living his own life in his own way and ignoring all conventions, may find time to gladden distant friends with letters that are letters, and may in so doing enrich the shelves of many happy students with volumes very dear to them. But the Fitzgeralds are rare in the world, are growing rarer every day. Everyone lives more or less at high pressure, the affluent as well as the needy; it is not in the ranks of the American Millionaires or in the Dukeries that a graceful ease, a lettered idleness, is to be found to-day. Perhaps some daring spirit who went and lived in a cottage like Thoreau, perhaps some determined woman who shut herself apart from the world like Harriet Martineau might find the time to write long delicious letters to their friends, and another generation would be enriched with a new Walpole or a new Sevigné. But if such daring adventurers found the time to write those letters, could their friends find the time to read them? Could the busy man, could the busy woman, with more to put into the day's round than ought properly to be accomplished within the orbit of any respectable week,—could they find the leisure to sit down and gravely read long pages upon pages of correspondence, however delightful, however freshly fancied, however charmingly expressed? It is much to be feared that in nine cases out of ten the new Sevigné or the new Walpole would be laid aside for a more convenient opportunity, and also that in nine cases out of ten that convenient opportunity would never arise.

"Before I was married, whenever I saw the children or the dogs allowed, or rather caused to be troublesome in any family, I used to lay it all to the fault of the master of it, who might at once put a stop to it if he pleased. Since I have married I find that this was a very rash and premature judgment." Such are the words of one of a series of bitter reflections upon marriage, in which Lord Melbourne indulged after his marriage to Lady Caroline Ponsonby. It is easy to understand from such a review of the case as is given in the Whartons' book, why Lord Melbourne should have penned such a passage. There could hardly have been two persons more unsuited to each other than William Lamb and Caroline Ponsonby. She afterwards accused him in her novel of Glenarvon of never taking her seriously, while on the other hand, her flighty way, and literary affectations must have tried him terribly. The Whartons do not seem to have known of Lady Caroline's encounter with Byron's funeral passing along the Northern Road, as she was coming out of the Brocket Gates for a morning ride, an encounter which so affected her nature, as to make a separation from her husband inevitable. There is a story told too, in the recently published Lord Melbourne's papers which deserves to be quoted here. At a dinner at Paris, Lady Caroline suddenly asked one of the party, in the hearing of the rest, whom he supposed she thought the most distinguished man she had ever known, in mind and person, refinement, cultivation, sensibility and thought. The person addressed suggested Lord Byron. "No," was the reply; "my own husband, William Lamb."

Let us make our bow to Lady Morgan before we say farewell to these Queens of Society. Lady Morgan is somewhat unfairly forgotten of late. She was very clever, her novel "The O'Briens and O'Flahertys," is one of the most remarkable Irish novels ever written. The fame she enjoyed in her day has been followed by a wholly undeserved neglect. If the republication of these papers serve to reawaken interest in her works, they will have done simple service.

JUSTIN HUNTLY M'CARTHY.

PREFACE TO THE SECOND EDITION.

IT would be vain to attempt anything like a reply to the numerous remarks, both public and private, that have been passed on 'The Queens of Society.' By some writers the choice of individual characters for this eminent position has been approved; by others, questioned; by several critics, absolutely denied to some of our most notable royalties. Now a disputed title is always an important point,—whether, as it regards great kingdoms, or arbitrary distinctions.

A 'Queen of Society' we hold to be one who, by the force of her reputation, her good management, her abilities, her manners, partly, and, even of her rank and fortune, commands around her a circle of persons of eminence, or fashion, or celebrity of some valid nature: this circle being dependent on the attractions, be they intellectual, or simply fashionable, of the fair monarch herself—contingent on her continuance in life, or, in what is much the same thing to a 'Queen of Society,' on her capability of receiving guests.

Taking the denomination in this view, we cannot agree with those who deny to Madame du Deffand the title; nay, it seems to us peculiarly her own. Blind, old, poor—not of that high rank which in France, in the last century, was still before the

Revolution, held in such reverence; with a more than sullied character, a bad temper, an *exigeante* disposition—Madame du Deffand managed to assemble around her a circle of the most intellectual and agreeable persons in Paris, a circle into which foreigners were eager to be introduced, and in which the sceptical old lady reigned absolute. She was as much a 'Queen of Society' in *her* way, in the Convent of St. Joseph, as the beautiful Duchess of Devonshire in Devonshire House, or, to bring the similitude more closely, as Mrs. Montagu in Montagu House. They were all queens, although their subjects were of a different stamp, and their thrones varied in outward splendour. The empire over the intellect was perhaps greater in the convent than in the palace.

Again, in respect to L. E. L., whose elevation seems to displease some of her contemporaries, it cannot be denied that by her gift of poetry, her remarkable conversational charm, her gaiety of spirits, and her great success in general literature, she, a poor unknown girl, commanded a position in society denied to many a rich and even a titled lady. It is pleasant to observe that women can thus raise themselves from obscurity to influence; and to reflect how completely genius and agreeable manners may supersede all necessity for rank and wealth, so far as an eminent position in the social world is concerned.

It is objected, also, that the queens are all too charming, too beautiful, too faultless, the annals too flowing, and eulogistic. We cannot assent to the criticism. Dark shadows rest on some of their thrones; and these have been distinctly marked. The scepticism of Madame Roland, the imprudence of the Duchess of Devonshire, the doubtful moral code of Madame

Récamier, not to mention many other cases, have all been the theme of sorrowful, if not of stern comment.

It is stated, also, that the materials for these volumes have been taken from works generally known, and that they have not comprised all those sources to which easy access might be had. If the volumes which form the staple even of *one* life were enumerated it would, we believe, by their number, startle even the contemptuous. In taking largely what contemporary writers have to offer of fact, or comment, we have only done what is done every day in common life. When we want to draw forth traits of character we generally apply to those who know, or who have known the subjects of our inquiries. Could the system of foot-notes have been adopted, Grace and Philip Wharton would have stood forth as indefatigable authors; but the pleasure in reading the work might, it was thought, be lessened by references which are apt to interrupt the narrative. Since no authorities have been given, the greater obligation is felt for any corrections, either through the medium of the valuable periodicals of the day, or in the various letters which have been received by the authors of the work. Aware of our weak point, namely, the absence of avowed authorities, yet conscious of sincere endeavours to be accurate—to be just, and to omit nothing well authenticated—the comments that point out errors are not viewed as attacks, or even as reproofs, but as welcome aids. Suggestions have been attended to, and a careful revision of the work has been made.

In accepting these, however, the writer of this preface begs to decline all advice conveyed in anonymous letters, of which a considerable number have been sent to Grace and Philip

Wharton. These mostly come from the far-off land, now in civil commotion.—America; some, however, have even been sent from New Zealand, one or two from Canada; all violent, upon some supposed slight to an ancestor or ancestress; all, in so far as the authors of the work can attest, mistaken.

Since the first edition of this work came out, 'The Autobiography, Letters, and Literary Remains of Mrs. Piozzi-Thrale,' edited by Mr. Hayward, have appeared. This work has thrown a new light upon the character of Mrs. Piozzi, and the author of her life, as one of the 'Queens of Society,' has profited by the publication in correcting some incorrect statements and impressions

PREFACE TO THE FIRST EDITION.

WHEN the guardian-demon of the unblest was asked how many monarchs he counted among the souls in his keeping, he replied, 'All that ever reigned.' So says fable; we are very far from intending to indorse it. But there may be some people who think that the monarchs of society—those uncrowned heads, whose dominions are the minds and hearts of their fellow-beings—present as few exceptions as those sovereigns who build up history. There may be many who imagine that the 'Queens of Society' have won their titles with no better qualifications than wit and beauty; that their very position has rendered them vain, if not imperious; and that they have lived in the world and for the world only. No opinion could be more erroneous; it is a libel on society to suppose its judgment so distorted; and a glance at the names of the women who have held this proud position will show that this is the case. Of the eighteen ladies whom we have selected as best fitted to represent this class, no less than six have been as celebrated for their literary talents as for their social position. Of these Lady Morgan and Lady Caroline Lamb wrote novels which were eagerly devoured in their day; the Countess of Pembroke and Mrs. Thrale were miscellaneous writers; L. E. L. was a charming poetess; and Madame de Staël may be justly held up as the greatest authoress of France.

Letter-writing, again, has been the province of six others, of whom Lady Hervey, Mrs. Montagu, and Madame de Maintenon are only of less celebrity than Madame de Sévigné and Madame du Deffand, always cited as *the* letter-writers of France, while Lady Mary Wortley Montagu holds the same place in this country. Seven again, have been eminent political leaders; one of them, indeed, Madame de Maintenon, though uncrowned having been virtually Queen of France; and though Madame Récamier and the Duchesses of Gordon and Devonshire may have had comparatively little influence on the fate of their respective countries, the same cannot be said of Madame Roland; while the names of De Staël and 'Queen Sarah' are historical.

Nor was it their talent only that recommended these women to the Electress-ships of their respective circles. Though society may do without a good heart, it will not dispense with that appearance of it which we call amiability of manner. With some few exceptions the 'Queens of Society' have been kindly, amiable, and even gentle people. While Sarah of Marlborough and Madame du Deffand were as notorious for their high tempers as for their wit, Madame Roland, L. E. L., Mrs. Montagu, and Mrs. Damer were all as amiable women and as thoroughly good-hearted as possible. Byron himself, never too liberal of his praise, has testified to the vast fund of good nature in 'De l'Allemagne,' as he calls Madame de Staël; Madame de Sévigné is a model of maternal affection; and Mrs. Thrale won Johnson — in spite of her faults—by the kindness she showed the poor invalid. We think those who remember Lady Morgan will readily add her name to the list.

The talents of society — wit, conversational powers, and a knowledge of the world—are, of course, necessary ingredients in the characters of these charming women; but that there was in most of them a depth of mind not always accorded to the other sex may be safely deduced from the fact that, with few exceptions, every one of them has been the intimate friend—often, indeed, the counsellor — of some great man. To run through the list before us: 'Queen Sarah' was no less the friend than the wife of Marlborough: Madame Roland was the friend of the leaders of the Gironde; Lady Mary both friend and foe to Pope; the Duchess of Devonshire the active partisan of Fox; Madame de Sévigné the intimate of the Arnaulds and La Rochefoucauld; Madame Récamier of Chateaubriand; Madame du Deffand of Voltaire and Walpole, of whom the latter was devoted also to Mrs. Damer; Necker received advice from, and Schlegel was the companion of, Madame de Staël; Mrs. Thrale was the friend of Johnson; Lady Caroline Lamb of Byron; Mrs. Montagu of Beattie; Lady Pembroke of Sir Philip Sidney; and Madame de Maintenon the consoler of Scarron, and the counsellor of Louis Quatorze.

These facts must necessarily add much to the interest of lives, which even apart from them, have no ordinary attraction. But perhaps the greatest interest to the general reader will be found in the varied phases of society in which these women moved. The history of society collectively remains to be written; but it is written disjointedly in the life of every man or woman who has taken a high social position. It is, indeed, only in these that we are introduced to scenes of past life, which history, fully concerned with monarchs, parliaments, and nations, cannot condescend to depict. The writers have therefore selected certain periods to illustrate by the lives in question. The profligate courts of Louis XIV. and Louis XV., the earlier and later periods of the French Revolution, the Empire, and the Restoration, are here touched upon in the memoirs of French women of society, while, for our own country, tnere is a life to illustrate every period from the reign of

Elizabeth down to our own times, from the Countess of Pembroke to Lady Morgan, although a chronological arrangement has, for certain reasons, not been followed.

It remains only to point out that while the selection has generally been made from women of irreproachable moral character, one or two have been chosen by way of contrast and by way of warning. The temptations of society are very great; yet how far more easy it is to attain the honour—if honour it be—of reigning in its circles, by strictly virtuous than by lax conduct, may be seen from the memoirs to which the reader is now introduced.

In many cases the lives of the ladies selected have been written at greater length by other biographers; in some, however, none but short notices, prefixed to their letters or works have hitherto been published, and in one or two, we believe, no consecutive memoirs have ever been written.

That the reader may not be misled, it should perhaps be stated that the mode of writing Lady Morgan's name is that adopted by herself

Lastly, the illustrations have been executed with especial attention to costume and known peculiarities of dress; and, whenever it was found possible, the artists have introduced portraits of the persons represented.

THE QUEENS OF SOCIETY.

SARAH DUCHESS OF MARLBOROUGH.

Queen Sarah's Birthplace.—La Belle Jennings.—'The Queen of Tears.'—The Handsome Englishman.—Marlborough in Love.—Privately Married.—Queen Anne upon Dress.—Yearns for Equality.—An Afternoon in the Seventeenth Century.—'Est-il Possible?'—Anne Flies from Court.—Colley Cibber as Footman.—Colley's Enthusiasm.—Mary of Orange.—The Model Queen.—The Cockpit.—Sidney Godolphin.—Sarah the Object of Calumny.—Marlborough to his Wife.—King 'Caliban.'—Marlborough Disgraced.—The Court in Full Dress.—The Royal Sisters.—Lady Marlborough Tabooed.—Royal Spite.—Cold Receptions.—The Little Whig.—The Churchills.—The 'Dictatress's' Insolence.—The Shorn Tresses.—Mrs. Oldfield, the Actress.—Whig and Tory.—Poor Relatives.—A 'Back-stairs' Conspiracy.—Queen Sarah Dethroned.—Takes Leave of Queen Anne.—The Building of Blenheim.—The Duchess's Economy.—Her Wonderful Shrewdness.—Death of Marlborough.—A Suitor for the Richest Peerage in England.—The 'Proud Duke.'—Anecdote of the Duchess of Buckingham.—The Duchess of Marlborough's Pet Aversion.—The Duchess as Portia.—'A kind of Author.'—'Old Marlborough' Dead.—'Old Marlborough' Buried.

STUNG by the aspersions cast on her by her political enemies, this celebrated woman, whom Pope has satirized under the name of Atossa, published her own Memoirs. 'I have been,' she wrote, 'a kind of author.' She penned with great spirit her own vindication; nor would she have condescended to do so, had not her best feelings been wounded by the impressions entertained against her by the widow of Bishop Burnet: so alive was this celebrated woman to the good opinion of others.

Yet, though even Henry Fielding, whose father, Edward, had served under the Duke of Marlborough, wrote a vindication of the 'duchess's character in general,' as well as an answer to the attacks upon her, it is strange that neither her birthplace, nor the spot where she died, have been positively known, even to the descendants of this beautiful, arrogant, all-powerful female courtier. The fact, perhaps, was, that those who succeeded to her loved her little; whilst 'Jack Spencer,' as he was usually styled, her reckless favourite grandson and heir, was not a man to search out for the annals of an aged grandmother, and still less to dwell upon the scenes of her death-bed.

She was born, however, as careful and recent researches have proved, in a small house at Holywell, near St. Albans; so called because the nuns of Sopwell, a monastery in the vicinity, used to dip their crusts in that well when too hard otherwise to be eaten; and on the 29th May, 1660, the future 'viceroy,' as this leader in fashion and politics was termed, first saw the light.

Her father, Richard Jennings, was a plain country gentleman, possessing land to the value of four thousand pounds, yearly, derived from his estate at Sandridge, near St. Albans, and other manors in Kent and Somersetshire : and her mother, Frances Thornhurst, was the daughter and heiress of Sir Giffard Thornhurst, of Agnes Court, in Kent. Sandridge, where once the family chiefly lived, is a straggling, uninteresting village : there seems not to have been any good house on the estate, until, sold by the extravagant grandson of the duchess, her darling spendthrift, Jack Spencer, a handsome house was built on it by a prosperous gentleman retired from trade.

Destined by fortune to affluence, Sarah Jennings was the youngest of three daughters : the two elder ones were Frances, who afterwards became Duchess of Tyrconnel, and Barbara, married to Edward Griffith, Esq. : two sons, John and Ralph, successively inherited the patrimonial property.

Sarah and Frances passed their girlhood during the tranquil period which preceded the death of Charles II., chiefly at Holywell. The opinions of men, were, even then, forming themselves into the three great political parties - - Jacobite, Whig, and Tory ; but those factions in which 'Queen Sarah' afterwards mingled so conspicuously were still dormant. Her father and her forefathers had been zealous adherents to the Stuart cause, but they were also strict Protestants.

Frances, who figured afterwards as the 'White Milliner,' early displayed those talents which, with her surpassing beauty, were likely to gain an ascendancy in the court of either of the last Stuart kings. England was then what France has since been termed—'*le Paradis des Femmes.*'

> 'Love ruled the court, the camp, the grove,
> And earth below, and heaven above.'

But of heaven the well-bred in those times thought but little: they were either tainted by French morals, or perverted by bigoted views of religion, which was mournfully mixed up with politics and party views.

It may, therefore, easily be imagined into what peril the two lovely sisters, Frances and Sarah Jennings, were consigned, when their parents, impelled by their devotion to the Stuarts, resolved to send them to court. Frances went first. She was one of those blonde beauties, with luxuriant flaxen hair—a bright, delicate complexion, pretty, and somewhat insignificant features, who seemed born to grace the gallery at Whitehall, and to be painted by Lely. She had no sooner shown herself in that dangerous circle, the avowed leader of which was Lady Castlemaine, than her youth and innocence were assailed by every idler of the iniquitous region. But she was shrewd, and, though a coquette, had a principle of virtue within her that kept her respectable, though it did not render her modest. La Belle Jennings, as she was called, had great wit, great penetration, great fearlessness in all she said, and she had courage even to turn to ridicule the compliments and addresses of James II., then Duke of York, who persecuted her with his admiration.

The sisters were nominally under the protection of Anne Hyde, Duchess of York; and at twelve years of age, Sarah Jennings entered the service of that intelligent though not irreproachable woman. Anne had the weakness of wishing to surround her own plain person with youth and loveliness, in order to challenge comparison with Katharine of Braganza, the queen of Charles II., an excellent princess, who had brought from Portugal some of the most frightful maids of honour that had ever set foot on English shores. It seems, however, that Anne Hyde had chiefly encouraged the very early admission of Sarah Jennings into her court, in order that she might be a playmate to the Princess Anne, afterwards queen; and this companionship, which produced in after days such signal effects, was continued not only after the death of Anne Hyde in 1671, but subsequently to the marriage of Mary of Modena, her successor, to James II.

Frances, precocious and vain, continued to flutter in the giddy court. Sarah was withdrawn from such influences. Anne, from her youth, was staid, if not prudish; and her mother, the Duchess of York, was one of the most sensible and prudent of women, and under her guidance Sarah enjoyed singular advantages.

But, during the year 1671 the scene in which Sarah figured was changed. Anne Hyde died, and the 'Queen of Tears,' as Mary Beatrix D'Este, was called, was selected for the bride of the royal widower, James.

This lovely princess, the adopted daughter of Louis XIV., became henceforth the mistress of Sarah; and during the twelve years that she continued to be Duchess of York, there was kindness on the one side, respect on the other. Mary Beatrix was, indeed, about the same age as the young maid of honour. Young and lighthearted, she soon obtained the affection of all classes: her brilliant complexion, her dark hair and eyes, the sweet expression of her countenance, her exquisite form and dignity, gained her the reputation of great beauty, which her portraits do not seem to verify.

Sarah lived occasionally, only, in the duchess's household; and, under the influence of her example, grew up into a prudent and well conducted woman, endowed with singular intelligence and ready wit. To these qualities were added a beauty so rare, and yet so enduring, that at the age of sixty, Sarah was still comely: 'a grandmother without a grey hair.' Her face was round and small, with soft, deep-blue eyes; a nose somewhat retroussé; a delicate, rosy mouth, on which no trace of *temper* had settled; a forehead white as marble; her hair was especially beautiful; blonde, thick, long, and glossy: her figure was perfect: even in a court famed for beauty, Sarah was considered surpassingly lovely.

It happened that on the marriage of the Duke of York to Mary of Modena, Colonel John Churchill was appointed one of his gentlemen of the bedchamber. He was the son of Sir Winston Churchill of Ashe, in Dorsetshire, where he had been chiefly brought up in seclusion, until, after becoming page to James Duke of York, he had obtained, at the age of sixteen, a commission in the army.

The young courtier was singularly handsome, and when Sarah first knew him was even then esteemed a gallant soldier. Above the middle height, with regular features, a noble brow, thoughtful eyes, and a mouth expressive of sweetness, Churchill might well attract the fancy of a young girl who must have seen him almost daily. His merits as an officer had even then been owned by Turenne, who had added to his praise of the young soldier the *sobriquet* of the Handsome Englishman; and then his manner, Lord Chesterfield has declared, 'was irresistible either by man or woman.' It was this, as that competent authority decides, that 'made his fortune.' Colonel Churchill, however, was, like many others, pushed on by interest. Although his family were Cavaliers of stern integrity themselves, they had not blushed to see Sir Winston's daughter Arabella the avowed mistress of James II. during his first marriage, and the mother of several children, amongst others of James Fitz-James, Duke of Berwick, whose family is still traceable in France. John Churchill is also generally believed to have been indebted to his cousin Barbara Villiers, Lady Castlemaine, for the means to appear at court, and for the royal patronage which led to an early promotion. She gave him, during the brief continuance of her mad passion for him, whilst he was only an ensign in the Guards, five thousand pounds (probably public money,) with which he bought an annuity from the Earl of Halifax.

It was at the age of twenty-four that Colonel Churchill became enamoured of Sarah Jennings. During three years their engagement continued; and even when their marriage took place, it was in privacy, the kind Mary Beatrix being the only confidante. They had met, first, at court; and when Sarah, then in her sixteenth year, saw the hero figure in a dance, her fancy was captivated. It is said that at that age he could scarcely spell. He excelled, however, in the courtier-like accomplishment of dancing. 'Every step he took carried death in it;' and Sarah, who was then the star of the court, felt that her heart was gone for ever. She immediately rejected the addresses of the Earl of Lindsay, and others, and accepted the eager love-suit of Colonel Churchill.

For some time their attachment could only be expressed by letters. Those from the duke, poor as was his orthography, displayed the most ardent tenderness. The replies he received from Sarah were, like herself, variable, petulant, and haughty. Nevertheless, after the fashion of men, Churchill loved her all the more. His family objected to the marriage; for Sarah's portion was scanty, and Churchill's patrimonial estate encumbered, like those of most of the landholders who had clung to the fortunes of Charles I. The estate of Sandridge, to which Sarah was coheiress, was also burdened by provisions for collateral relatives; so that the matter seemed hopeless, until Mary Beatrix offered pecuniary aid, and Churchill purchased with his ill-gained five thousand pounds the annuity from Halifax. But whilst all this was being arranged, the lovers, as is too often the case in long engagements, fell out perpetually. Once, indeed, matters went so far that Sarah begged of her lover to 'give up an attachment which might injure his prospects,' and declared that she should set off with her sister Frances to Paris, and so 'end the matter.' This spirited conduct, coupled with terms of abuse, in which Sarah was pre-eminent, brought matters to a crisis, and the lovers were forthwith united.

Still he continued to address his wife, by letter, as Miss Jennings, probably in order that she might retain her post. 'My soul's soul,' the brave soldier wrote to her from Antwerp, 'I do, with all my heart and soul, long to be with you, you being dearer to me than my own life.' Two years afterwards, when Churchill was made master of the robes by the Duke of York, the young couple continued in the service of their kind patrons, and with them and the Princess Anne visited the Hague and

Brussels. They went subsequently to Edinburgh, the journey to which lasted a month. In 1631, a daughter, Henrietta, afterwards Duchess of Marlborough in her own right, was born in London, and the domestic happiness of the young couple seemed to be complete. It is curious to find the great Marlborough, the terror of Europe, writing to his young wife about their child in these terms, thus affording a proof that the bravest hearts are often the tenderest:—

'I hope,' he says, 'all the red spots of our child will be gone against I see her, and her nose straight, so that I may fancy it to be like the mother, for she has your coloured hair. I would have her to be like you in all things else.' Whilst these domestic incidents were gladdening the father's heart, public affairs wore the darkest aspect. The Rye House Plot, and its woful results; the death of the Earl of Essex, who, like Raleigh, sought to avert his fate by suicide; the execution of Russell; all served to show the real character of James II., even before he ascended the throne, and induced Churchill to wish for retirement. He had now been created Baron Churchill of Eyemouth in Scotland, and his favour with his royal master daily increased. Lady Churchill, meantime, as Sarah was now styled, was winning the affections of the Princess Anne, then in maturer age. Anne had her own secrets to pour into the breast of her young confidante. She loved, as far as her placid nature could love, the Earl of Mulgrave, whose addresses to her had been refused by her father. George I. had looked at her with matrimonial intent, but left England without offering. Prince George of Denmark, a staid bachelor, ten years older than the princess, was the husband eventually selected. Without love on either side, there was sympathy. The prince was a Tory at heart; Anne inclined to those sentiments. He loved the pleasures of the table, and taught his wife to do so in time; and they formed as dull and respectable a couple as ever won the suffrages of society.

It may easily be supposed what a court these two illustrious personages must have around them, and how essential Lady Churchill's society was to the heavy-minded Anne. And yet the princess and her favourite were dissimilar. Anne was a martinet in trifles. Every one knows the anecdote of Lord Bolingbroke's presenting himself before her in a Ramillies tie, and her remark, 'that his lordship would soon come to court in his nightcap.' She had her servants marshalled before her every day that she might see if their ruffles were clean, and their periwigs dressed. In her reign her bust on the gold coin was draped by her command. She had a calm good sense, but few ideas beyond her nursery, Prince George, her evening's rubber of whist, and her favourite, in whom, indeed, all that Anne ever showed of heart seemed to be bound up. She was also a rigid, uncompromising Protestant; whilst Lady Churchill, who detested trifles, was a latitudinarian in religion, or rather, she could not bear to have the Church made the watchword for intolerance.

Anne was taciturn from having nothing to say. Sarah was sarcastic, reckless, and buoyant. She had been imperfectly educated, but had made the most of what knowledge she possessed. Playing at cards was the only diversion Anne could endure. The lively Sarah soon, therefore, grew weary of a court life. Still she was bound to the princess by many early associations; and, with regard to Anne, she did not insist upon subserviency. 'A friend,' she said, 'was what she most wanted.' For the sake of friendship she wished all forms laid aside. 'Your highness,' displeased her, so she proposed to the lady in waiting that when separated they should adopt less alarming titles. 'My frank, open, temper,' says Lady Churchill, 'led me to pitch upon Freeman,' and so the princess took the name of Morley: and from this time Mrs. Morley and Mrs. Freeman began to address each other as equals, made so by affection and friendship. But, unhappily, the affection was all on one side. In after life the duchess, though she allowed that Queen Anne possessed a certain majesty of deportment, depicted her as wearing a constant and sullen frown, showing 'a gloominess of soul and a cloudiness of disposition:' terms which one would not readily employ when referring to any one who had ever been the object of our genuine attachment. Yet there is something noble and spirited in the following sentiment, expressed by the duchess in her vindication: 'Young as I was when I became this high favourite, I laid it down as a maxim that flattery was falsehood to my trust, and ingratitude to my dearest friend.' Anne, on the other hand, begged of her not to call her 'highness' at every word, but to speak her mind freely in all things.

Henceforth, Lady Churchill remained in the household of Anne until faction turned their friendship into enmity. Lady Churchill, located at Whitehall, now became the star of that minor court, noted for dulness and respectability, which assembled in Anne's private apartments to play, whist, or quadrille, or to drink caudle after the birth of a young prince or princess. From this stately retirement, Lady Churchill witnessed the course of events; the death of Charles II., heart-broken by Monmouth's ingratitude; the accession of James II. During this period the beautiful Mrs. Freeman appears to have held aloof from masquerading, which was the fashion of the day. Her sister Frances, attired as an orange girl, had passed her basket round in the pit of the theatre under the very eyes of Mary Beatrix, her patroness, and, her disguise half suspected, had vaunted of the compliments paid her. But Sarah abstained from lowering herself; and though afterwards reigning over fashion as over politics, was little seen except in the performance of her duties.

Hyde Park was then only a country drive, a field, in fact, belonging to a publican. Sometimes the Princess Anne might be seen there, driving with her beloved Freeman, in her coach, panelled only, without glass windows, which were introduced by Charles II. There they encountered Lady Castlemaine and Miss Stuart, whose quarrel which should first use the famous coach presented by Grammont to the king was the theme of Whitehall. Sometimes from the groves and alleys of Spring Gardens they emerged, perhaps, into the broad walks of St. James's Park, between the alleys of which, cafés, such as those permitted in the gardens of the Tuileries, were resorted to by the gay and titled.. Sometimes the Princess Anne, followed by the haughty Freeman in her hood and mantle, descended Whitehall Stairs, and took her pleasure in her barge on the then calm and fresh waters of the Thames, beyond which were green fields and shady trees. These were all inexpensive plea sures; and both Mrs. Morley and Mrs. Freeman were economical. The princess's allowance from the privy purse was small, and Lord Churchill's means were moderate.

More frequently, however, the two friends sat in the princess's boudoir, then termed her closet, and in that sanctum discussed passing events with bitterness :—the dramatic close of the days of Charles II., who begged pardon of his surrounding courtiers for being 'so long a-dying;'—the accession and unpopularity of his brother James;—and, afterwards, the event that roused even Anne from her apathy and made her malicious—the birth of the prince whom we southrons call the Pretender.

Kind, gentle, and correct as she was, Mary Beatrix was secretly the object of Anne's dislike. A stepmother is born to be hated: dislike begets dislike; and Mary Beatrix was not wholly faultless in her conduct to the princess. Anne was then the mother of a son of two years of age, and William, Duke of Gloucester, as he had been created, was the heir presumptive to the crown. Doubts were raised: and Anne, touching on the subject of the queen's confinement, provoked her Majesty to throw a glove at her face, upon which the princess retired from court, and went to Bath; she was, therefore, as well as Lady Churchill, absent when the birth of James Stuart, afterwards styled the Chevalier, took place.

Hitherto Sarah, as well as her lord, had been wholly devoted to the Stuarts, and to that party, not then designated, until a later date, Tories, which holds to the reigning family, right or wrong. But Lord Churchill, attached to the Protestant faith, had ample reason, from the gross tyranny of James II., to withdraw from the court as much as possible, and to decline either new honours or offices of trust under that monarch.

One by one friends and courtiers deserted James II.: but Prince George of Denmark still remained near him during his flight to Salisbury. Whenever any fresh desertion took place, Prince George, with some diplomacy, merely exclaimed, '*Est-il possible?*' At last he went too. Upon hearing of his withdrawal, James, with a degree of humour which we would rather have expected from Charles II., exclaimed—'What! is *Est-il possible* gone too?' On his return, however, to his capital, James found that Anne had also fled: her apartments at the Cockpit in Westminster, were empty. 'God help me!' cried the disconsolate king; 'my own children have forsaken me.'

Anne had indeed, from a fear of being involved in disturbances which might injure the succession of her son, taken flight upon the return of *Est-il possible* to Whitehall. In the dead of the night she left her apartments, creeping down by the back stairs, in a hackney-coach, Lady Churchill accompanying her mistress; and protected by the Bishop of London, Dr. Compton, who had been Anne's tutor, they passed through the streets, and, unobserved, arrived at the episcopal palace, then in the city. On the ensuing day the fugitives went to Copt Hall, the seat of the Earl of Dorset: thence to the Earl of Northampton's, and then to Nottingham, where the country, and in particular the adherents of William of Orange, collected to welcome and support Anne. It must have been a simple cortège, of which Mrs. Morley and Mrs. Freeman now formed the main features: for the good Bishop Compton, firing up on the occasion, and recalling his youthful days, in which he had been a cornet of dragoons, rode at the front with a drawn sword in his hand and a pair of pistols at his saddle-bow.

Amid those who assembled at Nottingham was the famous Colley Cibber the dramatist, whose 'Provoked Husband' and 'Careless Husband' are among the most choice productions of a period rich in dramatic literature. Colley was then a young man, destined for Oxford: and his father, whose famous figures denoting Melancholy Madness and Raving Madness, of the size of life, in the Bethlehem Hospital, have never been excelled, was then usually working at Chatsworth, and altering the old Gothic pile into a Grecian structure. When Colley arrived at Chatsworth, he found that his father had gone to Nottingham to serve in the volunteer corps that had mustered for the protection of Princess Anne; and thither he also went. Now old Caius Cibber was by no means a hero, though the sculptor of heroes; and on beholding his son, full of ardour, he begged him to take his military duties on his young shoulders, and persuaded the Earl of Devonshire, who was the colonel of the corps, to allow of his having this substitute: so Colley, as he described it, jumped into his father's saddle, and figured away in the old man's regimentals.

Soon after this occurred, the corps were ordered to meet the princess on the London road, and to form a guard round her person whilst she entered Nottingham. The excitement in the town was very great, for a report prevailed that there were two thousand of the King's Dragoons in pursuit of the princess: but the cavalcade reached the Earl of Devonshire's quarters in safety. That night there was a supper. Anne was now the darling of the Protestant party; and all the persons of distinction in the town were eager to accept 'my Lord Devonshire's invitation' to sup with him. The guests were many, the attendants few; and Colley Cibber being well known to the Earl of Devonshire's *maitre d'hotel*, was pressed into the service. It must have been a singular and an animated scene. The Princess Anne, stately but heavy, was attended by two ladies of her bedchamber, both remarkable for their beauty; but Lady Churchill far outshone Lady Fitzhardinge, the other lady, in loveliness. As young Cibber, afterwards so noted for his delineation of a woman of haut ton in Lady Modish, stood behind Lady Churchill, his eyes were riveted by her graceful beauty. He could see nothing, hear nothing else.

'Being so near the table,' he wrote fifty years afterwards, 'you may naturally ask me what I might have heard to have passed in conversation at it, which I certainly should tell you had I attended to above two words that were uttered there, and those were, "*Some wine and water;*"' and these came from the 'fair guest' whom Colley took such pleasure to wait upon. 'Except,' he says, 'at that single sound, all my senses were collected into my eyes, which, during the whole entertainment, wanted no better amusement than that of stealing now and then the delight of gazing on the fair object so near me.' This was Lady Churchill, who sat unconscious of a gaze which the juvenile enthusiast described as 'a regard that had something softer than the most profound respect in it;' nor did he see why he was not free to express this admiration, 'since beauty, like the sun, must,' he thought, 'sometimes lose its power to choose, and shine into equal warmth the peasant and the courtier.' It was half a century after that evening that Colley, young still in fancy, described in those glowing terms the impression made on him by that brief interview. Lady Churchill was wholly passive in this flight of Anne's, although the blame of it was thrown on her by political writers. The metropolis, however, was in commotion when all was discovered. Every one believed that step to have been premeditated, since six weeks previously Anne had ordered a private staircase to be made. She had evidently seen the storm afar off. She returned, however, to Whitehall, to see her royal sister Mary occupying the apartments of Mary Beatrix in that palace, and William holding his court at St. James's, escorted by Dutch guards. This was a result which Lady Churchill does not seem to have anticipated, if we may trust her own account.

'I do solemnly protest,' she afterwards wrote, 'that if there be truth in any mortal, I was so very simple a creature that I never once dreamt of his (William III.) being king. Nevertheless, the responsibility was believed by every one to rest in some measure with Lady Churchill, since it was through her advice, it was thought, that Anne gave her consent to the crown being settled on William for life: whereas, after Mary, she would have been the rightful successor.

At this critical juncture, Lady Churchill wisely sought the advice of persons older and more competent to judge than herself. The widowed Lady Rachel Russell was still living at Southampton House, Bloomsbury, in deep and mournful seclusion. She sought her; and they consulted together, and, with the aid of Archbishop Tillotson, decided on the course to be adopted. It was in Southampton House, therefore, that edifice the sight of which had drawn tears from Lord Russell as he went to execution in Lincoln's Inn Fields, that it was resolved that Anne should henceforth turn from her father's cause, and embrace that of the Revolution. Lady Rachel was then in her prime; and the blindness which added to the sorrows of her old age, a blindness caused by incessant weeping, had not then commenced.

These preliminaries being settled, Lady Churchill endeavoured to like, as well as to acknowledge, the new queen who had succeeded the heroic, patient, and good Mary of Modena. But the court was indeed altered. Mary of Orange, on taking possession of her apartments at Whitehall, showed too plainly that she wanted feeling still more than the phlegmatic Anne. It was Lady Churchill's duty to attend her Majesty that day to the very rooms which had lately been occupied by Mary Beatrix, with her ill-starred infant son. Mary little suspected that the first lady of her sister's bedchamber was watching her with no friendly gaze. 'She ran about,' Lady Churchill relates, 'looking into every closet and conveniency, and turning up the quilts on the bed, as people do when they come into an inn, and with no other sort of concern in her appearance but such as they express:' and, although at that time Mary was gracious and even caressing to the favourite, Lady Churchill thought her behaviour very strange and unbecoming. Decorum, she felt, should have suggested some sadness of countenance, when Mary passed through the rooms, and paused to examine the very bed from which her father, King James, had been so lately driven. But these thoughts she kept to herself. Two days afterwards, the very hall of that palace whence James had fled, and at the gate of which Charles I. had been beheaded, witnessed the proclamation which made William king and Mary queen. In the present day, the faintest attempt to place a foreign monarch of another dynasty on the throne would produce revolution; in those, it was hailed as a refuge against despotism. Two days previously Lord Churchill having been created Earl of Marlborough, the aspiring Sarah gained another step in the course of her aggrandizement, and became the Countess of Marlborough. But she hated the hand whence this new honour came; and the reign of Mary was embittered to both the daughters of James II. by the incessant bickerings of the two sisters, and by endless disputes and affronts which Lady Marlborough did not attempt to soothe. She had abandoned, it is true, the friend and patron of her youth, the confidante of her marriage, Mary Beatrix; but she could not avoid feeling that Mary of Orange, with her cold virtues, would never replace that warm and fascinating patroness. The royal sisters too, it was soon perceived, did not assimilate. Mary was a model queen, a model wife; that unpleasant personage, a patron of excellence. She possessed what Pope calls, 'not a science, but worth all the seven, prudence.' She began to reform the court, to send away doubtful characters, to set an example of industry in needlework, and of regularity in public devotion as well as in private. She found fault, it appears, with Lady Marlborough's laxity in this last respect; and to hint a blemish in Lady Marlborough was to offend Anne mortally. Then Mary was an *esprit fort*, a great historian and politician, and a great talker; and she found her younger sister, from whom she had been separated for years, as silent as she was stupid, just answering a question, nothing more. William III. too, was intensely jealous of the popularity which Anne enjoyed, and which is sometimes the result of perfect insignificance of character in high station. There soon arose a pretence for disputes, and an outbreak followed of course.

The Princess Anne, as we have seen, lived in that part of Whitehall called from its entrance the Cockpit. St. James's Park, which, in the time of Henry VIII., belonged to the Abbot of Westminster, was bought by that monarch and converted into a park, a tennis-court, and a cockpit, which was situated where Downing Street now is. The park was approached by two noble gates, and, until the year 1708, the Cockpit Gate, which opened into the court where Anne lived, was standing. It was surmounted with lofty towers and battlements, and had a portcullis, and many rich decorations. Westminster Gate, the other entrance, was designed by Hans Holbein, and some foreign architect doubtless erected the Cockpit Gate.

The scene of the cruel diversion of cock-fighting was, indeed, obliterated before Anne's time, and the palace, which was one long range of apartments and offices reaching to the river, extended over that space.

The locality was pleasant enough. From her windows Anne could see the pleasant village of Charyng; Westminster Abbey, without the towers, stood in an open space, and the Park peopled with singing birds; and though merry King Charles was no longer to be seen there feeding his ducks, and talking pleasantly to everyone, there was a grand mall in fine weather, to which lords and ladies, shopwomen, Mohawks and roaring boys, maccaronies (or dandies) of both sexes repaired and sat, in gay dresses and periwigs, under the trees. Yet the Princess Anne was not contented: she had the bad taste to wish to remove to the very rooms once occupied by the Duchess of Portsmouth, mistress to her late uncle, Charles II., a personage who, with other disreputable ladies, had been routed by Queen Mary from the now saintly precincts of Whitehall. The difficulties and discussions induced by Anne's wish to remove, produced endless heartburnings, and ended in Anne's taking the duchess's rooms for her children's use, and remaining at the Cockpit.

Here, at this period, resorted the gay, the learned, the intriguing, attracted, not by Queen Anne and her dull consort, but by the grace, the wit, and busy political turn of Lady Marlborough. She stands at the head of those who have been 'queens of society,' for she governed the *beau monde* of her own time. It is true she was not in her climax until Anne was on the throne; but she was in the radiance of her youth when her friend Mrs. Morley dwelt in the Cockpit. Unlettered, she was the counsellor of her famous husband, the leading star of his ambition. Her plain, shrewd sense, without one grain of sentiment, riveted him. They had but one heart, one soul between them: whilst her loveliness, her dignified ease, her vivacity, fascinated a man of powerful understanding and noble qualities—the celebrated minister Sidney Godolphin.

The very name, Godolphin, signifying a white eagle, recalled in those days one of the heroes of the Great Rebellion, the ill-fated Sidney Godolphin. Like most others of Charles's adherents, the minister of Queen Anne belonged to an impoverished race, and it was even contemplated by his friends to place him in some trade. The young Cornishman had, however, all the shrewdness of the west countryman; and being a page to Charles II., when once in the precincts of a court he made the best of his opportunities. Nothing, however, in the public service so accorded with his inclinations as being made chamberlain to Mary Beatrix. He admired, he respected, he almost loved this young and amiable queen, and continued to befriend her until the close of his own career.

That career was a struggle between principle and affection. When James II. showed his true designs to his indignant people, Godolphin, like an honest man, clung to the standard of civil and religious liberty; but his heart was with his early patrons. Courageous, but tender-hearted, he set his party at defiance, accompanied James II. to the sea-shore, before his final departure for France, and continued to correspond with him, which he honestly confessed to William III., until the death of the exiled monarch. Godolphin was Lord Treasurer to James II., and he was retained in that office by William III. Although one of the plainest of men, he had attracted, early in her youth, Queen Anne's regard: he was now, according to slanderous report, the favoured lover of Sarah Countess of Marlborough. Deeply marked with the small-pox, his countenance was harsh; and no one could have imagined that Godolphin could weep like a woman when his feelings were touched, and that he was prone to sentiment. His smile, however, when it broke forth from his plain, hard features was most winning, and his eyes were dark and penetrating. Such was the man, to whose honour be it spoken that he ever cherished for Mary of Modena a romantic and generous devotion, and to injure whom, it was alleged by contemporaries that the wife of his friend and coadjutor, Marlborough, was the object of a passion by no means platonic. There existed at that period a paid regiment of writers, whose works were at once calumnious and adulatory. As 'Queen Sarah,' as she was now styled, was often the subject of the latter, so she sometimes became the butt of the former style of writing. Patronized by Dean Swift, amongst the venial defamers of the day, appears the notorious Rivella, *alias* Mrs. de la Riviere Manley, whose 'Atlantis,' 'History of Prince Mirabel,' 'Secret History of Queen Zarah and the Zarazians,' were thought worthy of being preserved by Swift among the state tracts. Rivella was a woman of abandoned character, the pupil, in her youth, of the infamous

Madame Mazarin, the confidante of the Duchess of Cleveland, and the tool, for party purposes, of the malignant Swift. It was her aim, of course at once to lower the Marlborough ascendency with the public, and to cut short an intimacy beneficial to all concerned, by tainting it with her foul and absurd aspersions; but Queen Sarah could not be aspersed. Her moral character was invulnerable. She rose superior to the assault, and retained the all-important friendship of Godolphin to her latest day. A woman of prudence and virtue has, in fact, a far greater latitude of action in her conscious innocence than those who dare not defy calumny. Marlborough was, indeed, continually absent; the very first campaign in Ireland tore him from his home. His letters were full of tenderness to her whom he left. 'Put your trust in God,' he wrote to his wife, in the very midst of his triumphs, 'and be assured that I think I can't be unhappy as long as you are kind.' And after the battle of Ramilies—' Pray believe me when I assure you that I love you more than I can express.' Yet Sarah had now passed the bloom of her youth, and her temper had lost its equanimity. Still the hero pined for repose with her. 'As God has been pleased to bless me,' he writes in another letter, 'I do not doubt but he will reward me with some years to end my days with you; and if that be with quietness and kindness, I shall be much happier than I have ever been yet.'

Lady Marlborough, was indeed, every way blessed: to please her, her husband now purchased the share in the family estate, from her coheiresses Frances and Barbara, and built a large mansion on the spot where she was born, called Holywell House, a stately structure, which she left only when Blenheim was given them by the nation, and in which some remember the old Lady Spencer, the mother of the beautiful Duchess of Devonshire, living in great comfort and suitable style.

Some clouds, nay some storms there were at times in this serene atmosphere; but these were almost essential to keep Queen Sarah alive, in the dull court of the Princess Anne. Like most spoiled women, she had one pet aversion, and that was King William, whom she called 'Caliban.' Other names that she gave him were not even so decorous as that offensive *sobriquet*. The dry, cold manner of William affronted her: the king despised talkers, and one of Lady Marlborough's greatest gifts was conversation. Then she hated his character, which, she thought, was exhibited in its true colours by William's eating up a dish of early peas all himself, whilst Anne, near her confinement, was dying to partake of them. 'Europe and the back stairs,' Horace Walpole remarks, 'shared in her mind in importance;' and whilst every-day incidents affected her mind to frenzy, it became hard to take a broad and generous view of affairs.

The court now assumed a formality that disgusted one who hated surface-piety. William, whilst Lady Orkney was his mistress, paraded virtue in the plainest of forms. His sententious remarks, his deep reserve, his chilling demeanour, formed a singular contrast with the easy politeness and mirth of Charles II., and the stately courtesy of King James. At Hampton Court, whither he retired with Mary, his 'Roman eagle' nose, his sparkling eyes—conspicuous on a face deeply seamed with the small-pox—his thin, small figure, made him look like a caricature of mankind. Like Napoleon III., he had the grand secret of hiding all he thought, and much that he felt. The royal actor on that stage whereon the pageant of royalty had of late passed so suddenly away, had the talent so much commended, for silence. The automaton monarch, however, broke the peaceful stillness, by his deep convulsive cough, and the weakness which was bearing him to the grave recalled the conviction that he was human.

Lady Marlborough now passed much of her time at Hampton Court, to which William was adding that mass of building which looks upon the gardens, and where he was planning, with a lingering fondness for his Dutch palace at Loo, the noble gardens upon the model of those of his regretted home. Amid the ornaments of the presence-chambers, none formed a more suitable embellishment than Queen Mary herself. She was every inch a queen, and far more agreeable in appearance than her sister Anne. Tall, majestic, with a fine open face—though weak-eyed—Mary moved with infinite grace. Fond of society, she endeavoured to obviate the impression made by the king's rudeness and taciturnity by talking herself, and by bringing around her those who could adorn the now exclusive circle of Hampton Court and Kensington. But she could not succeed in making the dull receptions of her court cheerful, or even endurable; for all the fashion, wit, and talent centred round Lady Marlborough.

Little did Mary love her sister Anne; yet she ascribed all the bickerings that now arose to the favourite, henceforth called the 'dictatress,' and resolved, if she could, to accomplish her dismissal. In spite of Lord Marlborough's great services to the crown, he had been detected in carrying on a correspondence bordering on treason with James II.; and a still more fatal error, he was also discovered to have told his wife of a design of William's to surprise the important port of Dunkirk. That project had transpired—and failed. It had been mentioned by Lady Marlborough to a Lady Oglethorpe; by Lady Oglethorpe to Frances Jennings, now Lady Tyrconnel; by *her* it was transmitted to the French court. Jean Bart, the pirate, a native of Dunkirk, had cut through the English ships which blockaded the harbour, and saved the town.

Marlborough was disgraced, and his wife was led to conclude that she would be forbidden the court; nevertheless, with her usual courage, emboldened also by the advice of Godolphin, she attended Anne, when the princess conceived it to be her duty to visit her royal sister at Kensington.

No details of the audience are extant; but it may be readily pictured to a mind conversant with that period. The interior of Kensington Palace was then dark and cheerless; the walls were oak panelled; the roof richly embossed. Beneath a canopy of state sat Mary, in her accustomed deep-blue gown, with flowing skirts, and a chemisette of point lace opening in the front of the bust. Her plump throat is encircled with a collar of pearls; her hair is flowing down her back: in front it is raised high on the head in a toupee form, intermingled on either side with pearls. She wears a 'commode' to set out her train, and has raised heels. Her aim is to be delicate and regal, for Mary has never worn her petticoats short since those days of youthful folly when she skated on the Scheldt with the

Duke of Monmouth, whom it was William's policy to allure to his Dutch court. In vain has she tried to model her dress strictly by the rules of modesty, though angry with Kneller for continuing to paint her in a costume which looks as if it were likely to drop off altogether.

By her side sits the king in a French peruke, which almost obliterates his face, except his eagle nose, and falls down to his small waist. He wears a field-marshal's uniform, with the star and garter, a costume rarely altered by him; and his cough might be heard, dry and asthmatic, even at the very entrance of the presence-chamber.

Courtiers of every grade, silver sticks and gold sticks, the grand chamberlain and pages, stand in their appointed places, some in waving flaxen perukes, called by wags, 'the silver fleeces,' others in frosted wigs, which had just begun to succeed the dark, curling perukes of Charles II. and his time. The higher the rank of each individual, the larger the wig. (Shame on Louis XIV., by whom this absurdity was introduced, and in whose reign even statues were bewigged!) The king's feet are mounted in high-heeled shoes, and buckles of diamonds, set in silver, shine on the step on which they rested. William's brow darkens as he beholds the princess enter, for he has heard that when the disgrace of Marlborough was announced to her, Anne had shed tears. She knew what was next to happen.

Near the king stands Bentinck, afterwards Duke of Portland, and once page to his Dutch majesty. Bentinck was one of Lady Marlborough's most powerful foes, for he had secured William's whole power of affection, by nursing him, at the peril of his own life, through the small-pox—as great an act of friendship in those days, when that scourge was wholly unmitigated, as can be conceived. Bentinck had taken the disease, and his placid face, seamed and disfigured, could never fail to recall to the king his act of devotion. To him we owe the taste of gardening which England, until his time, but little appreciated. Anne, when queen, never forgave his dislike of her dear Mrs. Freeman, and deprived him of his post as Keeper of Windsor Great Park. The princess, with her consort, Prince George, in his full dress as Lord High Admiral, may be easily pictured. The rubicund face of *Est-il possible* is now somewhat weather-beaten. He has lately distinguished himself fighting against his father-in-law's troops at the Battle of the Boyne; nevertheless, the king and queen treat the brave nonentity with no more respect, as Queen Sarah declares, 'than if he had been a page of the back stairs.'

Anne scowling, though Kensington could never have been too light, is handed by her consort with an air of injured innocence. There is a resemblance observable between the royal sisters, but the difference is the absence of intelligence and grace. Anne is clumsy in her stateliness; Mary is perfect in every attitude. Anne has a somewhat good house-wife air, and looks like the respectable mother of a family. Mary is a Stuart and a queen. As Anne, in a cinnamon-coloured gown, with a crimson train, a falling jewel on her brow, and her hair in thick short curls high on her forehead, moves heavily forward, a whisper runs through the presence-chamber. 'What! Lady Marlborough? and her husband dismissed from his command, and she the cause?' Yes, she is coming in all her matured beauty, with her light hair all in wavy curls on her head; one tendril intruding upon her brow whiter than snow. The hair, systematically careless, is thrown back so as to show the ears, and the delicate region of the cheek, the chin, the throat; and falls in tresses far away, undulating, glossy tresses over the left shoulder. Whilst all around are blazing with jewels, she wears not one: her dress is white satin, and could stand alone; but she, too, has a 'commode:' her white arm has a string of pearls round it, and that is all.

On the left side of the queen walks Lady Fitzhardinge, whom Sarah loved—a rare distinction—and who betrayed her friends to William, an event not rare in courts; and followed by the usual silver sticks, and the complement of pages, they make their way up to the Cloth of Estate amid the smiles and murmurs of all present.

The reception—to return from this ideal picture to fact—was perfectly freezing; and, early in the next day, Mary intimated to her sister that since she had allowed Lady Marlborough to go to Kensington with her, her 'lady of the bedchamber must not stay' in the princess's service: Anne's taking her 'was the very strangest thing ever done, and was very unkind in a sister, and would have been very uncivil in an equal.' She could pass over most things, but could not pass over Lady Marlborough's going to court on that occasion.

To this message Anne returned a calm but resolute reply, said to have been suggested by Godolphin. No answer was sent to it, except a messenger from the Lord Chamberlain to Lady Marlborough, commanding her to leave the Cockpit: that residence being in Whitehall, was considered within the queen's rights. The princess, thereupon, resolved not to separate from her friend, packed up, and went away also, accepting, for a time, the loan of Sion House from the Duke of Somerset.

So far Queen Sarah was triumphant; but even her spirits and health were affected by her husband's continued disgrace. 'Do, for God's sake,' Anne wrote to her, 'have a little care of your dear self. Give way as little to melancholy as you can. Try asses' milk.' And she was miserable at the necessity for Mrs. Freeman's being 'let blood.'

The feud between the two sisters went on for some time; but Anne was as obstinate as any Stuart. Lady Marlborough, meantime, lost her infant son, Lord Brackley; and the princess, taking a chair, braved royal anger, and went to see her. In vain did Mrs. Freeman offer to give up her post to ensure peace. Anne answered her offers in letters which her dear friend afterwards described as very 'indifferent both in sense and spelling,' with great repetitions of a few passionate expressions.

Anne's court, meantime, was almost deserted; and when she went to Bath, her uncle, Lord Rochester, wrote to the Mayor (a tallow-chandler), forbidding any respect to be shown to her; yet Anne was scarcely vexed. Her favourite's smiles or frowns affected her more than the tallow-chandler's not being allowed to light up Bath. 'Dear Mrs. Freeman must give me leave to ask her,' she humbly wrote one night, 'if anything has happened to make her uneasy. I thought she looked to-night as if she had the spleen; and I can't help being in pain whenever I see her so.' Mary even ordered that the text of the sermon at St. James's, where Anne went to Church, should not be put into her pew according to custom; but that 'noble design,' as Mrs. Freeman termed it, was dropped by the advice of ministers.

These woman-like disputes were going on when Mary was attacked with the small-pox, and died, owing to the mistaken treatment of Dr. Radcliffe. The two sisters never met more, and the audience at Kensington was their last interview.

After a time, when William's bitter anguish was somewhat assuaged, he was reconciled to the Princess Anne; and forthwith crowds were seen hastening to Berkeley House, and Queen Sarah was once more in her glory. How thoroughly she despised those who now caressed her as the 'dictatress' once more! How intensely diverted she seems to have been with the half-witted Lord Carmarthen's saying to Anne, as he stood by her in the circle: 'I hope your Highness will remember that I came to wait upon you when none of this company did;' and a burst of laughter shook the courtly assembly.

In spite of the reconciliation, however, William continued to show all the malice of a little mind towards his successor and sister-in-law. When Anne waited on his Majesty at Kensington, no more respect was paid to her than to any other lady, until this neglect was talked about, and then Lord Jersey saw her to her coach, but no one higher than a page of the back stairs ever came to meet her. Often was the princess kept waiting for an hour and a half. These annals of a wardrobe, as Horace Walpole terms them, are characteristic; and, as such, it is to be regretted that Hooke the historian, to whom the duchess intrusted the arrangement of her Memoirs, thought it prudent to cut out some of the most amusing and impertinent passages. Time, however, softened all these heartburnings; and William, now bitter soever his dislike to the Lady Marlborough, did justice at last to her husband. When the Duke of Gloucester, Anne's only surviving child, became old enough to require a governor, William confided him to Marlborough: 'Teach him, my Lord, to be like yourself,' were William's words to Marlborough, 'and my nephew cannot want accomplishments.' Bishop Burnet was appointed the little duke's tutor by Marlborough; and between them they so over-trained the poor hothouse plant, that in two years it ceased to exist.

Meantime, five daughters and one son seemed to fill up the measure of Lord and Lady Marlborough's felicity. But of all human sources of happiness, none excite so much hope, none often cause such bitter disappointment, as children. The son, Lord Blandford, died early; the daughters were beautiful and virtuous, but had tempers like their mother, and, as they grew up, there was little family union. Lady Henrietta Churchill, in her eighteenth year, was married to Lord Rialton, the eldest son of the minister Godolphin: she afterwards became Duchess of Marlborough in her own right, but died before her mother. Of her it is told that, being devotedly attached to Congreve, the dramatist, she had, after his death, a wax figure made resembling him, which was placed in his usual seat at her table, a cover always being laid for 'Mr. Congreve.' Henrietta's temper was not unperceived by her father, who deeply regretted the quarrels between his wife and daughters as the latter grew up.

Lady Anne, the second of the great Marlborough's daughters, and the loveliest, was married to Lord Sunderland, son of the disgraced minister, Sunderland, and through her descendants the titles and estates of the Churchills have been enjoyed by the Spencers. She was all goodness; but her union was infelicitous. Beneath a frigid demeanour, Lord Sunderland concealed fiery passions: with a cold heart, a republican in public, a tyrant in private life, he sought, when a young widower, the hand of Lady Anne Churchill, whilst such affections as he had were buried in the tomb of his first wife, Lady Arabella Cavendish. On this account Lord and Lady Marlborough long hesitated before they would intrust their best-beloved daughter to him. They were married, however, and Lady Sunderland became a leader of fashion; to compass which she must needs be a politician. 'The *little Whig*,' as she was called, from the smallness of her stature, used to wear her patches on the left side, whilst the Tory ladies wore theirs on the right; so that all society was divided by this social freemasonry. Lady Sunderland died at an early age of consumption.

Next came Lady Elizabeth, married to the Earl of Bridgewater:—

> 'Hence Beauty, waking, all her forms supplies,
> An angel's sweetness in Bridgewater's eyes'[*]

She also died of consumption, and was buried in Gaddesden Church, Hertfordshire.

Then came 'Angel Duchess Montagu,' Lady Mary Churchill, married to the Duke of Montagu; but, although Pope gave her that name, she seems to have been a complete shrew. Her mother and she were long at variance.

'I wonder you and your mother cannot agree,' said Marlborough, worn out, in old age by their squabbles; 'you are so alike.'

The daughter of the Duchess of Montagu, the good and gay Duchess of Manchester, was a great favourite of Queen Sarah's.

'Duchess of Manchester,' said her grandmother to her one day, 'you are a good creature, but you *have* a mother.'

'And *she*, too, has a mother,' was the ready, fearless retort.

For her daughters, the 'dictatress' procured so many places, that Queen Anne's court was said to consist only of one family. Yet, though they added lustre to her life, they were not the solace of her age.

The death of William III., in 1702, formed an era in the life of Queen Sarah. She was forty-three years of age, and her husband fifty-three, when, on Anne's coming to the throne, their prosperity was raised to the acme. Queen Sarah was now captivating as a wit, rather than as a beauty: yet her loveliness remained still; and her hair, preserved by the use of honey water, was abundant still, and untouched by time. Her haughtiness had now grown into insolence, and her temper was chiefly vented upon her royal patroness, whom for ten years she governed without a rival.

The courtiers, who had been weeping at the bedside of William, now rushed from Kensington to the more genial atmosphere of St. James's, which was crowded with loyal subjects, congratulating her whom they had deserted when she had held her court in the privacy of Berkeley House, and the coronation followed in a few months, when Lady Marlborough

---

[*] Pope.

was seen in all her glory, attending on the queen, who was carried in a low chair from the hall at Westminster to the abbey. Even then, the watchful courtiers observed that when holding the queen's gloves, or presenting them to her Majesty, the 'dictatress' used to turn away her head, 'as if she had an ill smell under her nose.' But Anne took this insolence passively, and heaped honours and pensions on her two favourites.

In the midst of all Lady Marlborough's triumphs, however, a blow came which might have chastened a less proud spirit. Her son, the Marquis of Blandford, caught the small-pox at Cambridge: the disease appeared in its most malignant form. His mother, now Duchess of Marlborough, hastened to him. The queen sent two of her physicians in one of the royal carriages to see him. For some time there was a slight, slight hope. In this suspense the great heart of Marlborough was poured out thus to his wife :—

'If we must be so unhappy as to lose this poor child,' such were his words, 'I pray God to enable us both to behave ourselves with that resignation which we ought to do. If this uneasiness which I now lie under should last long, I think I could not live. For God's sake, if there be any hope of recocovery, let me know it.'

A few hours after writing this letter, the unhappy father, unable to bear the delay of a reply, set off for Cambridge, where he arrived only in time to see his son expire. The youth was buried in King's College Chapel, the place where his prayers had been regularly and fervently uttered ever since his residence at college. Marlborough mourned like a father and a Christian; but he was summoned to the seat of war, and, in the excitement of battle strove to bear his loss, and to believe it for the best. It did not wean his wife from the world, in which her whole soul was fatally bound up. The bereaved couple were separated by the French war for many months.

The duchess was now for some years, if not queen indeed, the queen of society. Lord Somers and the Earl of Halifax, of whose poetry Horace Walpole observes, time has indeed 'withered the charms;' Pope, who satirized her as Atossa;

Gay, Steele, Addison, Congreve—all mingled in the circles which, in the Friary in St. James's, where Queen Sarah latterly resided, were assembled. The Duchess of Marlborough delighted in the society of Lady Mary Wortley Montagu, then a young and brilliant member of society. In after days Lady Mary and Lady Bute used to visit the duchess, and even sit by her whilst she was at dinner, or when casting up her accounts, which she did in the very midst of all her busy life. In the course of conversation with these two charming women, the duchess used to relate how proud the duke had formerly been of her luxuriant hair. One day, however, he offended her, and Sarah, in a fury, punished him. She cut off all those fair tresses, and laid them in a room through which Marlborough was obliged to pass, that he might see them, and be vexed. To her surprise, the duke took no notice of the loss of her locks. Years afterwards she found them, however, in a cabinet, amongst the most precious of his possessions, treasured up. At this point of her story the duchess used to melt into tears. The kind heart that had loved and pardoned her was, when Lady Mary Wortley heard the anecdote, in the grave; and the cold, undutiful members of the family alone remained.

Amongst the votaries of the duchess, Colley Cibber, in a scarlet and gold livery—for he was now one of the royal comedians, and styled a 'gentleman of the great chamber'—still admired the charms of the 'grandmother without a gray hair.' Mrs. Oldfield, the original Lady Betty Modish, was also admitted, frail as she was, into the aristocratic saloons then thrown open widely to talent. Here she learned to personate the woman of fashion. She was the mistress of William Maynwaring, who, at forty, had become attached to this first-rate actress with all the passion, and with more than the constancy of a first love. In vain did Maynwaring's best friends, and among others the Duchess of Marlborough, try to turn him from a connection so discreditable. Maynwaring was *ami de la maison* to the duke and duchess, and died at Holywell, after walking in the gardens there, very suddenly. He divided his property between Mrs. Oldfield and his sister, for which he was blamed by Swift, who knew not one generous sentiment, but defended by Sir Robert Walpole.

During the reign of Queen Sarah at court, Maynwaring had often warned her of the risk she ran in treating the queen with contemptuous familiarity. Dr. Hare, Bishop of Chichester, recommended self-control on still higher grounds, whilst the famous Dr. Garth was, in all emergencies, not only a physician but a friend. But nothing could pacify her implacable haughty spirit, and it brought its own reward.

Favoured so eminently by fortune, the duke and duchess had still their trials. Among the bitterest enemies of the Whig party was Dean Swift. He had set out in life as a violent Whig. When James II. left Whitehall, the dean declared that nothing would purify that ancient palace after the Stuarts had lived there.

> 'He's gone—the rank infection still remains,
> Which to repel requires eternal pains.'

The 'mad parson,' as Swift was called at Button's Coffee House, before his name was known there, excited the curiosity of many persons. The appearance of the 'Tale of a Tub,' in 1704, betrayed the renegade to his former friends. The 'Examiner,' conducted by Swift, Atterbury, Bolingbroke, and Prior, all Tory writers, made both the Duke and Duchess of Marlborough the objects of its skilful satire. The Whig party now began to decline, and in spite of the great victories of Ramilies and Blenheim, which ought to have reinforced Marlborough and Godolphin, a change of ministry took place, and Harley, Earl of Oxford, the very head and front of the High Church and Tory party, became prime minister. It is true that he endeavoured by every possible means to gain the favour of the power behind the throne—Queen Sarah; but whatever were her failings, she was fearlessly sincere—and she defied him : she would not bend to his flatteries, nor scarcely listen to him when he spoke.

The Duchess had, since the battle of Blenheim, become a princess of the German empire. Her pride was now almost too great for her attendance at court to continue ; she was becoming weary of her duties; but, although willing to go out, was by no means inclined 'to be turned out,' and possibly her reign would have endured until the last, had it not been for one fatal error in her tactics.

It is often poor relations, or humble friends, who prove the worst foes of the incautious.

One of the queen's dressers, by name Abigail Hill, had owed that post to the Duchess of Marlborough, to whom she was related. Abigail was the 'Becky' of Queen Anne's back-stairs. Her father had been a Turkey merchant, and had failed; and she had even been reduced so low as to become a servant to Lady Rivers; but her kinswoman had rescued her, and placed her in the queen's household.

The duchess's motives for this charitable act originated in that old-fashioned claim of consanguinity which is too often disallowed in the present day. Sir John Jennings, her grandfather, had had two-and-twenty children; and though he had an estate of four thousand a year, Mrs. Hill, the mother of Abigail, came in for a share of five hundred pounds only; and her husband having speculated, the family were reduced to indigence.

One day a lady ventured at Whitehall to tell the lofty Sarah that she had relations who were destitute. The dictatress, though by no means fond of parting with money, pulled ten guineas out of her purse, and sent it for present use. Mrs. Hill's eldest daughter, Abigail, after this became an inmate of the duchess's house at Holywell, and was brought up in a wholesome state of fear of her patroness. In due time Abigail was promoted to be one of the Princess Anne's bedchamber women or dressers; 'for,' the duchess states, 'as I found rockers (from the royal nursery) in King James's reign were promoted to that office, I did not see why she might not ask for it for poor Abigail Hill, whose younger sister was made laundress to the little Duke of Gloucester.' Another member of this indigent family was Jack Hill, who was at first put into the Customs, and afterwards rose to be a general, and commanded in the expedition to Quebec: nevertheless, this 'ragged boy, the honest Jack Hill, a good-for-nothing lad,' was afterwards, says the duchess, 'persuaded by his sisters to get up, wrap himself in warmer clothes than those I had given him, and go to the House to vote against the duke.'

The end might be conjectured, even if the often-told story of ingratitude and meanness on the one hand, and insolence and generosity on the other, had not been circumstantially told by the duchess in her 'Vindication.'

The queen and her favourite differed, it seemed, on several important points. Anne hated the idea of the Hanoverian succession, and pined to bring her brother back to England. Sarah was all for George I. and that dynasty, and showed her temper whenever Anne dared to rebel against her opinion. No sooner had she left the palace than Anne used to send for Mrs. Hill to confide to her how ill-treated she was. Mrs. Hill was willing to go all lengths, and to be a Jacobite heart and soul. Her manner was flattering and humble; and she had the additional advantage of being connected with Harley, Earl of Oxford, whose sentiments were Tory. In the midst of all this backstairs intriguing, Miss Abigail married, privately, Mr. Samuel Masham, the eighth son of Sir Francis Masham, baronet, and a groom of Prince George's bed-chamber. But though the Duchess of Marlborough was not informed of this secret union, Queen Anne was a confidante in the affair, and had even attended the ceremony secretly, as Queen Sarah found out from a boy who waited on the upper servants in Anne's household: 'back stairs,' again!

The deception had been carried on some time. Whenever the duchess went to see the queen, in stepped Mrs. Masham, with the boldest and gayest air possible. At the sight of her benefactress she stopped short, changed her manner, and dropping a solemn curtsey, with a—*Did* your Majesty ring?' retired with demure humility.

As the duchess was, as she expressed it, 'apt to tumble out her mind,' she did not scruple to express herself very openly when her suspicions were confirmed; and to her horror she found that the queen began to take her cousin's part. Offence followed offence: there was no reasoning with worthy Queen Anne, who had a habit of repeating the same thing over and over again, till Sarah was almost ready to rush from the room in a rage. Mrs. Masham had offended her Grace of Marlborough by never going near her; and when the duchess complained of this one day, the queen said that it was very natural Mrs. Masham should keep away, since the duchess was angry with her; and she was quite in the right. 'My cousin,' cried Sarah, 'has no need to be afraid, unless she is conscious of some crime.' Then Queen Anne began again—(this tiresome way of repeating the one idea in her mind had been inherited from her father)—'It was very natural, and she was very much in the right:' upon which, exasperated beyond measure, 'Mrs. Freeman,' as she was now only occasionally styled, got up, went away, shut the door of the closet, in which she and the queen sat, with such violence, that the very walls shook, and the corridor echoed with the sound.

Mrs. Masham, terrified, did at last call on the incensed duchess. Reproaches and recriminations proved that the poor queen was in the right: her interview made matters worse. During the ensuing Christmas holidays, the duchess made one more attempt to see the queen. They were still Mrs. Freeman and Mrs. Morley in words; but all confidence was gone. Queen Anne stood during the interview, as if to give a hint that it was to be short: and when they parted, merely gave her hand to the duchess, who stooped to kiss it. 'She took me up,' the duchess relates, 'with a very cold embrace, and then, without one kind word, let me go.' The duchess, nevertheless, made another effort. She wrote to the queen, promising never to name her cousin Abigail again, and begging her majesty, before she received the holy communion, to examine herself; quoting, also, passages from the 'Whole Duty of Man,' then the handbook of the religious world, and Jeremy Taylor; but, in spite of her lecture to Queen Anne, and her promise, she did not scruple to call Mrs. Masham, 'a wretch.'

Neither argument nor promises availed. The Duke and Duchess of Marlborough were obliged, by the influence of Abigail, to resign their offices; and from the moment of their retirement, Queen Anne ceased either to be great abroad, or respected at home. Henceforth, whenever Anne addressed her former favourite it was in the tone of command. Mrs. Morley and Mrs. Freeman had ceased to exist.

They met, however, once more. When Prince George of Denmark lay expiring, the duchess hastened to Kensington, and was present at his last moments. When all was over, the duchess, in the warmth of a generous heart, kneeling, entreated her Majesty to let her accompany her to St. James's, and to leave the scene of sorrow. Queen Anne was touched, but quailed at the idea of offending her 'poor Masham,' who was not in the room. She assented, however; but placing her watch in Sarah's hand, bade her retire till the finger should reach a certain hour; meantime to send Mrs. Masham to her. A crowd was collected outside the ante-chamber. The duchess, who perceived that all chance of regaining the queen's favour was at an end, resolved that the failure of her favour should not be disclosed to the expectant courtiers. She ordered them to retire whilst her majesty should pass through; she gave directions that her own coach should be ready for the queen's use: then she returned to the royal closet. 'Your Majesty,' said the lofty dictatress, 'must excuse my not delivering your message to Mrs. Masham: your Majesty can send for her to St. James's, how and when you please.' Then she gave her arm to the queen, who, looking to the right and to the left, afraid of wounding her 'dear Masham,' on whom she bestowed a glance of kindness, moved along the gallery. But no reconciliation ensued, and Queen Anne, when at St. James's, chose to sit in the very closet latterly occupied by Prince George, because the 'back stairs' belonging to it communicated with Mrs. Masham's apartment; and Abigail could thus bring to her any one with whom she chose to carry on political intrigues.

Well might Shakspeare's lines in his 'Richard II.,' in speaking of the farewell between Anne and her once dear Mrs. Freeman, be recalled:—

> 'And say, what store of parting tears were shed?
> Faith, not by me, except the north-east wind
> (Which then blew bitterly against our faces)
> Awak'd the sleepy rheum; and so, by chance,
> Did grace our hollow parting with a tear.'

Henceforth the duchess must be considered as the head of

the Opposition. Swift now attacked her more fiercely than ever in the 'Examiner,' and accused her of taking enormous bribes when in office, and of peculating as mistress of the wardrobe. When Queen Anne heard of these charges, she remarked: 'Everybody knows that *cheating* is not the Duchess of Marlborough's crime.'

Still Swift was in close alliance with the Masham faction, and directed against the Duke and Duchess of Marlborough those lines beginning—

> 'A widow kept a favourite cat,
> At first a gentle creature;
> But when he was grown sleek and fat,
> With many a mouse and many a rat,
> He soon disclosed his nature.'

The erection of a ducal residence at Blenheim henceforth occupied the duke and duchess's retirement. It was designed by Sir John Vanbrugh, an architect who was the object of Sarah's inveterate hatred. Vanbrugh built the Haymarket theatre: there he assisted Betterton as manager, and brought out two plays, 'The Relapse,' and 'The Provoked Wife,' at once witty and immoral.

Vanbrugh was completing Castle Howard, when he was engaged to build Blenheim. To his fantastic taste we owe St. John's Church, Westminster; not to mention his own residence now pulled down at Whitehall, of which Swift writes—

> 'At length they in the rubbish spy
> A thing resembling a goose pie.'

He was comptroller of the royal works, on which account, and being a man, on his mother's side, of good family, and of an agreeable exterior, he had been cherished in the society of the great. Having once been confined in the Bastille, and having been humanely treated, he built a house for himself on that model at Greenwich. He now began Blenheim, a work of which Swift says—

> 'That if his Grace* were no more skilled in
> The art of battering walls than building,
> We might expect to see next year
> A mousetrap-man chief engineer.'

The duchess and Vanbrugh began very soon to quarrel: she thought 'sevenpence half-penny per bushel for lime a very

* The Duke of Marlborough.

high price, when it could be made in the park,' and he did not hesitate to call her very foolish and troublesome.

She, in a manuscript letter, never yet published, taunted him with going down to Blenheim in a coach with six horses; whilst old Wren, she said, was carried up and down to the top of St. Paul's in a basket, and, though with ten times his genius, never grumbled. Vanbrugh, to do him justice, wished to restore the old Manor House of Woodstock (idealized by Sir Walter Scott). It was a picturesque building, quadrangular, with a court, and standing on an elevation near the then small stream, the Glyme, on whose banks old Chaucer wandered. Within the precincts of this tenement was the famous labyrinth, 'Rosamond's Bower;' and there was a gatehouse in the front of the ancient palace, from the window of which Queen Elizabeth, when a captive there, is said to have envied a milkmaid whom she saw passing, and to have written with charcoal those lines which are still extant, describing her wish for freedom. The Roundheads, too, had sheltered themselves in the Manor House. Yet in spite of all these associations, the duchess ordered the house to be pulled down, Godolphin, without one atom of taste, aiding her by declaring 'that he would as soon hesitate about taking a wen from his face as delay removing so unsightly an object from the brow of the hill.' Down, therefore, it went; and the hill being of 'an intractable shape,' as Vanbrugh said, was lowered. Among other relics found in the earth was a ring with the words—'Remember the Covenant.' It was given by the masons to Lady Diana Spencer. Blenheim was begun in 1705: in 1714 the shell of the building was not complete. It had then cost two hundred and twenty thousand pounds of public money.*

The duke and the duchess had begun to fear the enormous expense of living in such a palace, and to calculate about tons of coals and wax candles. When the Duke of Marlborough died, he left the duchess, however, ten thousand pounds, as the duchess said, to spoil Blenheim her own

* Since the first edition of this work appeared, the lamentable fire in the noble structure has taken place.—ED.

way; and twelve thousand a year 'to keep herself clean with, and go to law.' She finished the house, which altogether cost three hundred thousand pounds. The triumphal arch and the column were erected by her at her own expense. But a stout war was carried on between her and Vanbrugh, whom she would never allow to enter the house, even years after its completion. He consoled himself by calling her that 'wicked woman of Marlborough,' because she had seen through that remorseless jobbery which has ruined almost every national building in England.

The dictatress was, in fact, a woman of wonderful shrewdness. When the South Sea scheme was broached she predicted its fatal result. She had a great art of getting and hoarding money, yet she knew not one rule of arithmetic: when she added up, she set down her figures at random, as if a child had been scribbling on the paper; yet her sums, done chiefly in her head, always came right.

In 1716, the Duke of Marlborough was attacked by palsy, partly in consequence of the death of his favourite daughter, Anne, Countess of Sutherland, 'the little Whig.' His mind never recovered its tone, and his nerves were far more shattered by the duchess's temper than by his battles or the turmoil of politics. One day when Dr. Garth, who was attending him, was going away, the duchess followed him down stairs and *swore* at him for some offence. Vainly did the duke try the Bath waters. He recovered partially, and his memory was spared. It is therefore wrong to couple him, as he has been in the following lines, with Swift, who became a violent lunatic, and died in moody despondency :—

> 'From Marlborough's eyes the tears of dotage flow,
> And Swift expires, a driveller and a show.'

Marlborough was active and calculating to the last. Whilst at Bath, he would walk home from the rooms to his lodgings to save sixpence; yet he left a million and a half to his descendants to squander. When gazing at a portrait of himself, the great general is said to have exclaimed, "That *was* a man.' He lingered six years after his first attack, still, to the last, attending the debates in the Lords, and settling his money matters himself. He had one difficulty, *too much* money, and once wrote to a friend to help him. 'I have now,' he said, 'one hundred thousand pounds dead, and shall have fifty more next week; if you can employ it in any way, it will be a very great favour to me.'

As he was expiring, the duchess asked him whether he had heard the prayers which had been read to him.

'Yes, and I joined in them,' were the last words which the great Marlborough uttered. He sank to rest with her, whom, with all her faults, he had loved more than all, by his side.

The virtues of Marlborough were great; and one cannot but accord with Lord Bolingbroke, who, hearing his penuriousness spoken of, stopped the parasite who had hoped to please him by abusing a foe :—

'He was so very great a man that I forgot he had that vice.'

Swift, however, took care that it should not be forgotten. 'I dare hold a wager,' he said, 'that the Duke of Marlborough in all his campaigns was never known to lose his baggage.'

It is said that the great general scolded his servant for lighting four candles in his tent when Prince Eugene came to hold a conference with him. His habits were simple, like those of Wellington; his dress plain, except on set occasions; his table plain, too plain also, many thought, who would have comprehended ostentation better. He kept few servants, and he dreaded nothing so much as a numerous retinue; yet he was known to give a thousand pounds to a young soldier who wanted to purchase a commission. He was buried in the mausoleum at Blenheim, built by Rysbrach at the expense of the duchess.

She was now the richest peeress in England, with an income of forty thousand pounds a year; and not many months had passed after Marlborough's death before a suitor appeared in the person of a Whig peer, Lord Coningsby whose admiration appears to have commenced before the duke's death; when during the decline of the illustrious invalid, it was plain that Sarah would soon become a fine mark for the designing. 'Friendship,' however, had covered with its convenient garment his secret wishes: as a friend he and the duchess had corresponded: as a friend, four months after Marlborough had expired, he thus addresses the opulent widow.

'When I had the honour to wait on your Grace at Blenheim, it struck me to the heart to find you, the best, the worthiest, and the wisest of women, with regard to your health, and consequently your precious life, in the worst of ways. Servants,' he added, 'were very sorry trustees for anything so valuable, and the indifference of her Grace, when she lay ill, had lain dreadfully heavy on his thoughts ever since.' Then he reminds her of the loss her death would be to her two grandchildren, Lady Sunderland's children, whom she had adopted; and draws a parallel in his own case, saying that when he had himself lain on a bed of sickness, the idea of leaving his 'two dearest innocents' to trustees and guardians, who 'ten millions to one, that they would become merciless and mercenary, had almost killed him!' Of Lord Coningsby's 'dearest innocents' there were five, the eldest of whom had lately been created Baroness Coningsby, so that a little of the duchess's wealth would have been a great addition to this newly-acquired title.

The duchess, being now in her sixty-second year, was not, it is certain, taken in by this devotion. However, Lord Coningsby wrote again, and his letter has been disinterred by a worthy Dryasdust from amidst a heap of accounts and catalogues. This time she was his 'dearest, dearest, Lady Marlborough:' his despair at her intention of not going to London that winter: his desire to see her, if only for one moment; his hopes that she was going to make him the happiest man in the world, whilst he was to make her ('who was already the wisest and the best) the happiest of women' —end with a postscript, which was, perhaps, the only part interesting to the matter-of-fact duchess—

'There is no cattle or sheep, as your Grace desires, to be had till July next.'

Unhappily, Queen Sarah's reply to all this devotion has not

been preserved. We can imagine her reading the letter, swearing a little, and throwing it in with her bills, among which it has been found a hundred and fifty years after it was penned.

Charles Duke of Somerset, second duke of England, commonly called the 'Proud Duke,' offered to the still beautiful Duchess of Marlborough, within a year after the duke's death. This nobleman was a peer of the stamp of which one hopes the 'mould and fashion' are destroyed. Never did he condescend to speak to a servant; he conveyed his commands by signs. Never were his children allowed to sit in his august presence. It was his custom to doze a little in the afternoon, when he required that one of his daughters should stand by him whilst he slept. One day, Lady Charlotte Seymour, venturing to sit down, since she was tired, he left her twenty thousand pounds less than her sister. When he travelled, the duke ordered the roads to be cleared of all obstruction and idle bystanders. The duke was a widower of sixty-five, and his first wife having been a Percy, he thought he did her memory honour in offering his hand to the widow of Marlborough. He was, however, promptly refused. 'The widow of Marlborough shall never become the wife of any other man,' was the reply. He bowed to the decision, and begged the duchess to advise him whom to marry, as marry he would. 'Ask Lady Charlotte Finch,' was her counsel. He asked, and was accepted; but he never forgot the distinction between a Percy and a Finch. A gulf severed the two unequal families. The last duchess once tapped him familiarly with her fan. He turned round angrily, 'My first duchess was a Percy, and she never took such a liberty.'

Twenty-two long years did Queen Sarah survive her husband. She was the head of the Whig party who filled the saloons of Marlborough House, whilst the Duchess of Buckingham, the natural daughter of James II., was the 'queen' of the Jacobite circles. This eccentric lady, when her husband died, made as splendid a funeral for him as Queen Sarah had made for the defunct Marlborough, and when her son died, sent to borrow the funeral car which had carried the hero to the tomb.

'It carried my lord of Marlborough,' cried the duchess fiercely, 'and it shall never carry any other.'

"'Tis of no consequence,' retorted the Duchess of Buckingham. 'I have consulted the undertaker, and he can make me as good a one for twenty pounds.'

Each duchess despised the other. Pope's famous character of 'Queen Sarah' was shown to her by a friend (friends being the people who always show such *brochures*), as if it had referred to her Grace of Buckingham. But the shrewd old Sarah saw through it. 'I see what you mean,' she called out, as the friend went on reading; 'and I can't be imposed upon.' She gave Pope a thousand pounds to suppress the character.

Amongst other anecdotes told of the duchess's arbitrary acts in her old age, is the following unworthy trait. Her grandson, the second Duke of Marlborough, had embellished the Lodge in the Little Park at Windsor, made many improvements there; planted extensively, and formed a canal and a serpentine river. The old duchess hearing of this, set off from London, taking with her a number of men to destroy everything that had been done. She pulled up the trees, and cut and hacked everything she came near. She next proceeded to a piece of waste ground, which was, eventually, to become the property of Lord Sidney Beauclerc; but which had been enclosed by Justice Reeve. Here she caused everything to be pulled down, and destroyed. 'Sid the beggar,' she protested, nor none of his family should ever be the better for her; and told the justice he might go to law if he pleased. Not contented with this, she turned the duke, his guardian, out of the Little Lodge; and pretending that his duchess and her cousins (the eight Miss Trevors) had stripped the house and garden, she had a puppet-show made with waxen figures, representing the Trevors tearing up the shrubs, and the duchess carrying the chicken-coop away under her arm. The duke's offence had been his marriage into the Trevor family; Lord Trevor having been an enemy of his grandfather's.

Women of the duchess's character have always a pet aversion; and Sir Robert Walpole had the honour of holding that

THE DUCHESS OF MARLBOROUGH PLEADING HER OWN CAUSE.

post in her Grace's mind. Her latter years, after she had done with the 'Duke of Buckingham's widow,' as she called her, were passed in quarrelling with Walpole about a hundred thousand pounds she had lent to government; and with the Duke of St. Albans, about coming ad libitum into Windsor Park, of which she was ranger, under pretence of supervising what he called the fortifications, but what she termed 'the ditch around the castle.' The Duke's powers only extended to the castle and the forest; nevertheless, he had, the duchess said, besieged her in both parks, and been willing to forage them at pleasure.

It was the lot of the duchess to survive three of her lovely daughters: Henrietta,— Duchess of Marlborough, after her father's death, in her own right;—Anne Lady Sunderland;—and Elizabeth Countess of Bridgewater. Lady Harriet Churchill was married, after her father's death, to the minister, Pelham Holles, Duke of Newcastle. She died before her mother; and with the only daughter who survived her, Queen Sarah was in a state of perpetual warfare. The obligations of a courtier's life did not, perhaps, permit the duchess time to cultivate the affections, or to form the characters of her children, but she seems to have indulged her grandchildren with all the fondness that was never shown to their parents. One of the few objects she took pride in was the Lady Diana Spencer, Lady Sunderland's daughter. Though she detested Queen Caroline, the consort of George II., the duchess was pleased when her Majesty said, at a drawing-room, 'Tell my Dy to come back that I may bid her to hold up her head;' 'a thing,' said the duchess, 'I was always telling her to do.' Yet her Dy, who married Lord John Russell, the Duke of Bedford of Junius, only survived that union four years. There was another darling of the old dowager's heart, John, commonly called Jack Spencer, whom she styled her 'Torrismond.' Torrismond was more fond of the tavern, more frequently in the watchhouse, than became his rank, name and character: yet she still loved him, and hoped she might live to see him well married. In common with his elder brother, Lord Charles, he had squandered away the great sums left them, figured in all sorts of wild pranks, borrowed money from Jews at twenty per cent., and mortgaged his grandmother's jointure as soon as she died. She acted with great sense and forbearance; but at last an amicable lawsuit, as it was called, between the Jews and his grandmother, was brought to settle some disputed portion of the property. To the surprise of all, the aged duchess appeared in court to plead her own cause. The diamond-hilted sword given by the Emperor Charles was claimed by her grandson.

'What!' cried the duchess. 'Shall I suffer *that* sword, which my lord would have carried to the gates of Paris, to be sent to a pawnbroker's to have the diamonds picked out one by one?'

Jack Spencer died, after a profligate career, at six-and-thirty, because, as Horace Walpole says, 'he would not be abridged of those invaluable blessings of a British subject, namely, brandy, small beer, and tobacco.' His grandmother, nevertheless, left him a clear thirty thousand a year.

Lady Anne Egerton, the only child of Lady Bridgewater, was undutiful, according to the duchess's notions, and to be insulted and derided, of course. So Lady Anne's picture was blackened by her grandmother at once; and writing on the frame, 'She is blacker far within,' was placed in her grace's sitting-room, that all visitors might see it.

Wretched, however, from the frequent losses in her family, the duchess now began to say, that having gone through so many misfortunes, without being ill, 'Nothing but distempers and physicians could kill her.'

Her latter years were spent in resisting Vanbrugh's law-suits, and in compiling her Memoirs. These were put together from scraps she had written: such as the character of Queen Anne; the account of Dr. Sacheverell's deeds; her opinions of Halifax, Somers, Lord Cowper, Swift, Prior, and others. Lord Hailes wrote a manuscript preface to her 'Opinions.' At the age of thirty-two the duchess became as she said, 'a kind of author.' She published her Memoirs, and Nathaniel Hooke who wrote the 'History of Rome,' prepared them for the press. Hooke had suffered from the South Sea bubble, and was then, as he said, just worth nothing. He received four thousand pounds for his trouble; though he and the duchess quarrelled violently about religion whilst he was compiling the work.

At last the health of this remarkable woman began to fail. 'Old Marlborough' was dying, was the court news of the day. Her doctors said she must be blistered, or she must die. 'I won't be blistered,' she cried out; 'and I won't die.' She began to say that she cared not how 'soon the stroke of death came.' She still dictated to Hooke from her bed six hours a day, and played on a hand-organ, the eight tunes of which pleased her, she said, more than an opera. She had three dogs, whom she esteemed more than human beings. She was wrapped up in flannels, and carried about like a child, or wheeled in a chair; nevertheless, she continued to snarl and rail at the world, to hate Sir Robert Walpole and Queen Caroline, yet to remain a Whig, and to be as keen and as clear in all that concerned her immense property as ever.

She was alive to any depredation. Having sent a rich suit of clothes to be made by Mrs. Buda, a fashionable dressmaker, she missed some yards in her dress when it came home. She resolved to punish the fraud. Mrs. Buda had a costly diamond ring on her finger. The duchess pretended to admire this ring, and asked a loan of it for a pattern. In a few days she sent it to Mrs. Buda's forewoman, saying it was to be shown to her mistress as a pledge that a certain piece of cloth should be returned. The cloth came back, upon which the ring was placed on Mrs. Buda's finger, the duchess at the same time convicting her of her offence.

She was now fading slowly but surely away; bitter to the last. She seems to have rested much on the fact that she had never 'deceived any one.' She performed some generous actions. Child's bank being nearly ruined by a quarrel with the Bank of England, she drew a cheque upon the Bank of England, in favour of Child's, for a hundred thousand pounds.

Until the 6th of October, 1744, she was capable of transacting her own business; on the 18th of that month she sank to rest, at Marlborough House, aged eighty-four. She had been the favourite of nature and of fortune; but, as a wife and a woman, her character was at once wanting in sweetness and in elevation. She left, independent of many bequests, sixty thousand pounds per annum to each of her heirs.

Her funeral was, in accordance with her wish, strictly private. She was buried in the mausoleum at Blenheim. No mourning was to be given to any but the servants who attended at her interment. She did not, however, forget her poor chairmen, who had each twenty-five pounds. Her jewels must of themselves have been a fortune. Notwithstanding her conduct to Queen Anne, she left inscribed on the statue of that princess at Blenheim an epitaph full of eulogium. Her last sentiments, as far as concerned her own feelings, were those of a misanthropy which ill became one on whom so many blessings had been showered :—

'I think one can't leave the world at a better time than now, when there is no such thing as real friendship, truth, justice, honour, or, indeed, anything that is agreeable in life.'

MADAME ROLAND.

The Studious Child.—Her First Catechism.—Early Education.—In a Convent.
—Religious impressions.—Poor Ste. Agathe.—Grandmamma.—Religious
Doubts.—A Lazy Confessor.—Atheism.—The Spirit of the Age.—' A Bas
les Aristocrats.'—Manon's Portrait.—Her many Suitors.—Phlippon's Idea
of a Match.—Matchmaking.—Death of Madame Phlippon.—Manon writes
a Sermon.—A New Suitor.—Roland's History.—Phlippon Refuses.—A
Marriage of Reason.—Madame Roland as Nurse.—Brissot and the Girondins.—Brissot's Story.—Young Buzot.—The Meetings at Madame Roland's.—The King of Blood.—Robespierre's Ingratitude.—Dumouriez in
Love.—Madame Roland the Centre of the Girondins.—Ministers, no
Ministers.—Madame Roland's Famous Letter.—At the Head of Parisian
Society.—Anarchy Reigns.—The 20th of June.—The Inauguration of the
Republic.—Madame Roland at the Bar of the Assembly.—Conspiracies
Rife.—Roland Arrested.—Roland Escapes.—Madame Roland Arrested.—
Prison Life.—Madame Roland writes to Robespierre.—Prepares to commit
Suicide.—Her Letter to Her Child.—Her Trial.—Sentenced to Death.—
Before the Guillotine.—Reflections on these Deaths.—Let them Go.

ABOUT the year 1763 there lived on the Quai des Orfévres, on the banks of the Seine, at Paris, a jeweller of the name of Gratien Phlippon. His shop, filled with objects of art, is large, and gives evidence of a certain amount of prosperity. Phlippon is not strictly a jeweller, but an engraver; but as a restless and speculative man he has sought to enlarge his business, buys diamonds and other precious stones, which he takes care to sell at a good profit, and deals, too, in sculpture and engravings. He is a stout, healthy-looking man, active and loud-voiced, and intent on making money. While he sits in one corner of his room, receiving artists, giving directions to his apprentices, and himself plying the engraving-tool, there is not far from him a far more interesting character employed in a very different manner.

A little alcove adjoining the workshop has been turned into a miniature bedroom. There is here a tiny cot-bed, a small table, a chair, and a few shelves. By the table there sits a girl of nine years old, slight in figure, dark in complexion, with rich black hair, small sharp features, and very deep-blue eyes. Sombrely, almost solemnly, she is conning in that little corner a translation of 'Plutarch's Lives.' She has noticed that one of her father's young men, named Courson, leaves his books in a corner of the workshop, and from her hiding-place she has sallied out when no one was by and taken a volume stealthily to her little room. This she has repeated again and again, replacing the volumes when she has devoured them. The young man has perceived their disappearance; her mother, too, has detected her, but neither of them has said a word to her. Rather they are pleased to encourage this worship of books, and she is left in peace to wonder at the greatness of ancient Greeks and Romans, and to ask herself where such men are to be found in her own day. Nor is Plutarch her only joy: she has read the 'Adventures of Telemachus,' and been fired by the spirit of Tasso through a translation of the 'Gerusalemme Liberata;' but Plutarch is her especial favourite, and during Lent that year, when she was obliged to go to mass every day, she has carried it to church with her, and read it there instead of her mass-book. It is then that she receives those impressions which make her republican without knowing it. And such at nine years old is Marie-Jeanne Phlippon, destined in after years as the wife of Jean-Marie Roland, to be the centre of that band of fiery ambitious spirits who pulled down monarchy in France to raise up the guillotine, to which she who had encouraged them was herself to fall a victim.

Born in 1754, Marie-Jeanne was the second child of Gratien Phlippon and his wife Marguerite Bimont. Five other children were born to this couple, but all, including the eldest, died young, except this one precocious girl. Being sent into the country to be nursed by a worthy peasant woman near Arpajon, the little Manon (a *sobriquet* for Marie, equivalent to our Molly), as her parents called her, grew up healthy and strong, for that short but desperate battle of life she was to fight in after years. She gave early proof of a character which could be led by affection, but never driven by force. Her mother, a woman of good sense and delicate feelings, and far superior to her husband, whom she had married as a matter of duty, had no need to punish the little Manon. The single word *Mademoiselle*, pronounced with frigid dignity, was sufficient to recall her at any moment to obedience; and the child, thus addressed, would run and nestle at her mother's side and beg to be taken back to favour. But her father, who seems to have had a sharp temper, failed to bring her to her duty even by the application of the rod.

Once, indeed, when about six years old, she silently, and without a tear, suffered three severe beatings rather than take some medicine which she disliked. The child was ill, and the correction was so severe that it brought on a bad attack of illness, and from that time her father changed his system.

Her mother was a pious woman after the manner of her age and religion, and she early instructed her daughter in the mysteries of her faith. At the age of seven the little Manon was sent every Sunday to the catechising class, at which the curé of the parish, M. Garat, prepared the children for their confirmation. In a corner or side chapel of the parish church, the children were ranged on benches, the boys separated from the girls, while the priest sat on a chair in the midst of them. The collect, gospel, and epistles of the day were repeated one by one. Then came the portion of the catechism which had been the task for the week. Often the fond mothers would come and stand behind their children, and great was Madame Phlippon's pride when her little Manon answered the curé's questions in a manner which proved, even at that age, her mental superiority and especially the strength of her memory.

To this instruction was added that of masters in writing, geography, music, and dancing. To each of these studies the child applied herself with energy and delight, in her little room, and made rapid progress. In her love of reading she devoured everything she could get in the way of books. She found in her father's small library a folio edition of the 'Lives of the Saints,' and an old French version of the Bible. The heroic stories of the former were just suited to her peculiar mind, and the latter, with its quaint old-fashioned language, won her heart, and she returned often to it. When other books failed, she even studied a treatise on heraldry, and began, but could not quite digest, another on contracts! The Abbé Bimont, a brother of Madame Phlippon, and a gay, lazy, merry priest, undertook to teach her Latin, and the little girl eagerly consented. She used to go to him three times a week, but he was always either busy with parish affairs, or scolding the choristers, or breakfasting with a friend; and his niece, in spite of her zeal, never mastered the language.

At home her father taught her a little of his own art, though he had no desire that she should be educated as an artist. Still, she rapidly succeeded with the graving pencils, as with everything else, and would present her relations with specimens of her skill in the shape of flowers or complimentary verses neatly engraved on a well-polished plate. In return, she received a new dress or some such offering. Her mother, simple enough in her own person, was proud of arraying her only child in expensive clothes, far too good for her station in life; but had sense enough not to allow this to engender vanity in the little girl, and on week days would take her to market in the commonest attire, send her round to a neighbouring shop for parsley and lettuces, and expect her to do her share of the cooking.

The miscellaneous reading of this forward child did not, fortunately, raise up a self-confident spirit; on the contrary, it seems to have turned her thoughts from the material to the invisible world, and to have bred an anxiety and timidity of mind, well fitted to receive religious impressions. The 'Lives of the Saints' inspired her, too, with a longing to devote herself to the cause of religion. In her quiet retirement, she felt, even at the age of eleven, the high value of this life, this short, black line of time, so prominent in the bright endless stream of eternity; knew that now was the moment of free-will, now the day of choice, and resolved to make the most of it. She felt, and trembled before the presence of the all-pervading Spirit, and humbly hoped to appease Him.

The period of her first communion was approaching. The doctrine of transubstantiation gives to this sacrament a solemnity even greater than that which invests it in our faith. The strict Romanist held that there was no salvation for those who, being of an age to receive it, neglected to do so. The Church which could absolve readily from the greatest sins could find no pardon for neglect of her own rites. The preparation for an act of faith on which eternity depended was indeed of awful moment; and, impressed with a sense of this, the young girl was dissatisfied with her present life, and longed for the solemn shelter of a convent. One night she threw herself on her knees, and implored her parents to allow her to enter one for the period of her preparation. They consented, and made inquiries as to the best establishment in which to place her, fixing, at last, on that of La Congregation, which had a house in the Rue Neuve St. Etienne, in the Faubourg St. Marcel. Here she entered as a pupil in May 1765. The worthy sisters undertook gratuitously the education of thirty-four young ladies from the age of eighteen down to that of six. Here, among girls who had been sent hither by their parents after the custom of Roman Catholic countries, and who felt but little reverence or enthusiasm in the matter, the sombre child who now entered produced a favourable impression on the sisters. She was placed among the older girls, whom she soon equalled in their studies by unwonted diligence and quickness of apprehension. The calm seclusion of the cloister seemed to cheer and strengthen rather than depress her. The high-walled garden, jealously shut out from the busy, wrangling world beyond; the lofty, dimly-lighted chapel, filled with the swell of solemn music, when from time to time some high sweet woman's voice rose like an angel's above the deep murmur of the organ; the sober silence that reigned through the whole building, all brought out in full glow that peculiar feeling which in woman seems to take the place of actual religion. It was easy to believe that one loved God where there could be no temptation to love the world, and where all that was beautiful and majestic seemed to bring Him near to the humbled spirit. But then it required a certain piety and humility to be truly impressed with these effects. To many of her associates probably they were but tedious and commonplace. The little Manon was happy, too, in her confessor, a kind old man, with more sense than the majority of his class. Perhaps the explanation which Mad. de Sévigné gives for the attachment which women feel for their confessors, namely, that they would rather talk ill of themselves than not at all, may account in part for the affection which the young girl felt for this old man. In after years she could explain very sensibly the impression which all this made upon her.

'It must be confessed,' she writes, 'that the Catholic religion, though little suited to a healthy and enlightened judgment which subjects the objects of its belief to the rules of reason, is well adapted to captivate the imagination, which it strikes by the grand and terrible; while it takes possession of the senses by means of mysterious ceremonies alternately cheerful and melancholy. Eternity, for ever present to the mind of the sectarian, calls him to contemplation, and renders him a severe examiner of good and evil; while, on the other hand, the daily religious exercises and imposing ceremonies rather relieve and support the attention, and offer easy means of advancing towards the end in view. Women have a wonderful facility for performing these religious exercises, and investing ceremonies such as these with everything that can lend them beauty or effect; and the sisters of the convent excelled in this art.'

While she was at the convent a novice took the vows, and the scene so often described, and in which all possible accessories are brought into requisition to heighten the effect of youth, beauty, and gaiety, embracing voluntarily a spiritual death, had a deep effect on the young girl who witnessed it. With some few of the inmates of the convent she formed close friendships. Among these Angélique Boufflers, who went by the convent-name of Ste. Agathe, had been a victim to the vile system of sacrificing a daughter, that her proper portion of the family fortune might go to the sons—a system then even more common in France than now, and one but little better in principle than the female infanticide of India, at which a French mother would probably shudder sincerely enough. But we may ask of sensible people, which is the worse—to drown your little child at the age of one or two in the waters of the Ganges— waters, remember, whose sacred character gives, in the eyes of

Hindu mothers, a kind of sacrificial sanctity to the act—or to condemn them, after the enjoyment of a few years of sunny youth, to perpetual imprisonment, perpetual virginity, and a morbid hankering after active life—to condemn them to this against their wills, and to gild the gallows by the palpable lie that it is a religious life?

But Ste. Agathe had known her destiny from the first. It was the fate of poverty, and she must be resigned to it. After all it was not so very hard to a French girl, for there was but one alternative—forced celibacy on the one hand, or forced marriage, perhaps with a man she hated, on the other. No wonder, when French girls are subjected to such a life, they should console themselves after marriage with all that is frivolous and vain, if not absolutely sinful.

Ste. Agathe grew much attached to her little charge, to whom she gave a duplicate key of her cell, where the thoughtful child devoured such meagre works of devotion as were allowed to a convent miss. The good sisters, still fond of a joke, used to quiz Ste. Agathe on her affection for the little pupil—and why not? They had no one more important to quiz her about. Agathe was then twenty-four years old. Some thirty years later the Revolution released her from the imprisonment of a convent, but too late. It had become a second nature to her, and she was as miserable at leaving her ill-furnished cell as Pélisson was to quit his tamed spiders in the Bastille. Habit reconciles human beings to everything. Affection grows by and depends on habit. Offer them a palace and rob them of their relics, and are they happy? No; even death, which gives heaven in exchange for a wretched life, is looked to by even the most miserable of us with horror.

When, at the end of the year for which she had entered, the young Phlippon left the convent, she was grieved to the heart. She found, too, that her father was too much engaged in the affairs of the commune to which he belonged to attend entirely to his business, and her mother had to take his place, and could not, therefore, give much attention to her daughter. She transferred her, therefore, to her grandmother Phlippon, a good-humoured round-about little widow of sixty-five, who had failed once in trade, and come at last into a moderate fortune. Her sister Angélique lived with her—a meek, enduring, willing creature, with pale face, prominent jaw, and spectacles, who, without murmuring, filled the place of general servant to her more fortunate sister.

With this quiet couple, dwelling in the Ile St. Louis—a dreary, old-fashioned collection of moss-grown streets in the middle of the Seine—the future leader of the Girondists passed a calm life, quite happy if she could get a new book or a fresh nosegay from time to time. It was now the *Philothée* of St. Francis de Sales, 'the most loveable of all the saints,' as she confesses, and, we may add, always a great favourite with the women; now the Manual of St. Augustine, which led her thoughts back from the world into a realm of contemplation. But even now her mind, developing gradually, becoming weaker to imagine but stronger to reason, and apter to observe, began to ask, if not yet to doubt, and the controversial works of Bossuet encouraged the tendency. Does not real, sincere, manly faith imply a previous investigation? Can any of us say that we are *reasonable* believers, and have yet never doubted for a moment? Yet, too often the weak mind has not power to return from its doubts; too often mere inquiry overthrows all faith, and in women especially. In after years Madame Roland confessed that these studies were the first step to infidelity. She passed on to Jansenism, the mildest form of dissent from Romanism, and thence, as if naturally, to the philosophy of Descartes, just as Madame de Grignan, the daughter of Madame de Sévigné, the Jansenist, had before her, become a Cartesian. From Cartesian Madame Roland became Stoic; from Stoic, Deist; and from that she never returned.

How completely her mind was bent on reasoning at this period we may guess from her incapacity for singing, while she eagerly grasped the science of music. Her master was repeatedly saying to her, 'Put more soul into it. You sing a ballad as a man does the Magnificat.' To this Madame Roland with the egotism of an autobiographist, adds, 'The poor man did not see that I had too much soul to put into a song.'

The first thing which inspired a doubt of the truth of

Romanism was the universal damnation pronounced on all who did not adhere to it, whether they had it preached to them or not. This, indeed, is a great stumbling-block in the way of the success of that Church among civilized people, just as it is, perhaps, one of the secrets of its progress among the ignorant and superstitious; and unhappily those who dissent from it on this ground are not content to examine the more liberal doctrines of Protestantism, but fly off at once to philosophy or deism. Even at the present day immense numbers of nominal Romanists in France and Germany are Deists or Atheists; and at a time when the influence of Voltaire's writings was so great and general, it is not surprising that thinking men should have adopted the same course. The love of classical heroism, the admiration of the virtues of Socrates and of the superiority of many heretical writers, made it difficult to believe that perdition would depend on so little as the rejection or ignorance of the doctrines of Rome; and the moment this point was disputed by the inquirer, the Church might count him as lost to her.

To the cruelty of universal perdition succeeded the absurdity of infallibility, as an obstacle to blind belief; and one by one the arrogant assumptions of the Church of Rome were subjected to the test of reason. The young girl felt herself failing, and had recourse to her confessor, who, to save himself the trouble of going into controversy, supplied her with a collection of the defenders of Catholicism, such as Abbadie, Holland, and the Abbé Bergier. She read them and made notes on them, which she left in the volumes as she returned them to the curé. Here, too, she was introduced to the opposite party, and from the defenders themselves learned the doctrines of the accusers of her faith.

It is true that neither her reading nor the spirit of the age under a government which proclaimed by law that there was no God, ever brought Madame Roland to that terrible, hopeless, dreary goal where man, the impotent, the creature, the plaything of circumstance, dares to shout from the midst of his wretchedness that he is an Atheist, that he neither believes in nor cares for a Creator of the universe and a Protector of himself and his fellows. Her life was too pure and simple for such a creed. It has been doubted whether any man, tracking out truth patiently and with the humility attendant on the true student, ever does in his heart believe that there is no God. He may declare it in his works, or preach it openly; but there come moments when, in spite of himself, he trembles before that unknown Power, or in his weakness and misery turns to him for aid with too ready belief. Perhaps, indeed, the very word Atheist should be interpreted as one who lives without God, who *forgets* His existence, rather than one who, making that existence the subject of study, confidently *denies* it at last. The Atheist denies God in his life, but scarcely in his mind; and if we examine the cases of real or asserted atheism, we shall generally find that the lives of its assertors were such as to make them too glad to believe that there was no Judge to condemn them.

But Madame Roland, in later life, confessed that though not an Atheist, there were many unsolved and unsolvable questions on which, in the calm of a chamber and the impassibility of argument, she would agree with a partizan of atheism. Still her heart could never second her mind. 'In the midst of the country,' she wrote, 'and in the contemplation of nature, my heart, moved by it, rises towards the enlivening Principle which animates it, the Intelligence which orders it, the Goodness which in it supplies me with so many delights. And when,' she adds, in her prison cell, 'measureless walls separate me from what I love, and all the evils of society together strike me as if to punish me for having desired its highest good, I look beyond the limits of this life to the reward of our sacrifices and the happiness of meeting again.' One sees that this is not Christianity, nor, in our ideas, even religion; but it is the nearest approach to religion that a Romanist turned Deist can make.

'I could live with the Atheist,' she goes on, 'better than with the devotee, for he reasons more; but he is wanting in feeling, and my soul could not coalesce with his. He is cold to the most enchanting spectacle, and seeks a syllogism, when I can only give thanks.' We see in all this the influence of her reading. Voltaire had taught her to despise, as he himself sneered at, revelation. Rousseau, setting up a faith in the place of that which the other had knocked down, had bid her seek the true revelation in nature itself. It is strange that a woman of her sense should give to such writers the implicit faith which she refused to men like St. Paul and St. John; but this, too, was the fashion of the age. A novelty was demanded even in religion; and they got only a poor miserable revival of the deism of Greece, a faith—if it be a faith and not a feeling —which had turned out an utter failure.

Marie Phlippon seems to have wanted the courage to proclaim or maintain her opinions. Indeed, what Atheist does not feel some qualm in doing so? and she was not even an Atheist. She continued to observe the ceremonial of Christianity, on account, she weakly confesses, of her sex, her age, and her situation. Nay, perhaps, even her affection for her mother restrained her from an open avowal of her want of belief; and we gladly seize hold of such a symptom to show how little zeal there is in infidelity. Her life was morally faultless. She owns, that with the exception of a desire to please—the narrow ambition of a woman—she had no sins to confess to her spiritual father. She might, indeed, have added the worse fault of judging others.

She had already, urged probably by her reading, made many observations on the falsity of social distinctions. On one occasion, these followed on a visit which she made with her grandmother to a certain Madame Boismorel, who being above them in station, treated them with insulting condescension; on another, it was in accompanying a Madlle. d'Hannaches, a dry, disagreeable old maid, who boasted of her family tree, to the houses of certain people in authority, and noticing the attention paid to the birth and name of her companion, while she herself, the daughter of a mere engraver, was slighted. Then, again, she made one short visit to Versailles, where the old *régime*, with all its faults, called forth her contempt and disgust. 'I preferred the statues in the garden,' she says, 'to the people I saw there.' Lastly, even the relatives of her intimate friend, Sophie de Cannet, who in their small way were comparatively aristocratic, excited her indignation. One was proud, another so fond of money and so insensible to fame, that seeing the success of a tragedy, written by a relation of his, he exclaimed, 'Why did not my father teach me to write tragedies? I could have knocked them off on the Sundays.' Certainly the state of society at that time favoured the revolutionary sentiments which it produced; and while the despised working classes were meditating on the 'virtues' of ancient Greece, birth, rank, and wealth were running into greater extravagancies and more pitiful absurdities than ever.

But whatever her reflections on men and nature, Marie Phlippon had soon a most practical part to play in the world; and she who had hitherto been 'wedded in the spirit' to Socrates and Alcibiades, was now sought after by the butchers, bakers, and jewellers of her own class with a view to more substantial matrimony. Like the young ladies of the present day, who are all 'soul,' she seems never to have been positively in love. She confesses that at an early age she was captivated by the voice and face of a young artist, named Tuboral, who came to her father's shop on matters of business. Whenever, hidden in her little alcove, she heard his gentle voice, she would steal out, and pretend to be looking for a pencil or some other trifle which she was supposed to have left in the workshop. The young man, who was one-and-twenty, and had '*une figure tendre*,' blushed at seeing her more than she did, but as no intimacy arose nothing ensued from these little meetings.

Her appearance at seventeen—the marrying age in France—was of that kind which attracts Frenchmen, less on account of its beauty than of its interest. Her features though not ill proportioned, were not in themselves beautiful. Her profile was better than her full face, which was round rather than oval. The point of the nose was thick, and in the dilating nostril you saw more ambition than taste. The mouth was large, but the smile soft, and the expression gentle and kind. The brow was high, broad, and calm, as if enclosing a large brain. Above it the hair parted freely, and fell in long luxuriant curls over her shoulders. The eyes of a deep-blue, which looked in some lights brown, were full of thought and animation. The eyebrow was peculiarly elevated, dark, and full, so that it gave to the face an expression of frankness and loftiness combined with vigour. The whole frame of the woman had more strength than loveliness about it, the bust being full and high, the shoulders broad and manly, the figure slight, tall, and supple. But in the thoughtful and daring expression of the face was a charm, which in after years gave her a command over the wild spirits of the Revolution, and made even the men, who despised woman as a chattel, her willing servants.

Added to this face, she had a fortune of twenty thousand francs, being an only child; and it was natural that many suitors should seek her, some from admiration of herself and her talents, others from affection for her ducats.

At the age of eighteen, however, she was attacked by the small-pox; but though the illness was long and severe, her face on recovery, bore no traces of the disease. The chief effect of the attack was to interfere with those matrimonial projects which had hitherto been made for her.

These were so numerous that we need only cite a few instances. Her first admirer was her music-master, a Spaniard of colossal figure, with hands as rough as those of Esau. He announced himself as a noble of Malaga, whose misfortunes had driven him to teach the guitar, and employed a friend to make the offer for him. The ambitious father was not likely to listen to the proposal of a penniless teacher, and, after the manner of the day, ordered him never to set foot in the house again. A multitude of offers followed this one; and the jeweller, who enjoyed with a certain pride the popularity of his daughter, used to bring her the letters of proposal to answer: that is to say, she replied to them in her father's name, and he copied out her answers with his own pen. The next admirer was the butcher the family dealt with. His second wife had lately died, and he had amassed a fortune of some two thousand pounds, which he wished to increase. Accordingly, for about a whole summer he regularly met Madlle. Phlippon and her mother in their walks, dressed in a fine black suit with very good lace, and made them a dignified bow, without venturing to accost them. At length the usual manœuvring was effected through the medium of a person called Madlle. Michon, who boldly offered the butcher's fortune and business to the consideration of the ambitious jeweller. M. Phlippon's ambition was limited to a love of money; the butcher had it to offer, and he favoured his suit. But his daughter was not so easily won. Now that marriage was so much talked of, she made up her mind to wed a man of her ideal cast—a philosopher, or at least a thinker, some one above the common mould. This was all very well; but it is amusing to see the contempt which this girl, who fretted so angrily at the condescension of the well-born, felt for those of her own class. She confesses that she abhorred trade, and would never marry a trader. What she aspired to does not appear; what she finally accepted was indeed a poverty of choice. But to return: the butcher had wasted his time and worn out his clothes to no purpose. *Il fut congedié*, and there was an end to it.

An end, at least, to the hopes of the man of joints; but only a beginning to a difference of feeling between father and daughter, which later developed into absolute ill-will. Phlippon knew nothing and cared nothing for romance, learning, philosophy, or even feeling. He loved his daughter after a fashion; but like many a father, English as well as French, he wished to make that love an excuse for murdering her. He wanted to say to the world, 'See how anxious I am for my daughter's future comfort and ease; I will not let her marry any but a rich man.' But he knew well enough that that daughter preferred, as any girl of right feeling must do, to marry a man she could respect to all the ducats that butchers or jewellers could produce in the good city of Paris. Phlippon cared not a whisp for his daughter. That pretence was all sham. He cared only to have a wealthy son-in-law, a grand-son who should be an honour of wealth to his race, a connection in short, of which he could be proud; and in his vulgarity he could not be proud of high talents, fine honour, real breeding, and noble worth, but only of that eternal relay of gold louis and silver écus, which to his narrow mind represented all the rest. But why rail against Phlippon? Honest—yet as the event showed, not excellent—workman as he was, he did no more than half the fathers in England are doing this very day;

and those too. some of them, as proud as Lucifer, of birth and position. Just as the jeweller of the Quai des Orfèvres shut his door upon the needy music master, who had nothing but his guitar to offer, and hugged to his bosom the greasy flesh-monger, so my friend the baronet thrusts from his house the aspiring young tutor, and greets with a smile the wealthy representative of the great brewing firm of Malt, Barm, Kilderkin, and Co.; and my friend the baronet sees no vulgarity in so doing.

Marie Phlippon had not much romance in the matter. She knew well enough that she must marry a man whom she had no chance of loving before the wedding, but she wished at least to wed with one whose acquirements should be on a par with her own, who could understand her, and be a companion to her; and as she could not hope to discover much of such qualities from the slight intercourse which French manners permitted between herself and an aspirant for her hand and fortune, she was constrained to judge by circumstances rather than personal recommendations. So when a young physician, named Gardanne, was mentioned to her as a suitor, she rather caught at the idea, thinking that one of that profession must at least have a certain amount of instruction, and a certain knowledge of books. Hitherto she had often noticed that at church a pair of male eyes were fixed steadily upon her, or that in her walks with her mother a bow of peculiar meaning would be given by some stranger; and when after these tokens she saw her parents in anxious colloquy, she guessed what was the purport of these attentions. She was now to undergo another kind of manœuvre.

Walking one day to the Luxembourg with Madame Phlippon, she was suddenly stopped by her mother exclaiming that it was sure to rain, though the sky appeared calm enough. They happened—of course by accident—to be opposite the house of a lady friend, Madlle. de la Barre (it is generally a single lady of a certain age who undertakes these delicate transactions). They at once took refuge from the imaginary shower in this house, were served with a collation, and had not been seated many minutes, when, by pure accident, the young physician and a gentleman friend happened to call on the maiden lady. The doctor chatted away, ill at ease, cracked a bon-bon, and remarked that he loved *sweets*. This was considered a favourable sign, and papa Phlippon was ready to join their hands and pronounce a blessing at once; but his daughter did not encourage the bashful young doctor, partly because the wig, then worn by the faculty, gave him a ridiculous appearance. However, she expressed no repugnance this time, and the affair was on the point of being settled. It proceeded so far that the young lady and her mamma took the usual fortnight's journey to the country, in order to be out of the way while papa made inquiries into the character and position of the aspirant. This the worthy jeweller, who was not quite pleased with the match, did only too scrupulously; wrote letters of inquiry to Provence, the country of the physician, and even set people to take observations of his conduct at home. These movements came to the doctor's knowledge, and he was naturally indignant. The various go-betweens interfered, and as a simple consequence quarrelled; and so, one way or another, the young girl was relieved from the necessity of deciding for herself as to the wearer of the ugly wig.

New matches might soon have been put forward, and the same part have been played again and again, but for a terrible blow which now fell on the family. In the spring of 1775, when Marie was about twenty-one, her excellent mother was suddenly struck with paralysis. She had long been unwell, and had shown symptoms of unnatural languor and weakness. The attack was fearfully violent and ended in death. The daughter, mad with grief, lay ill for many days after this event. In losing her mother she lost all her family. Her father had never merited much affection, and he soon became utterly estranged from her. He had already taken to bad habits, from which his child had sought in vain to wean him. He passed his evenings, no one knew where, away from home, and was cold to his wife. Her death seemed to recall him for a time, but he soon relapsed into his old ways; and now that the restraint his wife had imposed was gone, became worse than ever.

Her mother's death left Marie to a solitude which she could only fill up by reading. Her father found little society at home. The daughter perceived that he needed it, and strove to make herself more a companion to him. But this was impossible. Phlippon caring for little but money and amusement could not enter at all into her ideas, nor she into his. He soon formed a connection with a person of bad character, wasted his money, and to make it good took to gambling. His daughter was left completely alone, but her mind seems to have taken a more religious tone after her mother's sudden death, and she read with avidity the works of Bossuet, Flétcher, Bourdaloue, and Massillon. She was vexed to find how much these celebrated preachers talked of the 'mysteries' of their faith, rather than of the high morals of Christianity, and she determined to try if a practical sermon were not easy to write. She wrote one on the love of one's neighbour, showed it to her uncle, the abbé, and received considerable commendation from him. What has become of this curious essay we do not know, but feel convinced that it would, if extant, have a peculiar interest, coming from the pen of a woman, who even in prison, with the guillotine waiting for her, could write in so masterly a manner as that of her Memoirs.

In the following December, however, began a new phase of her life. Her dearest friend at the convent had been Sophie Cannet, who living now with her family at Amiens, corresponded regularly with Marie Phlippon, and was on the most affectionate terms with her, whenever she came up to Paris. Sophie, lamenting the stupidity of the society at Amiens, had often talked to her bosom friend of one exception in the person of a well-informed and clever man of middle age, who however was not much at home, passing several months of the year in Paris, and often making longer journeys into Italy or Germany. To this person, on the other hand, she had praised the talents of her old schoolfellow, showed him her portrait, and raised in him a desire to make her acquaintance. At last one day in the winter of 1775 he told her that he was going to Paris, and offered to take a letter for her to her friend Marie. In this manner Marie Phlippon made the acquaintance of M. Roland de la Platière. The introduction from her bosom friend was a sufficient recommendation; but there was nothing in the appearance or manners of M. Roland to excite any feeling keener than respect. He was past forty, tall, thin, and yellow, with a bald head and rather stiff manner. When, however, he opened his mouth, he at once charmed the delicate ear of Marie Phlippon by the softness of his voice; and she confesses that attraction with her entered by the ears rather than the eyes. His conversation, though calm and simple, was that of a thinking man. He was fond of being listened to, and Marie had the rare and excellent gift of listening well. In short their minds had much in common; and the conversation of a man who had travelled and thought was an enjoyment which this young woman had rarely met with among the friends of her parents. For eight or nine months he repeated his visits, not indeed very frequently, but making long ones when he came. In the summer of 1776 he made a journey to Italy, and before leaving begged to be allowed to deposit his MSS. with Madlle. Phlippon, till he should return to claim them.

This peculiar mark of esteem was not lost upon her: and the MSS. left with her served to make her more fully acquainted with M. Roland's mind. They consisted of notes of travel, reflections, and outlines of works, and displayed strength of character, strict principles, austere probity, mingled with taste and learning. In addition to this he wrote her a series of learned letters from Italy, intended as notes for a work on that country, and utterly free from any touch of romance or mark of affection.

The previous life of Roland had been sensible rather than romantic. He was of a family which though in trade were rather proud of their claims to antiquity, a weakness from which the austere philosopher was not himself free, since in 1784 he attempted to revive his lost dignity by applying for letters of nobility. He was undoubtedly a vain man, as he proved in subsequent transactions; but of all vanity this pride of family was perhaps the most contemptible in a man affecting republican principles. He was the youngest of five brothers, and there were only two careers open to him—to embark in trade or take holy orders. He shrank from both, and to avoid being compelled to embrace a mode of life which he detested, he ran away from home at the age of nineteen. He arrived at Nantes, and engaged himself with a shipbuilder to go to India. Fortunately, perhaps, for his future fame. he burst a blood-vessel and was obliged to abandon the project. At Rouen he had a relation named Godinot, the superintendent of a large manufactory, and at his suggestion, Roland entered this establishment. He distinguished himself by his zeal, activity, and valuable head-piece, and worked up till he was himself appointed superintendent of a factory at Amiens. The government soon detected his abilities in matters connected with manufactures, and employed him to inspect those of Germany and Italy; and in this manner he was enabled to travel abroad, a rare advantage in those days among his fellow-countrymen.

After an absence of a year and a half in Italy, Roland returned to Paris, and renewed his visits at the house of Phlippon. Marie found in him a friend worth having. In his severe respectability she saw the *beau-idéal* of a philosopher, and as she had long since resolved to marry for mind rather than heart, she readily listened to the declaration of attachment which Roland at last uttered in her ears. She accepted for herself; but, with a self-denial which was perhaps the less trying, because her liking for Roland was purely based on esteem and admiration, and had nothing to do with love, she told him honestly how poor a match this would be for him in a worldly point of view. Her father had dissipated his fortune and hers, he was daily losing more than he made by his business, and had heavy debts to encumber him. Roland, very honourably for him, only insisted the more on the marriage. Though he was perhaps incapable of anything like a passion, and would have thought it unworthy of his dignity to indulge one, he was not insensible to the attractions of a handsome girl twenty years his junior, with a mind vastly superior to his own, and who freely returned his admiration. He returned to Amiens, wrote to the jeweller to demand his daughter's hand, and was bluntly and even insolently refused. Phlippon had never liked Roland, which perhaps was natural; he had seen in him a severe moralist, who would have no pity for his father-in-law's vices and follies: Roland was nearly of his own age, and he was jealous of his superior mind and character. Considering that the new applicant was in a far better position than the aspiring butcher, and was likely to rise higher still, and that his own daughter had nearly reached the (in France) hopeless age of spinsterhood, five-and-twenty, the refusal of Phlippon can be accounted for only by a very strong personal dislike of Roland.

The daughter, however, was old enough now to take the matter into her own hands. Though she could not marry against her father's wishes, she could take an independent step of another kind. From her mother's fortune she had saved about twenty pounds per annum, and resolving to live on this meagre income apart from a father with whom she could no longer agree, she retired to the Convent of La Congrégation, hired a small garret there, and set to work to parcel out her twenty pounds in such a manner as to cover the costs of her wants for a year. It can be well imagined that her economy was very severe. Her dinner, which she cooked herself, consisted of potatoes, rice, and a few vegetables, and with this she was fain to be content. In her garret she shut herself up with her books, receiving only the society of Ste. Agathe, her old friend of former days. Roland still wrote to her affectionately, but for six months did not repeat his proposal. He then came to Paris, and had an interview with her across the jealous grating of the convent door, and was more determined than ever to make this fascinating woman of spirit his wife. The independent position which she held as the inmate of a convent released her from her father's control, and she accepted, and was married to, the man whom she esteemed the most in the world. That there was little more than esteem on either side may be well conceived: and this match, founded on the basis of cold regard, would have been a failure but for the high moral principles of Madame Roland. She confesses that she 'often felt that similarity was wanting' between them: that if they lived quietly she had often 'very trying hours to pass,' and if they went into society she was 'liked by persons, some of whom, she feared, might affect her too closely.' The hard work which her husband exacted, and she willingly undertook, was the only safeguard against cherishing such thoughts as these; but the fact that they should often have arisen, proves how completely the union was one of reason rather than love.

Thus ended the girlhood of Marie Phlippon, much in the manner that one might expect—cold, rational, intellectual, and uncomfortable to the last, yet, in its very abnegation of comfort, grand and consistent with her whole character. Without, perhaps, knowing it, she was deeply ambitious, and she chose by instinct the path which should lead her to a clear field for her ambition.

The first year of their marriage was passed in Paris, the next two at Amiens. One child, a girl, was the whole fruit of it; but the birth of this child, and the delicate health of Roland, were two new ties to her husband, which even developed her esteem into something of wifely affection. In 1784 they moved to Lyons, where Roland had obtained a similar appointment to the one he held at Amiens. In the neighbourhood of this city was the Clos La Platière, the humble paternal mansion of the Roland family, who took their *surnom de noblesse* from it, just as if Smith, who has half an acre of kitchen garden in Hog-lane, or Jones, who has inherited a two-roomed cottage in Green Bottom, should appear in the London world as Smith de Hog-lane, or Green-Bottom Jones, Esq. This silly pretension is rare in England, though, we believe, common in Scotland, where every Thomson or Johnson gives himself an air of antiquity by tacking on to his name the 'of' some few yards of land or tumble-down manse. The Revolution tried to root out this vanity of the people in France, but in vain. The people who left 'Monsieur le Comte de St. Cyr' without any surname by the declaration that there were no more Monsieurs, no more Counts, no more 'de's,' no more Saints, and lastly no more *Sires*, were still prone to such little weaknesses as that with which Roland called himself Roland *de la Platière;* and in the present day no butcher, baker, or candlestick-maker, however republican in sentiment, retires from trade and buys a petty freehold without instantly claiming a 'de something or other to beautify his humble 'Vidal' or 'Lefèvre.'

In this quiet country nook, however, Madame Roland *de la Platière* came out in more amiable colours than she had ever appeared in. Always ready to sacrifice herself for the good of others, and discovering that she was the only person in the neighbourhood who knew anything of medicine, she was ready to obey the most extravagant claims on her time and trouble, and would go three or four leagues at any moment to relieve a sick peasant. In 1789 she passed twelve days without taking off her clothes once, attending by the bed-side of her husband, who was dangerously ill, and this devotion raised a new bond of affection between the husband and wife. In this year, too, the first echoes of the Revolution reached them in their retirement, and both sprang up joyfully to greet what they regarded as the emancipation of suffering mankind. Roland was soon famous for his opinions in Lyons; and that city sent him as her first deputy to the Constituent Assembly. On the 20th of February, 1791, Madame Roland returned once more to Paris, where for two short years she was to lead, and be the soul of, a new movement, which repaid her zeal, as it did that of so many other disciples, with the knife of the guillotine. Thus at the age of thirty-seven her private life, which would have left her without a name in history, ended: and she began the brief brilliant career which has surrounded with a halo of blood-red light.

The rise of the French Revolution is too well known to need a review here; but it is necessary to show how the Rolands were drawn into the circle of the Girondins, and came to take so leading a part in the movements of that party.

The soul and originator of it was Brissot, a man of some virtues, more vices, but faithful to the last to the cause of the republic. He was the son of a pastrycook at Chartres. Born a democrat (unless making tarts and brioches be claimed as the aristocratic part of the business of a baker), a democrat by principles, education, convictions, he had yet that same aristocratic vanity which induced Roland to add 'de la Platière' to his plebeian name. Brissot, ashamed of his, assumed the cognomen of De Warville. He received a good education, and turned to literature as a means of living. He had great talents, and a powerful pen, but he used both unscrupulously for money, writing on every possible subject with little regard to political principle, and even, so he was accused, inditing libels for the press. He was sent to London by Turgot on a secret mission, and there became editor of the 'Courrier de l'Europe,' a paper at that time bearing a not very good reputation. He was there associated with a set of foreigners of the worst character; and if the accusations against him be true, he himself sank so low as to embezzle sums of money, and to have led a vicious life in the purlieus of London. At the first symptoms of the Revolution he returned to Paris, and became the editor of a revolutionary paper, ' La Patriote Français,' and in this paper went so far, that even Robespierre, who at that time desired liberty and not anarchy, reproached him with kindling a dangerous flame. Brissot was attacked in the papers; his character and early iniquities exposed; and though he defended himself ably, and his courageous political stand made him friends, he was never quite exculpated. Madame Roland was among those who saw in him the bold leader of her own party, a zealous soldier of liberty, and refused to lend an ear to the stories of his former days. He had some redeeming points: a tender affection for a girl he had married, in spite of the opposition of his family, and a courage which he maintained even on the scaffold. Like Madame Roland, he believed in God, and confessed this belief by the side of the guillotine, adding that he died for it. She says of him: 'He is the best of mortals, a good husband, tender father, faithful friend, and upright citizen: his society is as agreeable as his character is easy: bold even to imprudence, gay, simple, ingenuous as a boy of fifteen, he was made to live with the wise and be the dupe of the bad.'

Brissot had from time to time sent Roland copies of his works, and an acquaintance was thus formed between them even before they met in the Constituent Assembly. Madame Roland was rather shocked at his want of dignity, so different from the sedate, old-gentlemanly bearing of her husband, and at that levity of manner, which the life of an adventurer invariably gives in time. But Brissot's courage and love of liberty were more than equivalents in the eyes of the Rolands for this levity of manner, and he became their intimate friend. He brought with him to their house a better man, and fellow-townsman, Pétion—afterwards called King Pétion, when, as Mayor of Paris, he sat in state at the Palais Royal—who had already achieved a name by his speeches. Pétion and Brissot were the friends of La Fayette, and sincere lovers of liberty.

Another intimate, and more than intimate, of Madame Roland was Buzot. Young, handsome, and even elegant, he had none of the coarseness, none of the ferocity, of the heroes of the Revolution. He was by nature a gentleman, gentle in manner, in heart, in hopes. Like Madame Roland, he had long groaned at the corruption of the court and aristocracy, and the degradation of the people. He longed ardently for the freedom of his country, but he would not buy it at the cost of blood and anarchy. She has drawn his character in the most pleasing colours: 'An impassioned observer of nature, feasting his imagination with all the charms she can offer, and his soul with the principles of the most touching philosophy, he seems made to obtain and enjoy domestic happiness. He would forget the universe in the pleasure of home virtues with a heart worthy of him. But once launched upon public life, he ignores all but the rules of severe justice, and defends them at the cost of all. Readily indignant at injustice, he persecutes it warmly, and will never make a compromise with crime. A friend of humanity, susceptible of the tenderest affections, and capable of the sublimest impulses and noblest resolutions, he comes forward as a republican; but as a severe judge of individuals, and slow in developing his regard for them, he gives it to few. This reserve, combined with the energy with which he expresses himself, has brought upon him the accusation of pride, and made him many enemies.' 'Buzot is the kindest man on earth to his friends, the most bitter opponent of charlatans.' He detested and opposed the excesses of the revolutionists, and in their turn they accused him of a partiality for royalism. He and Pétion perished even more terribly than those of their companions **who** mounted the scaffold. After the condemnation of the moderate Girondins, they took refuge, in company with Guadet, Barbaroux, and Salles, at the house of Madame Bouquey, at St. Emilion, near Bordeaux. Thence they were hunted by the soldiers, and rushed into the fields and woods. Barbaroux shot himself, and was dragged back, still half alive, to Bordeaux, where the guillotine put an end to his misery. The gleaners some days after found remnants of garments, clotted masses of tangled hair, bones, and flesh, about the fields. Whose were these? The wolves had been down from the hills. Had they devoured Pétion and Buzot, who had escaped the wolves of the Reign of Terror? None knew, but a silent belief that it was so, passed through the country. Buzot and Pétion were heard of no more. To be torn to pieces by wild animals was not much worse than to be massacred by their own kind. In one sense it was better. These men had loved their own fellow-men; they had never loved the wolves of the forest. It is better to die by a hated, than by a loved hand. Perhaps it was better to be torn to death bit by bit by wolves than to be carried to the scaffold amid the derisive jeers of the people they had sought to lead to better things.

The house of Madame Roland was chosen as a rendezvous for these patriots chiefly on account of its vicinity to their homes. They met there four times a week in the evening The quiet, modest wife sat apart at a little table, working, or writing letters, but listening with both ears. None of the party suspected that this gentle woman was to play so prominent a part in the drama of their power and their fall. She who had dreamed of liberty as a glorious reprieve, who had thought of a Platonic republic, of the establishment of a grand reign of free thought and noble laws, was shocked and almost disgusted at the levity and bravura of these new-fledged patriots, who spoke of the constitution as a game in their hands. Often she longed to be up and speaking boldly among them. The words of her own husband, so calm and unenthusiastic, irritated her to frenzy. She saw, or dreamed of, purer, bolder motives, and could not sit to listen to such worldly prudence. She was a woman, not a man. While they strove to be practical and real, she longed to be grand and ideal. Yet she had to curb her tongue, and to learn from them the worldliness of even a Republican. The example of antiquity, the theories of Plato, the dreams of her youth, must be quenched in the strong, vulgar necessity of the times. She listened and said nothing.

There came, however, a new man among this small circle, and his character inspired her with hope. Small, feeble, and angular in figure, with an ugly, but not hideous face, heavy brows, sharp eyes sunk deep within the forehead, yet glaring forth with a terrible fire; a small, sharp, impetuous nose, puffing at the nostrils with a wild anxiety; a large, thin-lipped mouth, without passion, with no token of sympathy or affection, and with a sneer grafted there from youth upwards, and a strong, selfish determination that seemed to ask all earth and hell for its own —for of heaven it had no ambition—Robespierre, the king of blood, the apostle of hate. came among these men with a dominant resolution.

In their meetings he was a silent listener. He gathered up the gist of all that was there proposed and advanced it as his own at the Assembly. Yet Madame Roland saw in him at the first a sincere friend of liberty. He was born at Arras, of an honest, respectable family. The bishop of the diocese defrayed the expenses of his education, little thinking he was preparing a man who should denounce all religion as childish. When he came to Paris there was nothing to recommend him. He was a poor speaker compared with the excited men of the day; talked bad French; and when he spoke at all, had all the obstinacy and determination of a man whose mind was made up and whose object was long since fixed upon. Biting his nails, and grinning calmly at all that passed, he waited for the more enthusiastic spirits to clear the way. They talked of the Republic. Robespierre asked what a Republic meant. Such a man, with some fine fancies of the beauties of liberty, but selfish and unsympathising, was just fitted to play the part he afterwards did play without respect for persons or care for friends. He was, in fact, incapable of friendship, as he was insensible to kindness. The man who sent Madame Roland to the scaffold had been offered safety by the same woman in the hour of need.

After the massacre of the Champ de Mars, he had been accused of conspiring with the originators of the petition of forfeiture, and was obliged to conceal himself. Madame Roland, who knew the young man's hiding-place, went to him to offer him an asylum in her own house. He was gone; but Madame Roland, believing him worthy of her sympathy, sought out her friend Buzot, and begged him to do his best to save the suspected man. Buzot agreed to do so, and in after years he, like Madame Roland, was the victim of his ingratitude.

Such society, if society it can be called, did Madame Roland, the daughter of the jeweller, receive in her salon, and watch with a yearning in their earliest struggles after liberty and reason. Roland had a good reputation among these men. He was disinterested, and true to the highest principles of freedom. He represented the almost old-fashioned ideas which had oozed up timidly under the *ancien régime*, the aspirations for a perfect republic or a pure constitution. He was calm, silent, secure as a rock, a philosopher rather than politician. He was, in fact, a safe man, one whom in days when every man's hand was against his brother could be trusted to perform the part his principles dictated without the ambition to shine. At times he was brilliant, but no one knew that his wife had inspired him; at times he was bold, but few guessed that Madame Roland had pushed him on. It was this secure character which led the Girondins to choose him as Minister of the Interior.

At the dissolution of the Constituent Assembly, the Rolands had returned to their seclusion at La Platière; but having once tasted the excitement of political life, they could not long remain in a small country village, and soon returned to Paris. In the mean time, Vergniaud and Brissot, the leading spirits of the Revolution, had overthrown first M. de Narbonne, and then M. de Lessart. The poor king, weak in his despair, and willing to make any concession to popular feeling, determined to choose a ministry from among his foes. The victorious party sought out men who were likely to serve without displacing them —tools not masters. They fixed on Roland for the interior, and Dumouriez for foreign affairs.

Roland was too vain to see the position in which his party

held him; but Dumouriez, less blind, was glad to use this office as a stepping-stone to a conquest over that very party. Dumouriez was a dashing, handsome soldier, who had passed his life in various adventures, all more or less romantic. An unfortunate love affair had been his first incentive to ambition. He had fallen desperately in love with a beautiful cousin; his father had forbidden their union. The young girl retired to a convent, and her lover took poison, which, unfortunately for his future name in history, did not take the desired effect. Awake to his folly, but not cured of his love, he sought relief in action. In Corsica, Portugal, and Poland he accepted missions which were half diplomatic and half military, and played more honourably with his sword than with his portfolio. He was told that his beloved one had given him up, and was about to take the veil, and out of pique entered on a new connection. On his return to France he was sent to the Bastille for having too well carried out his instructions, but after the imprisonment of a year his sentence was commuted to an exile at Caen in Normandy. Here in a convent he found again the cousin whom he had so long loved, learned that rumour had been false, that she had neither forgotten him nor taken the veil, and then married her. In time he was appointed commandant of Cherbourg; and it is interesting to learn that he first formed those plans of fortifying that harbour which the present Emperor has lately completed. By the time the Revolution broke out he had reached the rank of general, and was fifty years of age, yet gay and adventurous as ever.

Such was the man who, on being introduced to Madame Roland, thought to win more than her esteem, even her affection. But her keen observation detected his careless ambition. 'Beware of this man,' she said to Roland; 'he has a false eye, and must be mistrusted more than any one. He has expressed great satisfaction at your being called to the ministry, but I should not wonder if he got you turned out one day.'

Roland, however, trusted him implicitly. This staid philosopher entered on his duties with secret delight, and was resolved to show the king what a Republican was. He appeared at his first audience in a black coat, round hat, and dirty shoes. The king was disgusted, but Dumouriez turned it into a joke. The chamberlain pointed indignantly to the dusty shoes which had no buckles. 'Ah!' laughed Dumouriez; 'all is lost! No more etiquette; no more monarchy.'

Madame Roland now took her place as the centre of the ministry in its private councils. They met at her house every Friday, and the cats'-paws of the Girondist party elicited her contempt. There was De Grave in the war-office, a mild, sleepy man, walking delicately on the tips of his toes; Lacoste, a commissioner for the navy, a bureaucrat of the old school, cold, respectable, but narrow-minded; Duranton at the head of justice, a doting old woman; Clavière, the finance minister, irascible and self-opinioned; and, lastly, Dumouriez, with more talent but less principle than any of them. With these men, the actual holders of office, came those who were the real masters of the ground, the chiefs of the Girondin Club, Brissot, Pétion, Guadet, Gensonné, and Vergniaud; but Robespierre was no longer a visitor at Madame Roland's. His own ambition clashed with that of the moderate Girondins, who wished for a constitution while waiting for a democracy. He detested Brissot too, who from his small room on the fourth story, could quietly make or depose ministers. He saw that the government, which the nation supposed to be carried on in the Assembly, and the king's council-chamber, really existed in the unpretending salon of Madame Roland. He had withdrawn and joined the rival Jacobins, where he led on Danton, Marat, and Camille Desmoulins.

It was, however, Madame Roland who drove Dumouriez from her salons. She had the penetration to see that, clever and daring as he was, he was not sincere in his adhesion to the Girondins, and suggested to her husband suspicions of him, which were imparted to the rest of the club. The Girondins were all respectable in their lives. Dumouriez was openly profligate, and it was said that he wasted money, which had been granted for the secret service, on his own pleasures. The Girondins, fearful that this open immorality would bring opprobrium on the cause of liberty, in which they believed they were labouring, remonstrated with him at Madame Roland's. Dumouriez treated the matter laughingly, but did not again come to the house.

This first Ministry of the People, as it was called, was by no means successful. The ministers might be diligent, but, with the exception of Dumouriez, were unfit to cope with the royal party. The councils at the palace were turned into mere parties of conversation. The poor king, forced to give in on every point to his new ministers, contented himself with accepting the decrees, and then chatted and even laughed with his directors. Roland was delighted with his affability: but his wife who longed for the establishment of a systematic democracy, saw that all was merely a delay of the great crisis. She took a step which has been much blamed. She foresaw that the nation would one day call these trifling ministers to account. She wished to save her husband; and with this view persuaded him to take to the council, and read to the king, a letter which she herself dictated, and which, if produced in the hour of need, would prove to the country that Roland had protested against the king's delays. The occasion of it was especially the refusal of Louis to sanction the decree against the nonjuring priests. The country demanded it with threatening gestures. France was in a ferment greater than ever. The Revolution went on while the monarchy survived. The letter called upon the king earnestly to take the proper measures to pacify the people. As we read it, it was sensible and excusable; but it has been affirmed that Roland and his wife, in thus providing a future defence for themselves, laid up a protest which would criminate the monarch Roland was serving. His own party even viewed it in this light. The letter was read, but the king held out; his conscience forbade him to sanction a step which he held to be destructive of the church he belonged to. At last the moment that Madame Roland had foreseen arrived. The king remained inflexible, and dismissed from the ministry Roland, Clavière, and Servan. Roland rose in the Assembly, and read out his letter. It was applauded; the king was blamed more than ever. Roland left the chamber a hero, and affected to think he had fallen by his own boldness.

Thus ended Roland's first ministry and his wife's first movements in the Revolution. Her husband's fall increased rather than diminished her influence. In an apartment high up in a house in the Rue St. Jacques, the young spirits of the day, yearning, some for fame, some for power, some for the establishment of that democracy of which they had long dreamed, collected round her, attracted by her talents, her enthusiasm, and her beauty. She received the ministers and the leaders of the Gironde at dinner twice a week; but, with the same modesty she had always shown, maintained a reserve proper to her sex, for she was the only woman present at these meetings. Her female friends were always few, the wife of Pétion being amongst the most intimate of them. There was, in fact, little female society at this time. The court circles were too depressed to enjoy it, and the *bourgeoisie* were too intent on the struggle which was going on to care for merely social meetings. The gatherings of clubs in which stormy debates arose took the place of balls, parties, and the amusements of more peaceful times.

But of the political society of the day Madame Roland was the one centre. She was, in fact, almost the only woman who appeared in it, and every new 'patriot' made a point of being introduced to her. Though the Jacobins were rising rapidly into popularity and power, the Girondists still and for long after held the field. They represented order, the constitution, and the medium between the king and the country. Their position as a ministry made them the apex of all the society of Paris, and the person who rallied them was Madame Roland. It was a proud position for the jeweller's daughter, yet she can scarcely be accused of abusing it. Her counsels to Roland, the measures she concerted with his party, the impulse she gave to their movements, were all, if not good and right in the abstract, the best in her view. She contrived to act on the principles with which she set out—the desire for liberty, equality, and fraternity in her country, the hatred of old pride, the contempt for old prejudices, and the hope for new institutions which should inaugurate a perfect Republic.

Even if our space permitted us to follow Madame Roland

from the first ministry through the storms that now burst over France, and deluged it with a rain of blood, to do so would be only to recapitulate history. Madame Roland is from this period an historical character. Without any intimate friends but statesmen, actual or future, with no near relations left but her husband and daughter, she quenched her private in her public life. Madame Roland was now one of the Gironde faction, and in reality its soul. Her position as a woman gave her more power to move, more independence of action than the others had.

The times were critical. The Gironde, no longer connected with the monarch, now plotted to establish a liberal democracy, and Madame Roland was their most enthusiastic counsellor. The morality of this conspiracy need scarcely be discussed here. The right of nations to depose their sovereigns, and even to subvert the institutions of ages, may be admitted in a country which glories in its two revolutions. The right to do so by bloodshed, terrorism, and the lowest weapons of rebellion will not be admitted by the wise. It must first, too, be shown what a nation is, and proved that the nation, in its entirety, wills and effects the change. It cannot be admitted that a mob of the ferocious and unthinking, roused by the voices of demagogues, is a nation, or even a fitting representative of a nation. The Girondins had recourse to such a rabble, to the scum of Paris, to alter the whole constitution of France. They had recourse to the violent measures which this rabble, roused and let loose, could not be restrained from taking. Such a revolution, thus effected, was in fact nothing more than the most shameful tyranny to the rest of France. If France had wanted to overthrow the monarch, France would have done it in time. To impose the will of a furious mob on France was worse despotism than any French king had ever been guilty of. The Gironde knew what they were about: and their act was punished by the very hands they had employed. The hell-dogs they set upon the royal family turned on themselves when blood was wanting; and the Girondins were among the earliest victims of a reign of terror which they had first made possible.

The excuse, if any there be, for this conspiracy, was the danger of delay. Already the army under La Fayette and Dumouriez was being driven out of Belgium,—always a disastrous field for French armies,—and the Austrians, it was reckoned, would in six weeks be in Paris, the monarchy be reinstated with more absolute powers than ever, and all hope of a constitution—still more of the democracy—lost for ever. The king's refusal to sanction the decrees was looked upon as a shilly-shallying means of gaining time. He was in correspondence with the enemies of the Revolution. Peaceful means had already been tried; the decisions of the Assembly had been nullified by the king's scruples or obstinacy. There was but one alternative—to wait till Austrian bayonets should foist upon them the despotism they feared, and maintain, as they have since done in more than one case, a dynasty of *fainéant* Bourbons, or to strike at the throne itself. When we of 1860 look at the countries where the line of this family has been supported by foreign aid, and compare them with what France now is, we may well say with reverence that the Revolution, bloody and frantic as it was, was an instrument in the hands of a foreseeing Father to save one of the foremost nations of the earth from a degradation far worse than any slavery: we may almost excuse the violent measures to which the Girondins now resorted.

Whatever blame falls on the Girondins who had roused the faubourgs, the first movement was due to the Jacobins. The 20th of June, when a Parisian populace, numbered by thousands, and aided by a faithless soldiery, marched to insult one poor weak family, one man and one woman, in their home, was the contemptible triumph of such men as Danton and Santerre. The narrative of the next six weeks is the most bloody in a country where blood has never been spared to ambition.

At last arrived the 10th of August, the crisis of the whole movement, and the long-desired democracy was established. What did it bring to its instigators? A petty triumph, a new struggle, and then—death. Of these events Madame Roland was only a spectator. Doubtless she rejoiced over the fall of the monarchy, and perhaps her enthusiasm blinded her to the excesses of the conquerors. She received the chiefs of the movement at dinner as before; and so completely was she recognised as the centre of the Girondins that those who had no personal friendship for her were glad to be among her guests. After the triumph of Dumouriez over the Prussians, he dined at her house. Madame Roland had forgotten all their differences, and he sat between her and Vergniaud, and received all the congratulations of the 'patriots.' After dinner he went to the Opera, where he was received with acclamations. Danton was at his side, for Danton was now his friend for a time. Madame Roland arrived with Vergniaud. She opened the door of the box, but seeing Danton there retreated in horror. She could never forgive this man the sinister hideousness of his wicked face.

The Girondins, terrified at the effusion of blood which their own scheme had brought about, were yet overwhelmed with joy at the proclamation of the Republic. On the evening of that announcement they met in force at Madame Roland's. There were present twelve out of the twenty-one leaders of the party—Brissot, Vergniaud, Condercet, Pétion, Guadet, Gensonné, and Barbaroux were among them. They supped and drank with a kind of philosophic worship to the success of the great movement. Roland himself looked at his wife, whose enthusiasm was displayed in the brilliancy of her beautiful face, as if to ask if their ambition were not now complete, and nothing remained but to enjoy the realization of their dreams. All eyes turned on Vergniaud, the hero of the day. After supper he filled his glass, and proposed to drink to the eternity of the Republic. Madame Roland, always ready to invest great moments with the poetry of her fancy, bade him pluck some rose leaves from her nosegay and scatter them on the wine. Vergniaud obeyed, but with a saddened look. 'Barbaroux,' said he, turning to the young man, 'it is not rose leaves, but cypress leaves we should quaff in our wine to-night. In drinking to a Republic, stained at its birth with the blood of September, who knows that we do not drink to our own death? No matter; were this wine my blood, I would drain

THE INAUGURATION OF THE REPUBLIC.

it to liberty and equality.' A cry of *Vive la République* answered this toast.

The words of Vergniaud contained a terrible truth. No sooner was the republic proclaimed than the real motives of so many of its institutors appeared in their true light. Popularity and power for themselves were what they desired, and the liberty of the people was only a cry to ensure it. The Girondins and Jacobins began to tear one another to pieces. The lion and the tiger fought over the body of the elephant they had combined to kill. Robespierre, the cunning jackal, quietly devoured the prey while they were fighting, and looked forward to feasting on their very carcasses. A system of mutual accusation was established, and each party watched for the slightest pretext to assail the other.

Madame Roland, mere woman as she was, did not escape. One Achille Viard, a worthless adventurer, accused her in the Convention of a secret correspondence with the constitutional party who had taken refuge in London, for the purpose of saving the life of the king, an object which the Girondins, who saw how his execution would disgrace the republic, eagerly desired. She was called to the bar of the Assembly. Her beauty, her calm modest dignity, and the clear innocence on her face already extracted a verdict in her favour from the whole body. They listened in silence and admiration, while in a firm voice she asserted her innocence; and when she had done a general murmur of approbation rose from each and all, except her accuser, who stood silent with shame. She left the Assembly acquitted by acclamation.

But though she acquitted herself thus publicly, private calumny, circulated by her husband's enemies, continued to assail her. The long-desired republic brought her nothing but misery. A conspiracy to assassinate the Girondins had been discovered only just in time to save them; but the life of that husband whom she regarded as the grand pillar of liberty, was in perpetual danger, and she wished to leave Paris with him and her daughter for her country-house at Beaujolais, but was prevented by the pressure of the time. The Girondins, who represented moderation, were still supported by all the middle classes, and by the departments. Their assailants were the inhabitants of the low faubourgs of Paris, people who, scarcely worthy to be called men and women, longed only for blood and excitement, and were readily roused by the Jacobins and Cordeliers to denounce the lovers of moderation.

Conspiracy followed conspiracy against the lives of the detested party, who, though unpopular with the terrorist mob of Paris, which thronging into the Assembly, by their threats and presence made moderation and rational deliberation impossible, were thus supported by the respectable part of the community. These conspiracies, however, failed. They were one after another revealed to the Girondins, who were thus enabled to prepare themselves.

At last a well-organized plot for their assassination and secret burial was proposed in a meeting at the Archevêché, of which the infamous Marat was the captain. They were to be arrested in the night singly, taken to a house in the Rue St. Jacques, subjected to a mock trial, and then buried in the garden behind, while it would be reported that they had fled the country. A young Breton happened to pass the door of the Archevêché when the conspirators were assembling, and noticing that they were admitted on showing a private copper medal, he had the audacity to pull out a *piece de deux sous*, showed it carelessly, and was admitted. The plot which he thus learned he reported at once to the deputy of his department, who was a Girondin. He was persuaded to go again the next night in the same way, and did so successfully. But he was this time noticed and followed, and the next day his body was found floating down the Seine.

The failure of these plots of assassination decided the Montagne, and the whole insurrectionary party, to unite in a *coup d'état*, and force the Girondins to quit office in the presence of an armed force. They might now have been excused if they had fled to seek safety; but conscious that their strength could alone avert the anarchy and terrorism which would succeed their downfall, they resolved to be firm to the last. They met in silence in a small apartment in the Rue de la Harpe, and one woman, of whom Danton had said, 'Why do they not choose a man for their leader? This woman will destroy them; she is the Circe of the Republic;' this woman was among them, encouraging them with her bold words, making each ashamed in the presence of his fellow-men of any desire for personal safety at the sacrifice of their principles. Courageous to the last, they prepared not for deliberation, but for death.

The first step taken by the Insurrectionists was to arrest Roland. Six armed men presented themselves in his apartment, and read an order for his arrest from the revolutionary committee. Roland replied that he did not recognize the authority of that body, and refused to follow them. The men had no orders to employ force, and their chief leaving them to watch Roland, went to report his reply. It was now for Madame Roland's courage to display itself. She wrote a letter to the Convention, announcing the attempted arrest of her husband, and set off in a fiacre for the Tuileries, where that body sat, more tyrannical by far than its former inhabitants. The Rolands were detested by the 'people' of Paris, the frantic savages who thronged the streets, thirsting for blood. She knew it, yet did not shudder at the risk she ran. The Place du Carrousel was full of the armed populace, whom Henriot had collected for the grand *coup*. She passed through them boldly and made her way to the Tuileries. At the doors of the Convention the sentinels forbade her to enter; but she insisted in such strong terms, that they allowed her to pass into the room set apart for petitioners. Through the closed doors, she heard the contest going on, which was to end in the defeat of the Girondins. At last after waiting an hour, she managed to get hold of Vergniaud, to whom she told all. He persuaded her to give up the idea of reading her letter, and to return to her husband.

Meanwhile Roland had continued to protest against the presence of the five armed men, who had at last consented to leave him. When Madame Roland reached home she found her husband gone, but soon discovered that he was taking refuge in the house of a friend in the same court. She found him out, embraced him, and then returned once more to the

Tuileries. This time the Carrousel was quiet, but the cannon remained pointed at the palace, and groups of *sansculottes* were collected around them. She found that the sitting of the Convention was over, talked a while to some of the ragged loiterers, and mounted the fiacre again. A little dog claimed her protection by nestling in her gown. She took it with her, and thought that she, too, wanted protection now. She thought of the fable of an old man who, wearied with the persecutions of his own fellow-creatures, retired to a wood to cultivate the friendship of animals. At the post of La Samaritaine the cab was stopped by the guard, who expressed astonishment at a woman being alone so late at night. 'Alone!' replied Madame Roland: 'I am accompanied by innocence and truth; what more would you have?' The guard allowed her to pass.

There was not room enough in the house where her husband had taken refuge, and she was compelled to return to her own apartment. Weary with the excitements of the day, she threw herself on her bed, but had scarcely done so when she was aroused by a deputation from the commune asking for Roland. She told them he had left her and refused to say where he was. The deputation retired, and for an hour she slept well. She was roused by her maid, who told her that some gentlemen wished to speak to her. It was one o'clock in the morning, and she therefore guessed their errand easily. She came out of her room and listened, while a *mandat* was read for her arrest and imprisonment in the Abbaye. She refused to recognize the authority of the Commune, and deliberated with herself whether resistance would be of any avail. She resolved to sacrifice herself to her husband's safety, hoping that while she was being taken, he would have time to escape. A *juge de paix* arrived and put seals on all her effects. One of the armed men wanted to have them put on her piano. He was told that it was only a musical instrument, and thereupon pulled out a rule and measured it, evidently with a view to appropriation. She sat down to write a note to a friend to beg his protection for her daughter; but as the officer insisted on seeing the letter, she tore it to bits, which he scrupulously picked up and put under seal.

At seven in the morning she was forced to leave her home and her child. An inquisitive crowd had meanwhile poured into her rooms, and they now surrounded the fiacre in which she was placed, and shouted, 'A la guillotine!' 'Would you like to have the windows closed?' asked her guard, politely. 'No,' she replied, 'oppressed innocence must never take the attitude of guilt. I fear no one's looks.' 'You have more courage than many men,' said the guard, unable to repress their admiration. 'I groan for my country,' she answered; 'I regret the error which made me think it worthy of liberty and happiness. I appreciate life, but despise injustice and death.'

At the prison she was fortunate in a worthy and kind-hearted gaoler, who, with his wife, did everything in his power to soften the misery of confinement to her. But those of my readers—let me trust they are few—who know what it is to be in prison, if only for one day, will understand that no comforts or attentions can make up for the want of personal liberty nothing can remove the degradation of being in the power of others, often too, at the mercy of those who have none. No wonder, then, that at the suggestion of Grandpré, she wrote a letter to the Convention, not indeed complaining or succumbing, but protesting boldly against the illegality of her arrest, and demanding that an investigation should be made into it. The letter of course, brought no results.

It is curious now to note the spirit of this woman. She said to herself, 'Death must come, but I will live till the last moment.' She had brought in her pocket a volume of Thomson's poems, a work to which she was very partial. She was allowed to have books, and selected 'Plutarch's Lives' which had first made her a Republican, and Hume's 'History of England,' with Sheridan's dictionary, *that she might improve her knowledge of English.* Even in the cell, and in the very shadow of death, she was resolved to make the most of her mind. Her gaoler granted her many little alleviations. She was allowed to have flowers in her cell, and to receive visits from a few particular friends, from whom she learnt that her husband was in hiding in the neighbourhood of Rouen; and assured of his safety, she was the more ready to die in his place. She was enabled, too, through their medium, to place her daughter with a Madame Creuze la Touche, in whom she could confide. From these friends, too, she learnt that one after another of her party had been condemned and executed, and lastly that her own name was written on the black list of Fouquier-Tinville. This list was signed by Robespierre, the man who in urging the execution of the king had protested his hatred of capital punishment, had affected a disgust at the shedding of blood, and simulated grief at being forced by the most weighty considerations to insist on Louis's death. This man had been one of the earliest of Madame Roland's political friends; she had brought him forward in the political world, convinced that he was a well-meaning man. She had defended him in spite of the affectation of his manner, which disgusted her. She had tried on one occasion to save his life. He had been her guest time and again; her correspondent; her friend. He had enthusiastically entered into her aspirations for liberty, he had imparted to her his own. He was the man who signed her death-warrant.

Once during her imprisonment she was visited by a physician, who turned out to be a friend of Robespierre's, and as he offered to take a letter from her to that man, she wrote one. She reminded him in it of the fickleness of fortune, and bade him take warning by the evil reputation of Sylla and Marius, who had enjoyed popularity in their day. The letter was dignified and touching, yet she feared it might look like a prayer for mercy, and she would not receive that at the hands of Robespierre. She tore it up.

When all hope of justice was dead, she determined that posterity at least should acquit her, and began to write her life. A friend named Bosc visited her frequently, and she confided to him the sheets of those Memoirs from which this one has been chiefly drawn. He carried them out under his cloak, and two years after her death he published them under the title she had given them, 'Appeal to Impartial Posterity.' From time to time during the six months she was thus employed, she received hints which led her to believe that her hour was come; yet she wrote on hurriedly but brilliantly, with all the eloquence of oppressed innocence. It consoled her to recall the days of her quiet girlhood, and to contrast them with the short chequered career of her political life, and the gloomy end that was put to it.

But the weariness of captivity, added to ill-health, broke her spirit at last; and she obtained some poison, and prepared to put an end to her misery. She wrote then to her husband, 'Forgive me, excellent man, for taking upon myself to dispose of a life I had consecrated to you. Believe me, I could have loved it and you the better for your misfortunes, had I but been permitted to share it with you. Now you are merely freed from a useless object of unavailing anguish to you.' To her daughter she wrote, 'Forgive me, dear child, young and tender girl, whose sweet image penetrates my mother's heart, and shakes my resolution. Ah! never indeed would I have removed your guide from you, had they but left me to you. Cruel hearts! have they no pity for innocence? Let them go; my example will be with you, and I feel, I may confess, at the doors of the tomb, that that is a rich legacy.'

At this moment she felt keenly the want of that Christian faith which she had thrown away for worthless philosophy, which could give her no strength, tell her of no future, and assure her no relief. Yet she believed in God. Those who have called her an atheist, cannot have read her own words. At this moment her thoughts turned from the world which had so deceived her, where all was disappointment, all hollow rottenness, up to that God whom she had learned to see and to love in nature. 'Divinity, Supreme Being,' she prayed, 'Soul of the world, principle of all that I feel to be great, good, and happy; thou whose existence I believe in, because I must have sprung from something better than what I see, I come to join thy Spirit.' But that is all. How cold this half-doubtful belief, so scantily accorded! Is it not almost equal to the despairing infidelity of the dying soldier who exclaimed, 'Oh! my God, if there be a God, save my soul, if I have a soul!' We must pass in silence over this fearful doubting, we must be content to believe that, in these her last days, she did look forward to immortality, did feel that somewhere there was a better world than that, which around her flowed with blood in the name of outraged freedom. She recalled, then, her friends and servants, and wrote her last words. 'Farewell, thou sun, whose bright rays brought calm into my soul, as they recalled it to heaven; farewell, lovely lands, whose view has so often moved me; and you, simple inhabitants of Thézée, who were wont to bless my presence, whose brows I wiped, whose poverty I softened, and whom I nursed in sickness; farewell, farewell, quiet little rooms where I fed my soul with truth, charmed my fancies with study, and learned, in the silence of meditation, to command my feelings and to despise vanity.'

But she had still a duty to do, and to write a separate letter to her child.

'I know not, my little friend, if it will be granted me to see or write to you again. Remember your mother. These few words comprise all the best I can say to you. You have seen me happy in fulfilling my duties and making myself useful to the suffering. There is no other way of being happy. You have seen me in calm misfortune and captivity, because I had no remorse, and retained the memory and the pleasure which good actions leave behind them. There is no other way than this to support the ills of life and the changes of fortune. Perhaps, and I trust so, you are not reserved for trials like mine; but there are others against which you will need as much to battle. A strict and busy life is the only preservative against all dangers, and necessity as well as wisdom compels you to work seriously. Be worthy of your parents: they leave you a high example, and if you profit by it, your life will not be useless. Adieu, loved child, whom I nourished at my breast, and strove to imbue with my principles. A time will come when you will be able to judge of the effort I made at this moment not to be melted by the thought of you. I press you to my bosom. Adieu, my Eudora.'

But Stoic as she was, she was still a woman. The thought of this one being, who had been more her own than any other, was too much for her, and for her daughter's sake she resolved to live. She threw the poison from her.

She was at this time at the prison of St. Pélagie. She had

been set at liberty one day, and mad with joy had rushed to find her daughter and clasp her to her bosom. But it was only a cruel snare. At the very door of the house where her child was, she was re-arrested, and her prayers to be allowed to see her were unavailing. She was taken back again, not to the Abbaye, but to St. Pélagie.

At length, after an imprisonment of nearly six months, she was taken, in November 1793, to that fatal Conciergerie, from whence in those days no prisoner issued but for the guillotine. Here she was placed in a wretched cell, next to that in which poor Marie Antoinette had been lodged. She who had rejoiced over the fall of that unhappy queen was now seen in private moments to weep bitterly. Yet her courage did not give way. In the cells were lodged many of the Girondins who were yet to be executed; and when they were let out into the passage for exercise, she talked to them across the grating of her door, and encouraged them to look on death as a martyrdom. She rose now to the level of an orator, and in her misery and despair poured out bitter reproaches against the very men, who in the hall above were holding the mock trials of her friends. One by one she saw those friends depart never to return, and felt that her turn must be at hand.

It came at last. Before David the judge, and Fouquier-Tinville the public prosecutor, she was accused of being the wife of Roland, and the friend of his accomplices. She stood before them proudly. She was dressed simply, in white, and her long rich hair flowed in curls over her shoulders. Her face, while it had lost all its freshness from long confinement, was still beautiful in expression. This beauty had once melted a whole Assembly before which she was arraigned, but it served only to enrage her present accusers. That very morning Brissot, the founder of her party, had been executed. She could not hope to escape, yet was resolved to speak out, and defend herself to the country.

The court was at that time open, and the trials were attended by the dregs of the populace, who interfered with them at pleasure, and mingled coarse invectives with the impatient questions of the public prosecutor. The interrogatory was at first of little importance, consisting of questions about her early life and first connection with Roland. It then passed to inquiries about his colleagues, and lastly to such gross imputations on her character, that she burst into tears. After three hours of this public torture, she was dismissed, and returned to her cell.

Two days later she was again called up; and the interrogatory proceeded as before. When called on to tell what she knew of Roland's concealment, she steadfastly refused to say a word. 'There is no law,' she exclaimed, 'in the name of which one can insist on a betrayal of the dearest feelings in nature.'

'With such a talker we shall never have done,' cried Fouquier-Tinville, furiously; 'close the interrogatory.'

She turned on him a look of withering pity. 'How I pity you!' she said; 'you can send me to the scaffold, but cannot take from me the joy of a good conscience, and the conviction that posterity will acquit Roland and me, and devote our persecutors to infamy.' She was told to choose a pleader. She chose Chanveau, and retired, crying merrily as she went, 'I only wish you, in return for the harm you wish me, peace of mind equal to what I feel, whatever price you attach to it.' She ran down the steps eagerly. Her friends were waiting to receive her in the passage, and as she passed through them, she drew her finger across her delicate throat to show that she was condemned.

The tumbril had come and gone incessantly on the fatal day. It was in its last journey for that day, that it took up Madame Roland and an old trembling man, named Lamarche. The mob, revelling in blood, shouted, 'A la guillotine!' 'I am going there,' she answered; 'but those who send me thither will not be long ere they follow. I go innocent; but they will come stained with blood, and you who applaud our execution will then applaud theirs.' The mob answered her with the vilest insults and grossest epithets. Youth and beauty could no more excite admiration in their ferocious hearts, than the sight of trembling old age by her side could draw forth pity. Lamarche wept bitterly; but Madame Roland, proud of her fate, was unnaturally gay, and strove to cheer and encourage him. When they arrived at the Place de la Concorde, where beneath a huge clay statue of Liberty stood the guillotine, reeking still with the blood of her friends, she leapt lightly from the cart. The executioner pulled her by the arm towards the scaffold. 'Stay,' said she, feeling sympathy for her companion even at this moment. 'I have a favour to ask, though not for myself.' She then explained that the sight of her death would redouble the poor old man's misery, and begged that he might be allowed to die first. She heard the knife fall on his neck without a shudder, then bowing to the great statue, she cried, 'Oh! Liberty, Liberty! how many crimes are committed in thy name!' and mounted the scaffold firmly. In a few seconds her head, fair as it was, rolled into the basket prepared to receive it.

Thus at nine-and-thirty died this strange woman. There is more of warning than of example in her story.

Some days later some shepherds, trudging along a Norman highway with their flocks before them, spied in a ditch the body of a man. They raised it up, found it to be that of an old man, tall, thin, and stern even in death. In his heart was yet the stiletto which belonged to yonder sword-stick lying by, and on his breast was pinned a paper with these words on it: 'Whoever thou art that findest these remains, respect them as those of a virtuous man. After my wife's death, I would not remain another day upon this earth so stained with crimes.' This was Roland, who had thus destroyed himself.

What a fitting end to the lives of two 'Apostles of Liberty!' The one to die at the guillotine, the other to end his own life in an act of cowardice. Such be the end of all those who think to besiege liberty by a tyranny far worse than the power they overthrow—a tyranny of might and terror.

How different are these two deaths to the glorious ends of the Apostles of Christianity! Where is hope in the last days of Madame Roland or her husband? where is the true courage of faith? the one in despair, venting invectives from her cell, brazen to the world, yet weeping in private; the other talking of a 'world stained with crimes,' when he himself had first raised the criminals, first urged them on to acts of rebellion and anarchy. How different this conceit, too, with which he proclaims himself a 'virtuous man' to the humility with which a Christian martyr passed away! how different his wife's unrelenting hatred to the forgiveness the other sheds on his persecutors in the midst of his torments! How blank these deaths, without a future to look to! How utterly despairing these lives where all had turned out rotten, when there was no trust in a perfect life elsewhere, no longing for the land of that pure government, those public virtues, that perfect organization, which in their arrogance they had hoped to set up on earth! How truly consistent is the cowardice of suicide with such a cheerless creed! How naturally adapted is such an end to the arrogance which rejected revelation and sought to raise men into gods! Well might Roland take care that his suicide should be known to the world, and well might his wife write an appeal to posterity. What else, poor creatures, had they to look to? What comfort, what hope in the hour of death? None, but the cold justice of time, the acquittal of posterity. And posterity has given them their due. Yes, it is quite enough meed of praise for either Roland or his wife to say that they were better than any of their celebrated contemporaries; that their moral characters were irreproachable; that they did not abuse power when they gained it, nor seek it selfishly; that they were moved by pure principles, and took even their most mischievous measures in the belief that they were acting right. Compared with Marat and Robespierre they were saints: compared with the obscurest Christian who does his duty humbly in faith and hope, they stand out as demons. But their own age must judge them, for their faults were its own. Let them go.

LADY MARY WORTLEY MONTAGU.

Her first Debut.—The Kit-Kat Club.—Early years.— A Female Scholar.—Anecdote of young Burnet.—Lady Mary's Verses.—Dolly Walpole's Troubles.—Mistress Anne Wortley.—A Country Gentleman of the Seventeenth Century. Lady Mary on 'the World.'—Classical Flirtation.—Mr. Wortley.—A Doubtful Lover.—Love-letters.—Unsettled Settlements.—Lady Mary Elopes.—Her Appreciation of Scenery.—The Curate's 'Nightgown.'—Lady Mary's Beauty.—A Disgraceful Court.—'The Schulenburg.' —The King's Creatures.—Introduced at Court.—The Town Eclogues.—Anecdote of Lady Mary and Craggs.—Her Letters from the East.—Pope's Love for Her.—Travels to the East.—Arrives at Adrianopol.—The Beautiful Fatima.—Rambles about Constantinople.—Introduces Inoculation.—A Cooing Couple.—Lady Mary's Turkish Costume.—Quarrels with Mrs. Murray.—All about a Ballad.—The Twickenham Set.—The Quarrel with Pope.—Lord Fanny and Sappho.—Reply to the Imitator of Horace.—Odious Verses.—Lady Mary's Society.—Walpole's Description of Her.—Lady Mary at Louvere.—Her Disreputable Son.—In the Harpsichord House.—Death of Lady Mary.—Satirists.—Lady Mary's Character.—Her Portrait.

THIS liveliest, wittiest, severest, and—if we believed Horace Walpole, which we do not—*dirtiest* woman of her time, is celebrated for her charming letters, her Oriental travels, for being first the idol and then the abomination of Pope, and lastly, but by no means least, as a public benefactress, by introducing into this country, in spite of the most vehement opposition, the operation of inoculating for the small-pox. As a female humourist moving in all kinds of society, admired by all, abused by many, but whether with admiration or dislike, talked of by everybody, Lady Mary claims her niche in this work.

Her father was Evelyn Pierrepont, raised afterwards to the Peerage. Her mother, Lady Mary Fielding,* was first cousin to the father of Henry Fielding, the author of 'Tom Jones,' so that two humourists, male and female, are to be found in the same family at the same time. It is always troublesome when one is reading the life of one person to go back two or three generations to others who gave them little more than their

*Spelt sometimes Feilding.

name. Suffice it then to say of Lady Mary's mother, that she was daughter to William Fielding, second Earl of Desmond, and third Earl of Denbigh, whose fourth brother, John Fielding, was the grandfather of Richardson's rival. Her father, Evelyn Pierrepont, of Thoresby, was grandson to a certain William Pierrepont of the same place, who supported the party of Cromwell in the civil war, and was commonly known as *Wise William*. In 1706 this father was created, by Queen Anne, Marquis of Dorchester; and in 1715 George I. made him Duke of Kingston. By his first wife Lady Mary Fielding, he had three daughters and one son. The eldest of these was Lady Mary herself, born in 1689-90; the next was Frances, who married the Earl of Mar, who took so prominent a part in the movement of 1715; the next Evelyn, who married John Lord Gower. After giving birth to her only son, William, in 1692, the Countess of Kingston died, and thus Lady Mary Pierrepont was left in childhood without a mother. In reviewing her life and character, this fact must be taken into consideration, and proportionate allowance made for her.

Her father, the Earl of Kingston, was a fine gentleman and a bad father, the friend of beaux and wits; but not over affectionate to his children. This, too, must be considered.

Her first *début* in society was rather illustrious. She was eight years old, a pretty fair-haired child, with a good deal of spirit and not a little vanity. Her father was amused with the pertness, and proud of the pretty face of his little daughter. He was a member of the famous Kit-Kat Club, which was then held in Shire Lane (now Lower Searle's Place), which lies between Lincoln's Inn Fields and Fleet Street. This little street, so called because it divided the city from the shire, was always a nest for wits. Here lived old Isaac Bickerstaff, the Tatler, who met his club at the 'Trumpet' Tavern, which still stands, and here assembled the Kit-Kat Club. It was composed of thirty-nine noblemen and gentlemen who were devoted to the Hanoverian succession, and all strong Whigs. Its curious name was the subject of much discussion. Some said that the house in which it met was kept by one Kit or Christopher Katt, who concocted those incomparable mutton pies which always formed a part of the supper of the members, and which from him were called Kit-Kats. Others maintained that the maker of the pies was named Christopher, and his house had the sign of the Cat and Fiddle. Pope (or it may be Arbuthnot) found another derivation for the name in the following well-known verses:—

> 'Whence deathless Kit-Kat took its name
> Few critics can unriddle,
> Some say from pastrycook it came,
> And some from Cat and Fiddle.
> From no trim beaux its name it boasts,
> Gray statesmen or green wits;
> But from the pell-mell pack of toasts
> Of old cats and young kits,'

referring to the then fashionable system of toasting some celebrated beauty after dinner. The ladies approved of had the honour of having verses to them engraved on the glasses, and, in some cases, of their portraits hung up in the club-room. The members at the time of which we speak were all more or less distinguished. There was Marlborough himself; there were Sir Robert Walpole, the minister of George I. and George II.; Vanbrugh, known for bad plays and worse architecture; Addison; Congreve; Dr. Garth, who could run as well as prescribe, and beat the Duke of Grafton in a foot-match of two hundred yards in the Mall; the Dukes of Somerset, Richmond, Grafton, Devonshire; the Earls of Dorset, Sunderland, Manchester, and Wharton; Lords Halifax and Somers; Maynwaring, Stepney, and Walsh, and the Earl of Kingston, Lady Mary's father. Jacob Tonson, the bookseller, was their secretary, and Sir Godfrey Kneller painted all their portraits, of that peculiar size ever since known as a Kit-Kat.

It must have been difficult for thirty-nine men to find thirty-nine incontestable beauties whenever they might be called on to do so, and in such a dilemma, or perhaps to indulge a whim, the Earl of Kingston one day proposed his daughter as his toast. The company demurred, on the plea that they had never seen her. 'Then you shall see her,' cried the father, ready to carry out the joke. She was sent for, and received with acclamations, acknowledged to be a beauty, and even an incipient wit, and handed, like a pretty doll as she was, from lap to lap among poets, wits, statesmen, and rakes. The omen was auspicious, and the bon-bons and kisses with which she was overwhelmed were only the types of that admiration she was destined to receive later. In after life she remembered the incident, and affirmed that it was the happiest moment she had ever known.

How the next ten years of her life were passed we have no accurate information. She lived at the dull house at Thoresby in the 'plains of Nottingham,' or at Acton, near London, and seems to have been mainly occupied in cultivating her mind. She herself tells us that her education was 'one of the worst in the world,' from which, as from other passages in her letters, we may infer that Lord Kingston gave her little or none. This deficiency her own energy supplied. Fond of reading more than anything else, she eagerly devoured such books as were then to be found in country libraries, many of them ponderous folios of serious writing, among which we may perhaps include the romances of Mademoiselle de Scudery, ponderous enough surely, and certainly a serious undertaking, and the other so-called novels then in vogue, and translated into English. These twelve-volume works were no light reading, though the lightest of the day. They took a six-month or so to get through; and being full of high-flown sentiment, must have had a far more powerful effect on the young reader's mind than the three-volume novels, of which a young lady was heard to boast the other day that she could read two a day and four on Sunday. Reading was then decidedly more profitable than it is now. It was, in fact, a study, not a mere indulgence. With her brother William's tutor, Lady Mary is said to have studied French and Latin, but it is more probable that she taught herself the latter. Her diligence, her thirst for knowledge, and her intrepidity in tackling any branch of it, added to her wonderful memory, enabled her to acquire what other young ladies of her day, content with tapestry-work and tittle-tattle, never thought of attempting, and in after years the same spirit made of her a very decent Turkish scholar. It is possible that in these more masculine studies she may have received some aid from her uncle, William Fielding; but it is certain that Bishop Burnet, the author of the 'History of the Reformation,' and Bishop of Salisbury, inspected and assisted her classical studies. At the age of nineteen she translated from the Latin (for her acquaintance with Greek seems to have been too limited to admit of her using the version in that language) the 'Enchiridion' of Epictetus. This translation, made in a single week, shows considerable proficiency in Latin, and, as the work of a girl who was perhaps self-taught in that language, deserves to stand very high. She forwarded it to the bishop with a long letter, in which several quotations prove that she had even then read Erasmus carefully, requesting him to correct her errors in the translation, which he did. This letter is perhaps more remarkable than its enclosure, and shows that at that age the young girl had already acquired no small amount of useful wisdom, better still than her Latin and Greek. She speaks thus of the education of women in her day, and I fear that what she says applies pretty nearly to that of many of our own fair contemporaries :—

'We are permitted no books but such as tend to the weakening and effeminating of the mind. Our natural defects are every way indulged, and it is looked upon as in a degree criminal to improve our reason or fancy we have any. We are taught to place all our art in adorning our outward forms, and permitted, without reproach, to carry that custom even to extravagancy, while our minds are entirely neglected, and by disuse of reflections, filled with nothing but the trifling objects our eyes are daily entertained with. This custom so long established and industriously upheld, makes it even ridiculous to go out of the common road, and forces one to find many excuses, as if it were a thing altogether criminal not to play the fool in concert with other women of quality, whose birth and leisure only serve to make them the most useless and worthless part of the creation. There is hardly a character in the world more despicable or more liable to universal ridicule, than that of a learned woman: those words imply, according to the received sense, a talking, impertinent, vain, and conceited creature. I believe nobody will deny that learning may have that effect, but it must be a very superficial degree of it.'

The name of Bishop Burnet reminds us of an anecdote of his son Thomas, for a long time the scapegrace of the family.

The bishop, observing him one day to be unusually grave, asked him what he was meditating. 'A greater work,' replied the young man, 'than your lordship's "History of the Reformation."' 'Indeed! what is that?'—'My own reformation.' 'I am delighted to hear it,' quoth the bishop, 'though I almost despair of it.' The young man's meditation was not fruitless, and he lived to be Chief Justice of Common Pleas, and, what was better, a respectable man.

In such studies, industriously pursued, were the younger years of Lady Mary's life passed; but when her father resided at Thoresby, and surrounded himself with his jovial companions, it was her duty to entertain them at his table. According to the custom of the day, she had the arduous task of carving for the whole party, while the earl at the other end pressed his guests, if indeed they required pressing, to drink and be merry. This undertaking, which the etiquette of the day made imperative on the lady of the house, was so considerable that she was obliged to take her own dinner in private beforehand. We can well understand the nausea of such banquets to the young lady.

Though Lady Mary had none of the young-ladyism or sentimentality of girls of her age, we are not to suppose her either hard or masculine. Her mind, indeed, had a manly vigour which she had developed by books rarely read, and thoughts rarely indulged, by others of her sex; but her character and her tastes were perfectly feminine. On the one hand we find her not only devoted to, but even composing, poetry; on the other, cultivating the tenderest and most affectionate friendships with young women of her own age.

Of her verses there is not much to say, except that they are free from sentimentality; so free, indeed, that they never once speak to the heart, and therefore fail to fix themselves on our minds. They have the epigrammatic turn and love of antithesis which seem inseparable to the poetry of her day, their fair share of classical allusions, and an easy gracefulness of style. To this they unite strong sense and some satire, though not nearly so witty as that in her letters. She began to make verses early. At the age of twelve she composed a fair imitation of Ovid's Epistles, entitled 'Julia to Ovid;' at fourteen, again, she penned some verses to Truth. But the most celebrated of her metrical pieces are the 'Town Eclogues,' and the various addresses and ballads, of which we shall speak in the proper place. It may suffice to say, that, in spite of the temporary popularity of these, Lady Mary has no claim to be considered as a poetess. Her verses are only pretty and neat. They show no inspiration, no power, no loftiness of thought; but they are sufficient to prove the elegance of her tastes.

Her early friendships were among those of her own station. She had some intimacy with Lady Anne Vaughan, the only child of the Earl of Carberry, and, therefore, an heiress. This young lady was very unfortunate in her marriage with Lord Winchester, afterwards the third Duke of Bolton, who married her only for her money, and soon threw her over for the celebrated actress Polly Peachum (Miss Lavinia Bestwick), whom he married after the death of his wife. The most respectable of the maids of honour of Queen Anne, Mistress (that is, Miss) Jane Smith, the third daughter of the Whig Speaker Smith, and an intimate friend of Lady Suffolk, was another of her intimates. Then there came the volatile Dolly Walpole, the sister of Sir Robert, the minister. Dorothy was a merry, harmless Norfolk girl, one of a family of nineteen, with no fortune but her face, which proved one in time, and which made her the belle of her native county. Bred up at Houghton, she was brought by her brother, then Mr. Walpole, to London, with a view of finding a husband. Her brother's wife is described as an intriguing and not very amiable woman, who was determined that Dolly should make a good match. She was surrounded by admirers, of whom one, every way desirable, presently declared himself. His relations, however, little thinking that Mr. Walpole would one day be the right hand of two sovereigns, and have more in his power than the richest peer of the realm, inquired about the young lady's portion. Like most mercenary people, they were destined to be cheated. They found that she was dowerless, and therefore forbade a connection which some years later would have been worth thousands to them and theirs. Dolly, who was in love, was miserable. Mrs. Walpole was unkind to her; and so when Lady Wharton offered her a shelter in her own house, she readily accepted it. She was too ignorant of the scandals of town to know what an infamous character Lord Wharton bore, and that this step would be ruinous to her. Sir Robert happened to be out of town; but when on his return he learned where his sister was, he went to Lord Wharton's with his usual irascibility, and utter want of tact, and thundered for admittance, claiming his sister in no very polite terms. When admitted, he assailed Lady Wharton in 'Anglo Saxon' language, carried off his sister, and took her down to Houghton, to pass her time in penitence for her mistake. The incident furnished a pretty story for the scandal-mongers of the town, and poor Dolly's name was hawked about in no very agreeable manner. For three years she mourned, at Houghton, her lost love and her tarnished fame. At that time, however, Charles, second Viscount Townshend, who had been away as ambassador at the Hague, and was now a widower, returned to Raynham Hall, in the neighbourhood of Houghton, saw Miss Dorothy Walpole's pretty face, and, ignorant of the little story about Lord Wharton, fell in love with it, and proposed to the owner. He was accepted, and they were married in 1713. The match was ample compensation for the first love. Lord Townshend afterwards became a minister, and played a conspicuous part under George the First.

It is said that Lady Mary took some part in this affair, opposing Mrs. Walpole, defending the simple Dolly, and making herself obnoxious to her sister-in-law; and it is also hinted that this part may account for the animosity which Horace Walpole, Dolly's nephew, felt towards Lady Mary. Horace was always much attached to his mother, and he never forgave a foe of his family. There is no doubt that, for one cause or another, he never spoke well of the subject of this memoir.

But the best and most intimate of Lady Mary's friends was Mistress Anne Wortley, the sister of the man she afterwards married. The Wortley-Montagus united in themselves two of the oldest families in England. The Montagus, from whom are descended the ducal families of Manchester and Montagu, and the Earls of Halifax and Sandwich, date their arrival in England from a Norman follower of William the Conqueror with the uncouth name of Drogo de Monte Acuto. The Wortleys were a Saxon family of Yorkshire. The grandfather of Mrs. Anne Wortley and Mr. Edward Wortley Montagu was Sir Edward Montagu, of Hinchinbroke in Huntingdon, who, being high-admiral at the time of the Restoration, influenced the fleet to declare for Charles II., and was, in consequence, created Earl of Sandwich. His eldest son succeeded to the title. His second was Sidney Montagu, who married Anne Wortley, an heiress and daughter of Sir Francis Wortley, of Wortley in Yorkshire, whose surname thereupon he added to his own. The son and daughter of this Sidney were the husband and bosom-friend of Lady Mary. As for this Sidney himself, he is described as sitting in his ingle-nook, employed in the refined and delicate occupation of swearing at his servants, washing down his oaths with store of canary, while his brother, the dean, meek and mild, sat opposite to him, beseeching Heaven to pardon the blasphemies he had not the courage to reprove.

With Mrs. Anne Wortley Lady Mary corresponded affectionately and even passionately, when she had fallen in love with her brother, and meant for him all the endearments she lavished upon her. The following letter, written in 1709, is a good specimen of Lady Mary's style at nineteen, and of the usual epistolary style of the day, and is interesting as showing what were her studies and interests at that age :—

'I shall run mad. With what heart can people write when they believe their letters will never be received? I have already writ you a very long scrawl, but it seems it never came to your hands; I cannot bear to be accused of coldness by one whom I shall love all my life. This will, perhaps, miscarry as the last did. How unfortunate I am if it does! You will think I forget you, who are never out of my thoughts. You will fancy me stupid enough to forget your letters, when they are the only pleasures of my solitude. * * * Let me beg you for the future, if you do not receive letters very constantly from me, imagine the post-boy killed, imagine the mail burnt, or some other strange accident; you can imagine nothing so impossible as that I forget you, my dear Mrs. Wortley. * * * I am now so much alone, I have leisure to pass whole days in reading, but am not at all proper for so delicate an employment as chusing you books. Your own fancy will better direct you. My study at present is nothing but dictionaries and grammars. I am trying whether it be possible to learn without a master; I am not certain (and dare hardly hope) I shall make any great progress; but find the study so diverting, I am not only easy, but pleased with the solitude that indulges it. I forget there is such a place as London, and wish for no company but yours. You see, my dear, in making my pleasures consist of these unfashionable diversions, I am not of the number who cannot be easy out of the mode. I believe more follies are committed out of complaisance to the world, than in following our own inclinations. Nature is seldom in the wrong—custom always; it is with some regret I follow it in all the impertinences of dress; the compliance is so trivial, it comforts me; but I am amazed to see it consulted even in the most important occasions of our lives; * * * I call all people who fall in love with furniture, clothes, and equipage, of this number, and I look upon them as no less in the wrong than when they were five years old, and doated on shells, pebbles, and hobby-horses. I believe you will expect this letter to be dated from the other world, for sure I am you never heard an inhabitant of this talk so before.'

What she here says of dress reminds us that in after years she was described by Walpole, who saw her at Florence, as being very untidy, in a dirty mob, and with uncombed hair. That well-known anecdote, too, is of Lady Mary, which relates how, being once reproached with having dirty hands, she replied (it was at the French opera), 'Ah, si vous voyiez mes pieds!' That she was eccentric and indifferent to dress, there can be no doubt. It is rather to her praise than otherwise; but that she was dirty in her person we can believe only on the word of Horace Walpole, who hated her, and did not mind what he said about his foes. That she could dress well, when she chose, is no less certain; for her dress at court one evening was so pleasing, that the Prince of Wales, who admired her a little too much, called the princess from her cards to see 'how well Lady Mary was dressed.' 'Lady Mary always dresses well,' replied the princess in dudgeon, returning to her basset.

One afternoon when Lady Mary went to call on her friend Mrs. Wortley, she found in her room a gentleman, some thirty years old, leaning familiarly by the fire-place, and watching her as she entered with a keen critical eye. His face, in spite of the huge full-bottomed wig, then in fashion, was handsome and expressive—a shade thoughtful, but cold and terribly sensible. In his manner there was a mixture of Yorkshire bluntness and *méfiance*, with something of Norman dignity. He talked like a man of the world, with a touch of the scholar, which delighted her. He had evidently mingled with the humorists of London clubs, but he preferred classics. Keen observer as she was, she at once entered on that subject. Accustomed rather to despise women, and particularly young ladies, he was amazed and charmed to find one of so much sense and such unusual reading. He improved the occasion, and lingered in his sister's room longer than he had ever done before. Nor did he leave it willingly. Here were beauty, wit, and strong sense united in one person. He was not a philosopher, but he was not susceptible. It required fascinations as great as these to move him, and he was moved. This man was Edward Wortley-Montagu, commonly called Mr. Wortley, the brother of Lady Mary's bosom friend.

They talked of Roman heroes. Fancy a young lady and young man of to-day flirting over the classics! He mentioned an author, and she regretted she had never read his works. Some days after she received an edition of this author, in the fly-leaf of which were written the following verses:—

> 'Beauty like this had vanquished Persia shown,
> The Macedon had laid his empire down,
> And polished Greece obeyed a barb'rous throne.
> Had wit so bright adorned a Grecian dame,
> The am'rous youth had lost his thirst for fame,
> Nor distant India sought through Syria's plain ;
> But to the muses' stream with her had run,
> And thought her lover more than Ammon's son.'

We perceive from this very clear declaration that Mr. Wortley had not much facility of rhyming, whatever his classical attainments. But he was not without his attractions in the eyes of an intellectual woman. He had been well educated, if we mistake not, at Cambridge; had made the grand tour in 1703, and even extended his foreign experience beyond the usual limits by a residence of two years in Venice. Like most young men of family in that day, he had entered Parliament early. There he sat at different times for the city of Westminster, the city of Peterborough—both very influential constituencies—and the boroughs of Huntingdon and Bossiney. He was a Liberal and a progressionist, two very good qualities in this day, though then sullied by a necessary adherence to the Hanoverian succession. About the time of his meeting with Lady Mary, he had brought in a bill for the naturalization of foreign Protestants. Later he entered one for limiting the number of the officers of the House, and securing the freedom of Parliament; and this bill, which nearly affected the interests of the members, was agitated for five years, and eventually lost in 1713. In the same year, 1709, he obtained leave for a bill to encourage learning, and secure copyrights of books to the authors. Thus we can judge that he was a sensible, well-meaning man, as different from his father as gold from tinsel. He had other recommendations. His tastes or his whiggism brought him in contact with the humorists of those days. Addison was his intimate friend. Garth, Congreve, Maynwaring, and even Steele, were among his associates. Perhaps he had not much wit or humour himself; he seems to have dreaded it; but it is certain he had much sound sense, and was not altogether a common man. On the other hand he had just as much heart as was wanted for his career, a strong feeling of honour and no romance.

The events that followed upon this interview form the real romance of Lady Mary's life; and, whatever else may be said of her, her conduct in them attaches us to her. A romance indeed this love affair was, quiet, and apparently cold as it may have been. It was the old romance of a woman loving fondly a man who disapproved of her, and of her efforts to attach him in spite of natural modesty and a consciousness of his indifference.

That Mr. Wortley was much in love there is no doubt; but he set his own judgment against his own heart: he doubted if this girl, who appeared to be coquettish, vain, fond of the world and society, would be a suitable companion for a man of his quiet and serious tastes, or take sufficient interest in his political ambitions. He not only felt this, but openly told her what he felt in the matter, and treated her with a nonchalance which only increased her affection for him.

For some time after he had offered and been accepted, their intercourse was carried on through the medium of letters to and from his sister; but about 1711 Mrs. Anne Wortley died in the flower of her youth. Some time after this, Lady Mary wrote her first letter to Mr. Wortley—'the first,' she says, 'I ever wrote to one of your sex, and shall be the last.' She begins by excusing her boldness in writing to him at all, and then defends herself against a charge of frivolous tastes, which he seems to have made, and while endeavouring to conceal her love for him, pleads for his affection. 'You distrust me; I can neither be easy, nor loved, where I am distrusted. Nor do I believe your passion for me is what you pretend it; at least I am sure, was I in love, I could not talk as you do. * * * I wished I loved you enough to devote myself to be for ever miserable for the pleasure of a day or two's happiness. I cannot resolve upon it. You must think otherwise of me, or not at all.'

His complaints, doubts, and accusations continued, and at last she writes: 'I resolved to make no answer to your letter; it was something very ungrateful, and I resolved to give over all thoughts of you. I could easily have performed that resolve some time ago, but then you took pains to please me: now you have brought me to esteem you, you make use of that esteem to give me uneasiness; and I have the displeasure of seeing I esteem a man that dislikes me. Farewell, then; since you will have it so, I renounce all the ideas I have so long flattered myself with, and will entertain my fancy no longer with the imaginary pleasure of pleasing you. * * * You think me all that is detestable; you accuse me of want of sincerity and generosity. * * * There is no condition of life I could not have been happy in with you, so very much I liked you, I may say loved, since it is the last thing I'll ever say to you. This is telling you sincerely my greatest weakness; and now I will oblige you with a new proof of my generosity; I'll never see you more.'

But in his answer to this he says : ' I would die to be secure of your heart, though but for a moment ;' and seizing on this expression she again attempts to exonerate herself, and the letters that follow are much in the same strain, defending their writer from charges of coquetry, of inconstancy, of a love of society, and even of interested views. Yet he could not make up his mind to give her up. ' I see what is best for me,' he writes ; ' I condemn what I do, and yet I fear I must do it.' In this letter he asks for an interview, and gives us some insight into the manner of their meetings. He proposes that it should take place at the house of Mrs. Steele, the wife of Sir Richard, who was then Mr. Steele. ' You may call upon her or send for her, to-morrow or next day. Let her dine with you, or go to visit shops or Hide Park, or other diversions. You may bring her home, I can be in the house reading, as I often am, though the master is abroad.' Hyde Park, it may be noticed in passing, was then, as now, the great promenade of London. Horse-races and foot-races were often held in the ring, and in the afternoon the ladies drove round and round it in a cloud of dust ; ' some,' says a writer in 1700, ' singing, others laughing, others tickling one another, and all of them toying and devouring cheesecakes, and marchpane, and China oranges.' The lodge there was celebrated for its milk, tarts, and syllabub, to taste which was the regular accompaniment of the drive. At that time the Serpentine, which was not made till 1730, was represented by a couple of ponds, and the lodge in question was close to these.

But whatever doubts he had, Mr. Wortley at last made open proposals to Lady Mary's father, then Lord Dorchester. They were favourably received, and all went well till the settlements came to be discussed. Mr. Wortley disapproved of the foolish practice of settling property on a son unborn, who might turn out a spendthrift or a fool. Lord Dorchester replied that no grandchild of his should risk being a beggar, and would have nothing more to say to his proposals of marriage. The wisdom of this precaution on Mr. Wortley's part was shown in the sequel. His son turned out both fool and spendthrift, and something worse ; and the Wortley estates, if settled on him, would soon have been squandered upon the wretched creatures who from time to time passed as his wives.

Lord Dorchester, however, did not leave his daughter alone, and when a more complaisant suitor with a handsomer income offered himself, briefly commanded her to marry him. To disobey such an order was then the height of undutiful conduct yet so great was the disgust which Lady Mary entertained for the gentleman proposed that she ventured to write to her father offering not to marry at all rather than unite with him. The furious parent sent for his daughter, and told her that she must marry him at once, or consent to pass the rest of her days, while he lived, in retirement in a remote part of the country. Her relations all encouraged the match, and seemed to think her mad for wishing to love her future husband, assuring her she would be just as happy after marriage whether she loved him or not. What was a vow, taking at the altar before God in the most solemn manner, compared with a settlement on an unborn baby, a jointure for herself, and plenty of pin-money? What indeed, in that day, and, we fear, with too many parents even in our own quasi-religious times? She replied to her father that she detested the man proposed, but was in his power, and must leave him to dispose of her. Lord Dorchester took this as a consent, made the settlements, and even ordered the trousseau.

Lady Mary was in despair, and Mr. Wortley, now that his prize was likely to be snatched from him, closed his hands on it eagerly. He proposed that they should be privately married; Lady Mary was delighted, and at once consented, though not without fears at such a step. 'I tremble for what we are doing,' she writes. 'Are you sure you shall love me for ever? Shall we never repent? I fear and I hope.' Yet delay would be fatal, and so she quietly walked out of the house one day, and was married to him by special license in August, 1712. Of course the father was furious, and of course, I hear some worldly people say, the marriage turned out ill. This is not exactly the case, as we shall see. It was as happy, perhaps, as the majority of matches—for many years it was enviably so—and the fact that it ended in a very amicable separation late in life, only proves that this couple had more sense than some, who though continuing to live together, do so only to quarrel and make the separation of heart and feeling far greater than one of mere abode.

After their marriage, Mr. and Lady Mary Wortley resided in different parts of the country, but not much in London. Sometimes they were at Hinchinbroke, the seat of Mr. Wortley's grandfather, Lord Sandwich; sometimes in Huntingdon, for which Mr. Wortley was the member at that period; sometimes in Yorkshire, occasionally at Wharncliffe, one of the houses there belonging to the Wortley family, as it now does to their descendants. The scenery round the last place is said to be very fine after a Yorkshire model; and because Lady Mary does not fall into raptures about it, she is accused of a want of love of nature. We are not inclined to defend Lady Mary's tastes and character of mind in every particular, though we are disposed to think she was a much better woman than some of her contemporaries, especially Walpole, made out; but this complaint is sheer nonsense. That she had an eye for beauty, and could appreciate it, we may see from many of her foreign letters; that she did not care for that of Yorkshire is no great sin; other people have been and are indifferent to that not very comfortable county; and it may be allowed to prefer shady lanes, wooded ground, and rich pastures to the bleak hills near Sheffield. After all, her expression is merely that ' Wharncliffe had something in it which she owned she did not dislike, odd as her fancy might be.'

Her letters to her husband, who frequently left her a long time alone at this period, are among the best proofs that she was not that vile, worldly creature which Walpole, who invented freely when he could not find legitimate abuse for those he disliked, tries to make her out. We here see the simplicity of her character. She is evidently weary without her husband, and is thrown among dull people, yet she makes the best of it, and is content to talk of her walks on the terrace and friendship with a robin-redbreast. Later she is anxious about her boy, who is ill; and later still, she makes a complaint, for the justice of which we have no direct evidence, but which is written in a touching manner. She reminds her husband that he has been absent from July to November; that he writes seldom, and then coldly; that he never asks after his child; and that when she was ill he expressed no sympathy and no sorrow. As all this was written without affectation or show of misery—a luxury to some women—we may believe that there was cause for her complaint. The letter having no date, had been dated by Mr. Wortley himself. Does not this tell a tale? The passionless man was smitten in his conscience: he was willing to note the time when such complaints were made against him he may even have been touched by them.

Her letters at this period, though far less spirited and less clever than those written from abroad, are interesting, as giving us glimpses into the then state of affairs. Thus in 1714 she describes how the king was proclaimed in York, and an effigy of the Pretender dragged about the streets and burned, and how the young ladies of the neighbourhood were in constant fear of the threatened invasion. Another letter gives us a hint of how Parliament was 'elected' in those days—perhaps, we may add, in these too—'I believe there is hardly a borough vacant * * * Perhaps it will be the best way to deposit a certain sum in some friend's hands, and *buy some little Cornish borough*.' In another she amuses us by the description of a love affair between a very high-church young lady of forty and a curate with a 'spongy nose' and a squint. She points out the curate going about in a dirty 'night-gown' (dressing-gown), to the happy spinster, who blushes and looks prim, but quotes 'a passage from Herodotus, in which it is said that the Persians wore long night-gowns.' Fancy consoling one's self for a lover's appearance by comparing him to a Persian!

But Lady Mary was not always engaged in such rural observations. On the accession of George I., her husband was made a Commissioner of the Treasury, and she came up from Yorkshire to stay in London. She was introduced at court, and her wit and—if we may call it so—her beauty made a great impression there. The coarse, heavy king was struck with her; the brutal, vulgar prince of Wales polluted her with his leers, and disgusted her with his admiration. She was at the age of her prime, four-and-twenty, and married. Her face, though not absolutely beautiful, had something most attractive in it. Pope, who had seen her as a girl, and was in love with her, wrote verses to 'Wortley's eyes;' and if her portraits are not the basest flatterers, her expression was precisely that to captivate and enthral a man of mind. There was no languor, no weakness, and yet no boldness in it. It betrayed an independent spirit, where a lofty self-respect, which was not vanity, united with a contempt for the follies and vices of the world, as she knew it. There were thought, dignity, eminence in her look, and her bitter, unflinching wit did not give it the lie. The face was a pure oval, the head freely set on a neck which might have been longer. The nose was sharp and very slightly *retroussé*, the mouth small, well formed, and firm set. The celebrated eyes, if not very large, were very bright, and the fair, fresh complexion added somewhat to their brilliance. She was beautiful by youth and expression; in old age she is described as a hideous hag, and the fire of the 'Wortley's eyes' had become too keen and bitter to redeem the wreck of the face. After all, if we look up the women whose beauty has gone hand-in-hand with their wit, and made tempests in many hearts, we shall find that they have rarely possessed perfect features, and that the mind has indeed been the real beauty of the body. So it should be.

The court of George I. was the worst in the history of England: it was every whit as vicious as that of Charles II., without the redeeming quality of elegance. All was gross and vulgar, from the heavy German monarch, who could pass whole evenings cutting out paper, to his minister, Sir Robert Walpole—almost the vulgarest man ever in a British ministry—and down to the wretched German underlings who had followed the Hanoverian to England. Not content with mere vice, the whole court was a kind of speculation. Those in power bought and sold the places of confidence they ought to have carefully distributed, and that unblushingly. Every one sought to make his or her fortune out of the miserable nation upon which the Hanoverian had been foisted. The king's mistresses amassed wealth by the sale of their depraved influence; the king's ministers were little better; women were given appointments which could only belong to men; ladies at their birth were made cornets or ensigns in the army, and received pay up to a marriageable age. There was not even the semblance of religion which invested the court of Louis XIV., where preachers could at least speak freely and did speak freely: the clergy, especially the bishops, were little less corrupt than the courtiers.

The king was surrounded by Germans, who looked upon England as a rich windfall, out of which they would make the most they could. They themselves had not wit enough to laugh at their dupes, but their English *protégés* did it for them; and Walpole treated poor old Marlborough with insolence, from which his fame as a soldier, if nothing more, should have protected him. The king spoke no English, and never tried to learn either our language or our institutions. He left all to his ministers—*tant mieux*—and amused himself in the company of Madame Schulenberg, whom he created Duchess of Kendal, and who was nearly sixty when he brought her over. It was then that England saw the representatives of her so-called 'noblest' families catering for the favour of this low person, and even marrying the illegitimate offspring of the king for the sake of court grace. Lord Chesterfield, the greatest beau and wit of his day, was not ashamed to ally the blood of Stanhope, which he affirmed was the surname of our first parents, *Adam de Stanhope* and *Eve de Stanhope*, with that Countess of Schulenberg; while Lord Howe, the father of the celebrated admiral, was quite delighted to secure the daughter of the other 'lady,' the Countess of Kielmansegg.

The best of this was that Chesterfield was duped, and very rightly punished. The old friend of his Majesty had not come to England to make money for an English earl, and the douceurs which she had received for a royal smile or a promise of a place were carefully despatched to her Vaterland, that the noble race of Schulenberg might for ever bless the sacrifice she had made of her virtue. Chesterfield, disgusted, got rid of his wife as soon as possible, and thanked Heaven that the fair Melosina— such was her name—presented him with no heir to sully the line of Adam de Stanhope and Eve de Stanhope with a bar sinister.

The Duchess of Kendal, though thus antique, very ugly, and very thin—in fact, a witch—possessed immense influence over the heavy mind of the King of England. Fortunately for this country she was too stupid to use this influence on her own responsibility. She contented herself with turning it in that direction from which the highest bribe was forthcoming; and so well known was this supremacy, and the mode of commanding it, that even foreign ambassadors recommended their governments to treat with her; and Count Broglio, the French minister here in 1724, openly hints in his despatches that the 'Schulenberg' must be bribed. The king was easily managed. He had not much conversation, and did not like to be bothered. He passed his evenings from five to eight in the charming society of this ancient Laïs, engaged in the intellectual pastime of cutting up paper. Except when an opposite fit came over him, he readily gave in to his 'friend's' suggestions. The other follower of his Majesty, the Countess of Kielmansegg, who was created Countess of Darlington, was many years younger than the favourite and was overpoweringly stout as the other was painfully thin. She did not make a rival of the Schulenberg, being persuaded that such influence as she possessed was sufficient to make her fortune. She was moreover, much cleverer than the other person, and much connected with the Whig ministry. She had wonderful powers of conversation for a German, and could be very agreeable when she chose. The king was indifferent to her, and only lounging in her apartments for the pleasure of smoking his pipe at ease. He was essentially the man for a German beer-garden, and would have made a good figure in the faubourgs of Vienna, but he was scarcely suited for the throne of such a country as Great Britain. But we English are a strange people; and while we dread a French invasion as the end of all things, we are quite content to invite a dirty and vicious band of vulgar Germans to come and rule over us and rifle our pockets.

The king was surrounded by Hanoverian creatures, who lorded it finely over the English nobility, who were obliged to kiss their feet. There were Baron Bothmar, who had been an agent in London for the elector during the last reign; Bernstorf, who had come over with him, and possessed considerable influence, and, in conjunction with Walpole, managed to get large sums of money into his hands; Goritz, another baron, but more respectable than the rest; Robethon, a French adventurer, to whom Lord Townshend was indebted for his place; and even a couple of Turks, Mahomet and Mustapha, who had been taken prisoners in the war in Hungary, and were now very useful in guarding the king's person and assisting him in affairs in which none but infidels (or Hanoverians) accustomed to the idea of a seraglio would have consented to take a part. To complete this virtuous and charming court, there was young Craggs, an Englishman, the son of a footman, risen into power by the lowest services rendered to the Duke of Marlborough. Young Craggs had got into the elector's favour through the influence of a *third* mistress of his Majesty, who did not accompany him to England, the Countess Platen, who was pleased by the handsome face of the youthful John Thomas. It was Craggs senior who confessed that when getting into his carriage he had always an effort to prevent himself getting up *behind*.

To manage such a band, all of them engaged in making the most possible money out of England, a rich bully like Sir Robert Walpole was indispensable. His character is well known; and it is a comfort to find that his colleagues in the ministry, with only two exceptions, Pulteney and Stanhope, all despised and hated, while they could not but fear him. But it is horrible to find Englishmen and English ministers joining with these rapacious foreigners in spoiling the country, selling places and receiving bribes; still more horrible to find that English ladies of high rank were ready to sell their honour to such people, as the Countess of Suffolk did to the Prince of Wales, a brute who, as Lady Mary tells us, 'looked on all men and women he saw as creatures he might kick or kiss for his diversion.' It certainly makes us smile at the gullibility of John Bull, to find that after denouncing the vices of the Stuarts, he invited over a yet more corrupt set to take their place; and that the main recommendation to the Hanoverian succession should have been the 'religion' of that family.

To this atrocious court was Lady Mary introduced at the age of four-and-twenty, a wit and a beauty. Now surely it is something to her praise that while half the court ladies of her own station were following the example of their august master, though often without the temptations which she must have had, Lady Mary, this monster of corruption as she appears in Walpole's letters, should never have succumbed to them. In the present day it is indeed no praise to a woman to be virtuous, because it is simply what we expect of her, and to be the reverse excludes her from the society of all classes. But when vice was the fashion, and a *liaison*, as it was charitably called, rather exalted than debased a woman, we may at least think passably of one on whom the peculiar smiles of royalty and the attentions of an heir to the throne had no effect but nausea. Lady Mary has left us an account of the court she frequented, which shows, if we take into account the tone of her day, how completely she despised its wickedness; and had she written novels à la Thackeray instead of simple letters, Lady Mary would be hailed—as 'Michael Angelo' is—as the bold satirist of the follies, if not the reformer of the vices, of society.

One work she did produce about this period which, though poor compared with the satires of Pope, entitles her quite to rank near him: this was the 'Town Eclogues,' written in 1715, and published in the following year. They consisted of six poems, one for each day of the week, entitled respectively, 'Roxana, or the Drawing-room;' 'St. James' Coffeehouse;' 'The Tête-à-Tête;' 'The Basset-table;' 'The Toilette;' and 'The Small-pox.' These poems excited a great deal of attention, as the characters portrayed in them were traced to well-known living personages; but reading them now that all the personal interest is passed, we can only say that they are clever, well-turned, somewhat rough, and almost too plain to be finely satirical. The coarseness with which they are replete was a common fault of the day, and was almost refined by the side of Pope and Swift, while, to judge from the letters of other ladies of rank, her contemporaries, Lady Mary did not exceed the licence allowed, even to women, in writing.

An anecdote, which she has related of her court days at this period, has been so often repeated that perhaps it would be wrong to omit it here. On one evening passed at court she wished to escape in order to keep some important engagement. She explained her reasons to the Schulenberg, who told them to the king, but his Majesty was too much charmed with Lady Mary's wit—and well the heavy German may have been so—to allow her to depart. At last, however, she contrived to run away. At the bottom of the stairs she met Craggs, the footman's son, who asked her why she was decamping so early. She told him how the king had pressed her to stay, and without replying he lifted her in his arms and carried her up the stairs into the antechamber, there kissed her hands respectfully, and left her. The page hastily threw open the door, and re-announced her. She was so confused by this sudden transportation, that she told the king, who was delighted to see her come back, the whole story. She had just finished when in came Craggs. 'Mais comment, Monsieur Cragg,' cried the king, ' est-ce que c'est l'usage de ce pays de porter les belles dames comme un sac de froment?' The secretary, confused, could say nothing for a minute or two, but at last recovering himself, muttered, 'There is nothing I would not do for your Majesty's satisfaction;' an answer which was well received.

From this corrupt court Lady Mary escaped to one where there was less corruption, because there was less pretence of either honesty or morality. The Turk had few vices, because his easy religion allowed him many indulgences. The Protestant monarch had many, because his religion, which he cared little for, allowed him none. The Turk could go to the Mosque with a free conscience; Madame Schulenberg went regularly to her Lutheran chapel in the Savoy, but we may question whether the reading of the seventh commandment was not trying to her ears.

In 1716 the embassy to the Porte became vacant, by the removal of Sir Robert Sutton to Vienna. The post was a very important one at that epoch, as it was to England that the Continent looked to settle the differences between Turkey and the Imperialists. That the mission was intrusted to Wortley may be taken as some proof that his talents had recommended him to the ministry. He resigned his situation in the Treasury, and set out in August on a journey which was then hazardous and difficult. It was daring in his wife to accompany him, and her doing so shows that she was still much attached to her husband. Few ladies ventured upon eastern travel, and she was even supposed for a long time to have been the first Englishwoman who had done so; but this was not the case, Ladies Paget and Winchelsea having both accompanied their lords in their respective embassies. However, Lady Mary was the first woman who wrote any account of her travels in those regions, and her letters from the East attained great celebrity. At first, indeed, they were looked upon as exaggerated and replete with 'travellers' tales;' but Mr. Dallaway, who travelled the same route and lived at the same palace at Pera, has vindicated them from this imputation. They were first published in 1763, without the cognizance of her relations, edited, it is supposed, by a Mr. Cleland. She had given a copy of them to Mr. Sowden, the English chaplain at Rotterdam, and it appears that two English gentlemen whom he did not know called upon him one day and requested to see the letters. They had contrived that he should be called away; and when he came back, he found that they had decamped with the books, which, however, they returned the next day with many apologies. To that edition a preface was appended, written in 1724 by a Mrs. Astell, a strong-minded lady, who upheld the 'rights of women' and was delighted to have a person of so much wit as Lady Mary belonging to her own sex. The letters are addressed chiefly to the Countess of Mar, her sister, to Mrs. Thistlethwayte, Mrs. Skerrett, Lady Rich, other ladies belonging to the court, and to the Pope. She appears to have travelled from Rotterdam to the Hague, Nimueguen, Cologne, where she writes, ' I own that I was wicked enough to covet St. Ursula's pearl necklaces,' and wished she herself converted into dressing-plate;' to Nürnberg, after passing Frankfort and Würtzburg. Here she makes an observation which is probably made by every English traveller, with much satisfaction, contrasting the cleanliness and order of the Free Protestant towns with the shabby finery of the rest; and tells us that in a Roman Catholic church at Nürnberg, she had actually seen an image of our Saviour in 'a fair full-bottomed wig very well powdered.' From Nürnberg they passed on to Ratisbon, whence taking boat they proceeded down the Danube to Vienna. Here she received one of Pope's extravagant love-letters, which rather than lose a friend she allowed him to write to her, replying in a jocose strain, which did not show much reciprocity of feeling. In this letter Pope says: 'I think I love you as well as King Herod could Herodias (though I never had so much as one dance with you)'—fancy Pope dancing !—' and would as freely give you my heart in a dish, as he did another's head.' He bears a high testimony to her wit and mind. 'Books have lost their effect upon me; and I was convinced since I saw you, that there is something more powerful than philosophy, and since I heard you, that there is one alive wiser than all the sages.'

In all her letters Lady Mary shows the same powers of observation, mingled with a keen sense of the ridiculous. She sees everything, and describes all she sees; but like a good traveller she takes more notice of the people than of the country, and does not weary her reader with a description of hotels they are not likely ever to enter, and dinners they have not eaten. Many touches here and there prove how little change 150 years make in the character of a nation. Thus she describes the extravagant dressing of the Viennese ladies, their hair piled up over a roll of stuff to an enormous height, and 'their whalebone petticoats of several yards' circumference, covering some acres of ground.' Surely the latter part of this description might have been written just as well in the month of January, 1860. At Vienna a German count made Lady Mary a declaration, and when she replied somewhat indignantly, added with perfect *sang-froid*, 'Since I am not worthy of entertaining you myself, do me the honour of letting me know whom you like best among us, and I'll engage to manage the affair entirely to your satisfaction.' So much for Viennese morals, which have not altered in a century and a half any more than Viennese petticoats.

Mr. Wortley's instructions delayed him about two months at Vienna, and the travellers thence proceeded to Prague, and thence through Dresden, Leipsic, and Brunswick, to Hanover, where they made a halt, to return to Vienna in January, 1717.

At last, at the end of January, the couple started on their perilous journey eastward. However, its perils proved to have been much exaggerated. The terrible Tartar soldiers who ravaged Hungary, killing everything, down to innocent cocks and hens, that they came across, did not molest our travellers. The weather, indeed, was bitter, but sables, and the fur of Muscovite foxes, kept out the cold. Inns there were none; but it is one thing to travel as an ambassador, and another to voyage as a nobody; so the envoy extraordinary and his wife were everywhere well received; and all went on smoothly enough for her ladyship, though probably the Turks, who talked to her, may have been uneasy and wondered if the women of England were not all men.

Lady Mary's letters during this period are very amusing, and her naïve descriptions of things, as she found them, are really the best ever written about the East, not even excepting Eliot Warburton's. Thus, when she goes to the bath, she not only uses her eyes, but her mind. She finds that the frequent contemplation of the nude figure destroys the interest we feel in the human face. Judging from the way we examine the beauties of animals, this is quite comprehensible; and we quite forgive Lady Mary for adding a sigh over the natural sensuality of mankind, which she believes would be twice as great, if civilization had not introduced clothing, an argument which will not readily be admitted. Near Belgrade, again, she passes the field of Carlowitz, still reeking with the blood of the Turks, defeated by Prince Eugene. She looks with horror on the mangled corpses strewn about the field, and without bursting—as is the modern fashion—into a storm of declamation, quietly deplores the evils, and laughs at the 'necessity' of war. 'Nothing seems to be plainer proof of the *irrationability* of mankind (whatever fine claims we pretend to reason) than the rage with which they contend for a small spot of ground, when such vast parts of fruitful earth lie quite uninhabited. It is true, custom has made it unavoidable; but can there be a greater demonstration of want of reason, than a custom being firmly established so contrary to the interest of man in general? I am a good deal inclined to believe Mr. Hobbes, that the *state of nature is a state of war;* but thence I conclude human nature not rational, if the word means common sense, as I suppose it does.'

The grand signior, as the sultan was then called, was at that time at Adrianopol. At Sophia, on her way, she visited a Turkish bath, which she describes in full—the ladies reclining on the sofas, unencumbered with any costume, while attendants combed and dressed their hair and so forth; and how they were quite satisfied, on seeing one stiff hideous portion of her dress, so hated by men, and known only to civilization, that her husband had locked her up in iron in a fit of jealousy.

Her letters from Adrianopol are full of most interesting descriptions, written in the easiest and most unpretending style, and, inasmuch as she was a woman, and therefore admitted where men are excluded, more interesting than any eastern travels ever written. The belief, so general in England, that she was admitted to the seraglio, has been clearly disproved by Lady Louisa Stuart, the writer of the 'Anecdotes' appended to Lord Wharncliffe's edition of Lady Mary's works; but wherever she could go, Lady Mary doubtless went, with plenty of courage and yet more curiosity.

At Adrianopol and elsewhere, Mr. Wortley lived in the greatest possible magnificence, the English government being quite alive to the value of *effect* upon the Turks. He travelled with three hundred horses and a retinue of one hundred and sixty persons, besides his guards. These last were Janissaries; and Lady Mary's letters contain many interesting notices of those now extinct functionaries. The grand signior and his ministers, she tells us, were quite in their power: 'No huzzaing mobs, senseless pamphlets, and tavern disputes about politics,' influenced the Ottoman government; but when a minister displeased the soldiery, in three hours' time, his head, hands, and feet would be thrown at the palace door, while the sultan sat trembling within.

Of the Turkish ladies, their dress, their habits, and their morals, Lady Mary had many opportunities of judging; and pronounces them the most free, rather than the most enthralled, women of the world. At Adrianopol she visited the Sultana Hafiten, the widow of Mustapha II., and Fatima, the wife of the Kyhaia, or deputy to the grand vizier. The latter she affirms to have been far more lovely than any woman she had ever seen at home or abroad. 'I was so struck with admiration,' she writes, 'that I could not for some time speak to her, being wholly taken up in gazing. That surprising harmony of features! that charming result of the whole! that exact proportion of body; that lovely bloom of complexion, unsullied by art! that unutterable enchantment of her smile! But her eyes! large and black, with all the soft languishment of the blue! * * * After my first surprise was over, I endeavoured, by nicely examining her face, to find out some imperfection, without any fruit of my search, but my being convinced of the error of that vulgar notion, that a face exactly proportioned, and perfectly beautiful, would not be agreeable; nature having done for her with more success, what Apelles is said to have essayed by a collection of the most exact features to form a perfect face. * * * To say all in a word, our most celebrated English beauties would vanish near her.'

At length, in the month of May, 1717, the embassy left Adrianopol, after a residence there of about six weeks, and proceeded to Constantinople, where it was lodged in a palace in Pera. Here, wrapped closely in her *feregee* and *asmack*, the adventurous Englishwoman rambled about the city of minarets, seeing all its wonders, and observing narrowly the manners of its inhabitants. Its mosques, its baths, its palaces, its Babel of foreigners, all were described in an easy lively style; and at a time when there were so few books of eastern travel, and those mostly of a very formal character, it will be understood that these letters were read in England with avidity. Her position, as wife of the ambassador of Great Britain, admitted her into the highest native society, as far as a woman could enter it at all; while her knowledge of Turkish, which she learned from one of the dragomans of the embassy, and her interest in classical antiquities, enabled her to give a literary value to her letters. On the other hand, the reader of them will be shocked by what he will perhaps consider their occasional coarseness; but it must be remembered that the manners of her day permitted even a woman to speak openly of many things now passed over in silence; and certainly her descriptions, if sometimes too graphic, give us a more thorough knowledge of the people and the scenes she painted, than the more delicate productions of modern days.

In the month of October, however, Mr. Wortley received letters of recall, countersigned by his friend Addison; and her stay in Constantinople was therefore limited to about a year.

On the 6th of June, 1718, Mr. Wortley and his suite prepared to return to England, but not by the route they had formerly travelled. They now took ship through the Levant round to Tunis, and Lady Mary was delighted by the sight of all the celebrated haunts of Greek lore. After a short stay at Tunis, they sailed for Genoa, passed though Piedmont, stopping at Turin, crossed Mont Cenis into France; and, after short halts at Lyons and Paris, reached England in October, 1718.

Lady Mary Wortley Montagu brought back with her a great reputation as a traveller, and the valuable knowledge of inoculation, which she was determined to introduce into England. She had observed the practice in the villages of Turkey, where it was generally performed by an old woman with a good-sized needle. She had a very natural horror of the small-pox, which had carried off her only brother, to whom she was tenderly attached, and had visited herself in a very severe manner. Of the effects of this attack she wrote a description in one of her 'Town Eclogues,' in which Flavia laments the destruction of her beauty. Fortunately, however, the disease left few traces on her face; but one of its effects was to destroy her eyelashes, thus impairing the softness of the expression, and giving her eyes that fierce look which worked such a spell over Pope, who has immortalized them.

Her first trial of the cure which she had thus discovered was made, with great magnanimity, on her own son, with whom it succeeded admirably; and with a patriotism which entitles her to the gratitude of the country she determined, on her return, to introduce it into England. This was no quiet, no pleasant task, for, instead of a national benefactress, she was hailed as a demon. The faculty prophesied disastrous consequences; the clergy preached against 'the impiety of thus seeking to take events out of the hands of Providence;' and the ignorant and foolish declaimed against her. Yet the repeated success of the operation brought it, though gradually, into favour; and Lady Mary had the courage and the patriotism to persevere. A commission of four physicians was deputed by government to watch the effect of it upon her own daughter; and when this was found satisfactory, poor Lady Mary had to endure the fresh persecution of too much popularity, and her house was turned into a species of consulting place for every one who could claim the slightest acquaintance with her, until, in the course of four or five years, the safety and advantages of the operation were firmly established. Certainly this zeal of Lady Mary's shows a better heart than the partisans of Pope and Walpole will allow her; and whatever her character may have been, she deserves a high place as the introducer of an operation, which, until the discovery of vaccination, was the rescue of many thousands of lives, and which, but for her courage, might have remained untried to this day.

On her return Lady Mary became a great favourite at court, especially with the Princess of Wales, afterwards Queen Caroline; but she had not been long in England, when, at the persuasion of Pope, she retired to a house at Twickenham, where he was then decorating his well-known villa, making, among other things, a subterranean grotto, decorated with looking-glasses—surely the last piece of furniture the hideous little man should have coveted. Lady Mary gives a curious reason for her retirement from London. Mr. Hervey, afterwards Lord Hervey, celebrated for his effeminate character and some mediocre poetry, was then recently married to the beautiful Mary Lepell, whose life, under the title of Lady Hervey, is given in this volume. 'They visited me,' writes Lady Mary, 'twice or thrice a day, and were perpetually cooing in my rooms. I was complaisant a great while, but (as you know) my talent has never lain much that way: I grew at last so weary of those birds of Paradise, I fled to Twick'nam, as much to avoid their persecutions as for my own health, which is still in a declining way.' Yet in after years it was these very people, her partiality for whom brought about her quarrel with the author of the 'Dunciad.'

Mr. Wortley bought the house that Pope had recommended to them, and Lady Mary was chiefly occupied in the alterations they were making in it, the education of her little daughter, and the society of Pope, Gay, and Swift, who were all at Twickenham.

It was here that Pope induced her to sit, or rather stand, to Sir Godfrey Kneller for her portrait in her Turkish costume, which she describes in one of her letters. This dress was truly magnificent, and became her figure *à merveille*. The trousers were of thin rose-coloured damask, brocaded with silver flowers; the slippers of white kid, embroidered with gold. 'Over this hangs my smock of a fine white gauze, edged with embroidery. This smock has wide sleeves, hanging half way down the arm, and is closed at the neck with a diamond button ; but the shape and colour of the bosom are very well to be distinguished through it. The *antery* is a waistcoat made close to the shape of white and gold damask, with very long sleeves falling back, and fringed with deep gold fringe, and should have diamond or pearl buttons.' Then came a *caftan*, of the same stuff as the trousers, and reaching to the feet. It was confined by a broad girdle, studded with precious stones ; and in this was stuck the dagger with a splendid jewelled hilt. The *talpac*, or head-dress, of fine velvet, was, again, covered with pearls or diamonds, and beneath it the hair drawn up from the face hung down behind at full length, braided with copious ribbons. The attitude of queenly dignity which Lady Mary assumed in this costume is very graceful; and her fine figure is set off by it far more than it could have been by the stiff fashions of her day.

Little Pope was in raptures as Sir Godfrey drew the portrait in crayon, to finish it off at his leisure; and we may imagine him hovering about the artist, gazing first at the original and then at the likeness, and already jotting down the following verses, which he gave to his idol, on this occasion :—

> 'The playful smiles around the dimpled mouth,
> The happy air of majesty and truth,
> So would I draw (but oh ! 'tis vain to try,
> My narrow genius does the power deny,)
> The equal lustre of the heavenly mind,
> Where every grace with every virtue's join'd;
> Learning not vain and wisdom not severe,
> With greatness easy, and with wit sincere,
> With just description show the soul divine,
> And the whole princess in my work should shine.'

Very different these lines to the brutal satires he afterwards vented on this 'princess.'

To all gifted with a fine vein of satire, let Lady Mary's quarrels be a warning. She not only lost friends by her uncontrollable wit, but by the bitterness with which she attacked her foes has left posterity in doubt which party was to blame. It was the custom of her day to write ballads on every occurrence in society; and Lady Mary was by no means singular in this indulgence. These productions were hawked and sung about the streets, but seldom traced to their authors, though Lord Hervey and Lady Mary, known to be both poets and satirists, had much of the odium attached to them. It was one of these squibs which gave rise to the first of her many quarrels. A certain Mrs. Murray, for a long time one of her most intimate friends, had had a most disagreeable adventure, which, for a time, was the talk of the town. One of her father's footmen, named Arthur Grey, had, in a drunken fit, one night entered her room, presented a pistol at her head, and declared his solemn intention to gratify the passion he felt for her. Her cries roused the household, the man was seized, tried at the Old Bailey, (where Mrs. Murray was compelled to appear as a witness,) and condemned, on the charge of attempted burglary, to transportation. Two ballads, if not more, appeared on the oc casion. As Mrs. Murray was very pretty, and of winning manners, it was possible to take a romantic view of the incident, and this Lady Mary did in a poem entitled 'An Epistle from Arthur Grey, the footman, to Mrs. Murray;' describing the passion which he had hopelessly entertained for his mistress, and the despair in which he had had recourse to violence. There was nothing in these verses to offend Mrs. Murray, except the mere fact of their giving additional notoriety to an event which ought to have been forgotten. To say the least, it was bad taste on Lady Mary's part to write them. But side by side with these appeared a ballad, which was in every way infamous. Mrs. Murray believing Lady Mary to be the author of both poems, withdrew from her society. The ballad-writer was foolish enough to ask for an explanation, and stoutly denied the authorship of the second piece. Mrs. Murray was not satisfied with this denial, and at a masquerade singled out Lady Mary, attacked her grossly, and hinted at impropriety in her conduct. According to her own account, Lady Mary did not retort, but met this attack with gentleness. However this may have been, the acquaintance could not continue, and Lady Mary had the public odium of scurrility.

Lord Hervey was by no means the best friend Lady Mary could have. His effeminacy and fastidiousness were so well known that she herself said of him that 'this world consisted of men, women and Herveys;' and it is related that when once asked to take beef at dinner, he replied, 'Beef! oh, no—faugh! Don't you know that I never eat beef, or *horse*, or any of those things?'

In addition to this Lord Hervey professed to be a sceptic, and he was certainly a man of bad moral character even for that age. On the other hand he had a fascinating manner, plenty of natural wit, the advantages of a polished education, and—what, perhaps, had more influence with Lady Mary than all the rest—some acquaintance with the Continent. He was already known as a poet; and his 'Four Epistles after the manner of Ovid' were much admired. Gay, and a pleasure seeker, he appears still to have been capable of serious thought, at least sufficient to compose a deistical pamphlet. At Richmond he had met his wife, among the rather brilliant than respectable ladies who thronged about the Princess of Wales, such as Mrs. Howard, Mrs. Selwyn, Miss Bellenden, and Miss Howe. With these ladies Pope,

> 'The ladies' plaything and the muses' pride,'

as Aaron Hill wrote of him, was a great favourite. The Herveys became intimate with him at Richmond, and thus with Lady Mary herself.

Probably this set of wits at Twickenham exemplified the proverb of our copy-books about familiarity and contempt. Certainly they appear to have indulged the first in far too great a degree, and certainly the second came in its wake sooner or later. Lady Mary especially laughed at both Pope and Hervey. She was at Twickenham what the princess was at Richmond, the centre of the same circle when it moved a little farther up the Thames, and she was surrounded by Gay and Swift, Chesterfield, Bathurst, and Bolingbroke, besides Pope and Hervey. Pope's temper was none of the best. Like all satirists, he could not stand being made a butt, however good-naturedly. His mean appearance made him very lonely and morbid with any woman whose affection he wished for, as well as esteem. There is no doubt that Pope was in love with Lady Mary. Though his letters are almost too extravagant to be called love-letters, of which they are sometimes the parodies, at least as coming from a man with a keen sense of the ridiculous; yet many touches in them betray that the fancy he had entertained for her, when a girl, had ripened into something like passion when she was a married woman. Lady Mary allowed him to write these declarations to her, perhaps thinking that neither he could be vain enough nor the world so silly, as to believe she would return them; but what man is not vain when he finds the slightest possible encouragement? It is said, that, at last, he made her a declaration in person, which she, unable to control herself, received with a burst of laughter, rude enough though well deserved. Pope never forgave it, and ceased to visit her. This is one story told to account for their subsequent quarrel.

On the other hand it is related that Pope was jealous of Lord Hervey, with whom Lady Mary became very intimate, and who, though so effeminate, was very handsome in face: and as for effeminacy, there is scarcely a man of any note of that day who may not be charged with it more or less; unless, like Beau Nash and Sir Robert Walpole, he were a mannerless bully. That Pope, with his morbid character, was jealous of John Lord Hervey, is possible enough; nevertheless it is only fair to give his own version of the story, which is, that he cut his old acquaintance 'because they had too much wit for him.' The subterfuge is too evident. Did Pope, would Pope, ever admit that anyone had too much wit for *him?* or, admitting it, would not his vanity have prompted him to accept the fight? On another occasion that great poet—for such even his enemies confess him—ascribed the quarrel to a wish on the part of Lord Hervey and Lady Mary to get him to write a satire on certain persons, of whom he did not think ill enough to accept their propositions. Very good, Mr. Alexander Pope! but was this excuse of thine anything more than an excuse? Strong, terrible as thou wert, we know thee a liar, all the world knows it; and Johnson confesses that before Lady Mary Wortley, thou retreatedst with ignominy. There are, however, few tasks less thankful than raking up the embers of a dead poet's life. There are always plenty of people to defend the poet on the strength of his poetry; and perhaps it is best so. In seeking for the cause of this quarrel, we only seek to exonerate a woman, who really, as women go, was a great deal too good for the bitter, peevish, unannealed author of the 'Dunciad.' Look through the case as we will, we can find little or no blame attaching to Lady Mary; and knowing the morbidness of Pope's character, we are not at all disinclined to attribute all the blame to him. At any rate, Lady Mary asserts that their quarrel was 'without any reason that she knew of;' but there was clearly no love lost between them, at least on her part; since, on the publication of 'Gulliver's Travels,' she writes: ' Here is a book come out, that all our people of taste run mad about; 'tis no less than the united work of a dignified clergyman (Swift), an eminent physician (Dr. Arbuthnot), and the first poet of the age (Pope), and very wonderful it is, God knows; great eloquence have they employed *to prove themselves beasts*, and show such a veneration for horses, &c.' This was written in 1726, and we think it sufficient and very satisfactory proof that at that time Lady Mary and Pope were at variance.

These quarrels of authors, however, can yield us little profit. These two never made it up. They 'flayed' one another in the most disgraceful manner. Pope began it, in his 'Miscellanies' (1727, where he attacked Hervey; but it was not till 1732 that he published his great satire, 'An Imitation of the Second Satire of the First Book of Horace,' and certainly as good as, if not superior to, the original. In this Lord Hervey was well ridiculed as 'Lord Fanny,' and Lady Mary was bantered under the title of 'Sappho.'

The 'Imitation of Horace' will probably live, but who cared for it in those days? Great as Pope was, it was personality that then won the day; and there was more personality in the answer to these verses than in the verses themselves. In short, the 'Verses to the Imitator of Horace' made more sensation, inasmuch as they revealed the secret of a quarrel between the Wortleys and Herveys on the one side, and the most avaricious man of his day on the other. Now, as to the authorship of these verses there is much doubt. One says 'twas Lord Hervey, another 'twas Lady Mary, wrote them. Wilson Croker, the serpent of critics,—a man therefore, to 'go upon'—has pronounced that they are more Hervey's than Wortley's, and more Wortley's than Hervey's — no paradox, meaning withal, that Hervey wrote them and Wortley made them her own. Certainly they are too good for the lord and too bad for the lady; whether fathered by the one or mothered by the other, they are a disgrace to both parents and god-parents. Pope was not only not spared in them, but those physical defects, which he could not help, and about which he was morbidly sensitive, were attacked in a ruthless and cruel manner Thus they begin :—

' In two large columns on thy motly page.
Where Roman wit is striped with English rage;

> Where ribaldry to satire makes pretence,
> And modern scandal rolls with ancient sense.
>
> * * * * *
>
> Thine is just such an image of *his* pen,
> As thou thyself art of the sons of men,
> Where our own species in burlesque we trace,
> A sign-post likeness of the human race,
> That is at once resemblance and disgrace.
>
> * * * * *
>
> Hard as thy heart and as thy birth obscure.'

This last line was disgraceful, and Hervey or Wortley, whichever wrote it, ought to have blushed to taunt the poet with his origin; yet, probably, he heeded no such sneer. Then come allusions to his appearance—

> 'But how should'st thou by beauty's face be moved,
> No more for loving made than to be loved?
> It was the equity of righteous Heav'n,
> That such a soul to such a form was giv'n.'

A sneering threat, equally ungenerous, follows:—

> 'But oh! the sequel of the sentence dread,
> And whilst you bruise their heel, *beware your head*.
>
> * * * * *
>
> And if thou draw'st thy pen to aid the law
> Others a cudgel, or a rod, may draw.
>
> * * * * *
>
> If limbs unbroken, skin without a stain,
> Unwhip't, unblanketed, unkick'd, unslain,
> That wretched little carcase you retain;
> The reason is, not that the world wants eyes,
> But thou'rt so mean, they see, and they despise.'

Yet there was some truth in the last lines, for Pope *was* hated.

> 'But as thou hat'st be hated of mankind,
> And with the emblem of thy crooked mind
> Mark'd on thy back, like Cain by God's own hand,
> Wander, like him, accursèd through the land.'

To these odious verses Pope replied in prose and again in verse, yet more cruel than Hervey's or Wortley's. Lord Hervey was a valetudinarian, and almost supported his existence by means of asses' milk, and Pope accordingly calls him

> '——that mere white curd of ass's milk.'

So the quarrel went on. Doubtless Pope's genius and bitter

ness won the day, but what a poor triumph it was! The man who ridiculed mankind, had not the strength of mind himself to despise the effusions of poetasters like Hervey and Lady Mary, and retorted in even a vulgarer tone than theirs. But perhaps the worst part of the business was, that Pope, with mean cowardice, tried to get out of the scrape by lies. Even Johnson, his admirer and biographer, admits that in his retreat before Lady Mary Wortley he was mean. He soon after attached himself to the opposite party in politics, of which he now became an ardent upholder, and could therefore never forgive Hervey for being his opponent. He attacked him under the name of *Sporus*, and that ably; but while we admire Pope's wit, we cannot but regret that a man of such noble genius should have been guilty of such petty spite.

Of Lady Mary's position during this period, little need be said, because any reader of any memoirs of those days must have met her name frequently as a leader of society. Besides her house at Twickenham, she had one in Cavendish Square, where she received on Sundays the whole court society of London, keeping those whom she liked to supper. Among her intimates were Sarah Duchess of Marlborough and Henry Fielding. She naturally thought more of the former than of the latter, though she was too little a truckler to the spirit of the time to care much for rank. There was rather a certain exclusiveness of caste, a pride of superior understanding and acknowledgment of things, which made the line so marked between the 'upper' and 'lower.' Everybody, more or less, could say with Lady ——, when looking at her lady's maid— 'Regardez cet animal, considérez ce néant, voilà une belle âme pour être immortelle.' If this was the pride of the day —and its stupid blindness, for so it is—we wonder there was not an English revolution in 1789, or even before; but we may still wonder: there are people who think like this to-day, and there is no revolution.

For twenty years Lady Mary Wortley Montagu held court in Cavendish Square, or at Twickenham. Her keen sense of right and wrong disgusted her for English manners of that day and no wonder. Her plain speech, which **certainly** spared neither affectation nor pretence, made her many enemies among people who were, in addition to their vices, both affected and pretentious. She longed to be away from this world of folly, and sought for peace. She believed she should find it on the Continent, and tried to persuade her husband to live abroad.

Whether Mr. Wortley really intended to follow his wife or not, cannot be ascertained; though from an expression in a letter he wrote to her shortly after her departure, it would seem not; for he there says, 'I wish you would be exact and clear in your facts, because I shall lay by carefully what you write of your travels.' It is, however, probable that neither of them at this time contemplated more than a temporary separation, which Lady Mary's ill-health, and Mr. Wortley's advanced years, tended to make permanent. But there seems not the slightest cause for ascribing their separation to incompatibility of temper, or any other estrangement. She wrote to him from her first stage in England, and again from Dover, and from that time they continued to correspond very frequently, and quite as affectionately as two sensible people, of whom the one was more than sixty and the other just fifty, could be expected to do.

Lady Mary left England, then, on July 26, 1739: reached Calais; traversed France, which she found vastly improved in twenty years; and passing through Piedmont and Lombardy, reached Venice in September. She had wished for her comfort to travel incognito; but found this impossible. Wherever she went, she was received as a great celebrity; and writes: "I verily believe, if one of the pyramids of Egypt had travelled it could not have been more followed. At Venice she pitched her tent, living in a palazzo on the Grand Canal, and mingling with the highest society of the place, until the following August, when she made a tour through Italy. At Florence she met Horace Walpole, then a young man of three-and-twenty, travelling through Europe. His description of her, though as exaggerated as all his remarks about her, is too amusing to be omitted. 'Did I tell you Lady Mary Wortley is here? She laughs at my Lady

Walpole, scolds my Lady Pomfret, and is laughed at by the whole town. Her dress, her avarice, and her impudence must amaze any one that never heard her name. She wears a foul mob that does not cover her greasy black locks, that hang loose, never combed or curled; an old mazarine blue wrapper that gapes open and discovers a canvas petticoat. Her face swelled violently on one side, * * * partly covered with a plaster and partly with white paint, which for cheapness she has bought so coarse that you would not use it to wash a chimney.'

When we add that we have left out one part of this description, as too indelicate to reprint, the coarseness of this account will be admitted. The words left out contain an imputation which could not in any probability have been true, which inclines us to doubt the veracity of the whole. Of her dress we have spoken before. Of her 'impudence,' we can only say that Lady Mary was always very plain-spoken, and her candour in condemning affectation to its face may have offended Walpole, who was not always quite free from it. The accusation of avarice, which Walpole repeats in other letters, seems to have been generally credited at the time, though we have no proofs of it. Mr. Wortley was probably very careful of his money, as he left at his death a very large fortune; and Pope, after his quarrel with Lady Mary, speaks of him as 'old Avidien,' in reference to his parsimony. It is probable that his wife's eccentric habits and indifference to dress may have brought the character given to her husband upon her. At Lady Walpole she might well laugh; but as for scolding Lady Pomfret, who was her intimate friend and correspondent, she can only have done so in a most friendly manner, to judge from her own letters.

But we may offer, as a contrast to this description, one given by a clergyman who met the original shortly afterwards, namely, the Rev. Mr. Spence, the author of 'Spence's Anecdotes.'

'Lady Mary is one of the most shining characters in the world, but shines like a comet; she is all irregularity, and always wandering: the most wise, the most imprudent; loveliest, most disagreeable; best natured, cruellest woman in the world, "all things by turns, but nothing long."

Whatever Walpole thought of this celebrated woman, he was 'particularly civil to her,' as Lady Mary herself confesses. which he had no other reason to be, than that he found her agreeable. The truth is, that Horace, in his letters, would say almost anything of those of whom he could do so without danger, for the sake of appearing witty, and Lady Mary is not the only person who has been wrongfully held up by him to the world in a most atrocious light.

After wandering from Florence to Rome, Naples and Genoa, Lady Mary settled at last, in 1742, at Avignon. This place she left in 1746 on account, she tells us, of the number of the 'Scotch and Irish rebels' (meaning the supporters of Prince Charles Edward in 1745) who were crowding there, and who, as Lady Mary was a stanch Hanoverian, made the place very unpleasant to her. A perilous journey through the north of Italy, where the Spanish army met the travellers on their route, brought her to Brescia in Lombardy; and for the next twelve years she lived chiefly at the little watering place of Louvere, on the Lake of Isco in Austrian Lombardy, and at the foot of the Tyrolese mountains. In this charming, and at that time retired spot, the waters of which seem to have done her good, she lived away from the world, with which she kept up no more connection than that of letters, addressed chiefly to her husband and daughter, who also sent her out parcels of the new English books. She seems to have passed her life chiefly in reading and writing. She commenced a history of her times, but foolishly burnt all but a fragment, sufficient to make us regret the loss of the rest, as it gives a most amusing and authentic account of the court of George I. But even in this calm retirement she was not without her cares. The reckless, disgraceful conduct of her son, who appears to have been guilty of every enormity he could conveniently commit, caused her great anxiety. While at Avignon, his mother had seen him, and endeavoured to make a good impression on him, but in vain, as he insisted on returning to Paris, where his conduct had been so bad that he was even imprisoned with a Mr. Taaffe, a disreputable Irish member of Parliament, and devoted friend of Madame de Pompadour, for robbing and cheating a Jew at cards, which, to say the least, showed an amount of sharpness that he was not generally celebrated for. In fact, his mind was very weak, and it is evident, from Lady Mary's letters, that she was afraid he would become insane. He was frivolous and almost childish in his extravagance. In 1751, Walpole, writing from London, says of him: 'Our greatest miracle is Lady M. Wortley's son, whose adventures have made so much noise; his parts are not proportionate, but his expense is incredible. His father scarcely allows him anything,' (this is not true, as may be seen from a letter of Lady Mary's—Vol. ii. p. 325 of Wharncliffe's Edition), 'yet he plays, dresses, diamonds himself, even to distinct shoe-buckles for a frock, and has more snuff-boxes than would suffice a Chinese idol with a hundred noses. But the most curious part of his dress, which he has brought from Paris, is an iron wig: you literally would not know it from hair. I believe it is on this account that the Royal Society have just chosen him of their body.' Lady Mary's letters on the subject of her son show an amount of feeling which the 'cruellest woman' of her day had often been denied to possess.

At Louvere Lady Mary entered more into Italian society than she had ever done before, and this was the more possible, as it was not sufficiently gay to interfere with her retirement. Her letters are full of descriptions of Italian life at that period; and most interesting are her accounts, most amusing her adventures. We regret that we have not space to give extracts from her letters written at this period, but we must notice one adventure, which has been most libellously interpreted by Walpole. For some time she was kept a prisoner by an Italian count in his own house, where she had gone to make a visit. Probably he expected to obtain a ransom from her relations; but as she does not mention the subject in any of her letters or papers, it is difficult to arrive at the real state of the case. To show how shamefully Walpole could malign those whom he did not like, we must mention that he accounted for this detention by an improper *liaison* between the count and Lady Mary. Unfortunately for his character for veracity, the lady was at that time sixty-one years of age; and it may well be asked, if such a connection was at all within the bounds of probability.

In 1758 Lady Mary finally settled at Venice. In 1761 Mr. Wortley died, leaving, says Walpole, a fortune of half a million, of which a thousand a year was left to his son for life and twelve hundred a year to his widow. The main part of the property descended to the daughter, Lady Bute, the wife of the then minister. The conduct of Mr. Wortley and his wife to their son has been aspersed: but considering his disgraceful behaviour, it appears that they acted very well in leaving the bulk of the fortune to his sister.

Lady Mary now returned to England, and took an apartment in George Street, Hanover Square. This was in a house, the rooms of which were shaped like a harpsichord. She writes: 'I am most handsomely lodged. I have two very decent closets and a cupboard on each floor.' She was received enthusiastically and with much curiosity, for her fame was established. Walpole gives the following account of her. 'I went last night to visit her. * * * I found her in a little miserable bedchamber of a ready furnished house, with two tallow candles and a bureau furnished with pots and pans. On her head, in full of all accounts, she had an old black-laced hood, wrapped entirely round, so as to conceal all hair or want of hair. No handkerchief, but up to her chin a kind of horseman's riding-coat, calling itself a *pet-en-l'air*, made of a dark green (green I think it had been) brocade, with coloured and silver flowers and lined with furs, bodice laced; a foul dimity petticoat sprigged, velvet muffeteens on her arms, grey stockings and slippers. Her face less changed in twenty years than I could have imagined. I told her so, and she was not so tolerable twenty years ago that she needed have taken it for flattery, but she did, and literally gave me a box on the ears. She was very lively, all her senses perfect, her languages as imperfect as ever, her avarice greater. She entertained me at first with nothing but the dearness of provisions at Helvoet, with nothing but an Italian, a **French**, and a Prussian, all men-servants, and something she calls an *old* secretary, but whose age, till he appears, will be doubtful. She receives all the world, who go to homage her as Queen Mother' (Lord Bute was at that time prime minister), 'and crams them into this kennel. * * * She says she has left all her clothes at Venice.'

But Lady Mary was suffering from that most terrible disease, cancer in the breast. For a short time she contrived to receive her many friends, and many of the curious, who were not her friends, but anxious to get a view of the famous wit and oriental traveller. The disease had been rendered dangerous by her journey; and after some ten months' residence in England, she died at the age of seventy-two on the 21st of August, 1762.

She is said to have left *one guinea* to her worthless son. She also left her letters behind her. Walpole says: 'I doubt not they are an olio of lies and scandal.' They have turned out not to be the former; and as to scandal, they contain perhaps less than any letters of that day, which was, in every sense, a scandalous one.

Lady Mary filled a useful place in this life. In spite of her enemies, no improper conduct has ever been brought home to her. She hated and despised the vices of her age, and her plain speaking may have done some good in making them ridiculous. She was eminently a satirist, and, perhaps, the greatest female satirist that has ever been. She attacked things evil fearlessly. Some people are cursed by too great readiness for hate. These are evil and their natures demoniacal. Others, with less passion and more sense of justice, are cursed—for in this world it is a curse—with too quick a perception of evil. They detect the fiend at once, and can see only with bleared gaze the angel struggling with him. They attack the evil, but cannot join in the purer triumph of the good. Pure enough themselves, they yet want sympathy with the pure. Their interest is not in the enjoyment of good, but the assault of evil. Warlike spirits, they almost despise the Christian humility of the patient and the hopeful. They would see the world perfect, yet when perfect they would not enjoy it, because there would be no more imperfection to assail. They rarely love, never praise. Such spirits are useful, are almost necessary in an evil world, where it is important to rouse the indignation of the passively good. But they are not lovable, and they often degenerate into mere cynics. The isolation in which their contempt of hypocrisy—the commonest vice of mankind—leaves them at last, sinks into a morbid selfishness. They have few friends, and even of these they cannot help seeing the faults. People like these are happy only in complete solitude or in the company of the utterly harmless; and it is often touching to see with what tenderness your bitter satirist will caress a child, seeking from its ignorance the love he has cut off from himself in the world.

There are many such characters among the great men of this world, and most great characters have a touch of dogmatism. It is in the nature of genius to assert itself strongly. In some it takes the forms of vanity: in others of bitterness. But this character is rare among women, who, as a rule, would rather be loved, though all the world were damned, than save one soul by making themselves disagreeable. Lady Mary was an exception to this rule of womankind. She showed at an early age how thoroughly she despised the meaner qualities of mankind.

Her love of her husband was founded in conviction that he was free from all affectation and hypocrisy—his very openness in telling her of her faults endeared him to her. She always knew her own faults, though she would not always confess them. Her so-called cruelty, especially to Pope, was based on the same grounds. A vainer woman might have been flattered by the love of the greatest poet of his age. Lady Mary could not help seeing his weak points, and despised him for them. Say what we will of Pope, we must own him a coward. His very satire wanted elevation. It was that of despair, of bitterness, rather than of indignant justice. He did not write as one that would thrust down evil proudly, but as the viper which wriggles to the heel it hates, to poison it. He left his venom in many a conscience, but he was neither feared nor admired, only hated. After all, there was much to love in Pope, much to pity, much to excuse. But Lady Mary would not see it; and that the scourge of society, the man who said that those who did not fear God, should at least fear *him*, should be guilty of the evil passion he entertained for her, may well have made her despise him. It is something to say for her that whatever she may have written in verse, and with his own weapons, she seldom spoke ill of him in her letters. She seems to have forgotten, if not forgiven, him.

In Lady Mary herself there is much to love. Though married to a man of no lovable character, she was a faithful wife. She was an excellent mother to her daughter, Lady Bute, and tried to be so to her worthless son. Walpole's assertion that she ill treated her sister, Lady Mar, has not been proved, and her affectionate letters to her scarcely permit us to credit the possibility of her doing so. With all her contempt for littleness, she was a warm friend, though an unsparing enemy. Her introduction of inoculation under much opposition is some proof of the general benevolence that was in her, and we cannot read her letters without seeing that she could appreciate the good as well as detect the evil in mankind. There is something very attractive in her eccentricity; and her contempt of her own appearance certainly exonerates her from all charge of vanity. But perhaps there are two portraits which do her more justice than any review we can now take of her character—the one painted in a few words by Mr. Spence, as we have already quoted it, and the other in miniature prefixed to Lord Wharncliffe's edition of her letters. The latter especially, the writer confesses, has made a very favourable impression on him.

GEORGIANA DUCHESS OF DEVONSHIRE.

Her Parents.—The Duchess when a Girl.—The Duke and the Lustres.—Devonshire House.—Prince Charles Stuart.—An Atrocious Nobleman.—Sheridan.—The 'Maid of Bath.'—Fox.—The Gambler and Herodotus.—The Ladies' Canvass.—The Duchess and the Butcher.—Fox Elected.—Mrs. Crewe.—The True Blue.—The Smile that Won.—Scandal about the Duchess.—George the Third goes Mad.—'The Weird Sisters.'—Burke and Fox.—Death of Fox.—Lines on his Bust.—Death of the Duchess.—Lady Elizabeth Foster.—Report relative to her.

NOTWITHSTANDING the purity of morals enjoined by the court of George III., the early period of his reign presents a picture of dissolute manners as well as of furious party spirit. The most fashionable of our ladies of rank were immersed in play or devoted to politics: the same spirit carried them into both. The sabbath was disregarded, spent often in cards, or desecrated by the meeting of partizans of both factions; moral duties were neglected and decorum outraged.

The fact was that a minor court had become the centre of all the bad passions and reprehensible pursuits in vogue. Carlton House, in Pall Mall, which even the oldest of us can barely remember, with its elegant screen, open, with pillars in front, its low exterior, its many small rooms, the vulgar taste of its decorations, and, to crown the whole, the associations of a corrupting revelry with the whole place,—Carlton House was, in the days of good King George, almost as great a scandal to the country as Whitehall in the time of improper King Charles II.

The influence which the example of a young prince, of manners eminently popular, produced upon the young nobility of the realm must be taken into account in the narrative of that life which was so brilliant and so misspent; so blessed at its onset, so dreary in its close—the life of Georgiana Duchess of

Devonshire. Descended in the third degree from Sarah Duchess of Marlborough, Georgiana Spencer is said to have resembled her celebrated ancestress in the style of her beauty. She was born in 1757. Her father, John, created Earl Spencer in 1765, was the son of the reprobate 'Jack Spencer,' as he was styled, the misery at once and the darling of his grandmother, Sarah, who idolized her Torrismond, as she called him, and left him a considerable portion of her property. Whilst the loveliness of Sarah descended to Georgiana Spencer, she certainly inherited somewhat of the talent, the reckless spirits, and the imprudence of her grandfather, 'Jack;' neither could a careful education eradicate these hereditary characteristics.

Her mother was the daughter of a commoner, the Right Honourable Stephen Poyntz, of Midgham, in Berkshire. This lady was long remembered both by friends and neighbours with veneration. She was sensible and intelligent, polite, agreeable, and of unbounded charity; but Miss Burney, who knew her, depicts her as ostentatious in her exertions, and somewhat self-righteous and vain-glorious. She was, however, fervently beloved by her daughter, who afterwards made several pecuniary sacrifices to insure her mother's comfort. The earliest years of Lady Georgiana (as she became after her father was created an earl) were passed in the large house at Holywell, close to St. Albans, built by the famous Duke of Marlborough on his wife's patrimonial estate. Aged people, some fifteen years ago, especially a certain neighbouring clergyman, remembered going to play at cards in this house; and the neighbourly qualities of Lady Spencer, as much as her benevolence to the poor, endeared her much to the gentry around. She exercised not only the duties of charity, but the scarcely minor ones of hospitality and courtesy to her neighbours. Before the opening of railroads, such duties were more especially requisite to keep together the scattered members of country society. Good feelings were engendered, good manners promoted, and the attachment then felt for old families had a deeper foundation than servility or even custom. As Lady Georgiana grew up, she displayed a warm impressionable nature, a passion for all that was beautiful in art, strong affections, and an early disposition to coquetry.

Her character spoke out in her face, which was the most eloquent of all faces : yet it was by no means beautiful if we look upon beauty critically. There were persons who said that her face would have been ordinary but for its transcendant loveliness of expression. Unlike the fair Gunnings, she was neither regular in features nor faultless in form, yet theirs was baby-beauty compared with hers. True, her hair inclined to red, her mouth was wide, but her complexion was exquisite; and the lips, ever laughing, were parted over a splendid set of teeth, an attribute rare in those days when the teeth were often decayed in youth. She had, too, a charm of manner natural to her, and a playfulness of conversation, which, springing from a cultivated mind, rendered her society most fascinating. 'Her heart, too,' writes Wraxall, her contemporary, 'might be considered as the seat of those emotions which sweeten human life, adorn our nature, and diffuse a nameless charm over existence.'

A younger sister, Henrietta Frances, afterwards Lady Duncannon, and eventually Countess of Bessborough, was also the object of Lady Georgiana's warm affection; and although Lady Duncannon was very inferior to her in elegance of mind and personal attractions, she equalled her in sisterly love.

During the middle of the last century, literature was again the fashion among the higher classes. Dr. Johnson and the Thrales, Miss Burney, Hannah More, still clustered at Streatham: many of our politicians were, if not poets, poetasters. It is true, if we except the heart-touching poems of Cowper, the Muses were silent: the verses which were the delight of polished drawing-rooms were of little value, and have been swept away from our memories of the present day as waste-paper; but a taste for what is refined was thus prevalent, and thus affected the then rising generation favourably.

Lady Georgiana Spencer had, however, a very few years allotted her for improvement or for the enjoyment of her youth, for in her seventeenth year she married.

William, the fifth Duke of Devonshire, at the time when he was united to Lady Georgiana Spencer was twenty-seven years of age. He was one of the most apathetic of men. Tall, yet not even stately, calm to a fault, he had inherited from the

Cavendish family a stern probity of character, which is always has a certain influence in society. Weight he wanted not, for a heavier man never led to the altar a wife full of generous impulses and of sensibility. He was wholly incapable of strong emotion, and could only be roused by whist or faro from a sort of moral lethargy. He was, nevertheless, crammed with a learning that caused him to be a sort of oracle at Brookes's, when disputes arose about passages from Roman poets or historians. With all these qualities, he was capable of being, in a certain sense, in love, though not always with his lovely and engaging first wife.

Miss Burney relates a characteristic trait of this nobleman: it was related to her by Miss Monckton. The duke was standing near a very fine glass lustre in a corner of a room in the house of people who were not possessed of means sufficient to consider expense as immaterial; by carelessly lolling back, he threw the lustre back, and it was broken. He was not, however, in the least disturbed by the accident, but coolly said, 'I wonder how I did that!' He then removed to the opposite corner, and to show, it was supposed, that he had forgotten what he had done, leaned his head in the same manner, and down came the second lustre. He looked at it with philosophical composure, and merely said, 'This is singular enough,' and walked to another part of the room without either distress or apology. To this automaton was the young Lady Georgiana consigned; and the marriage was, in the estimation of society, a splendid alliance.

Her animal spirits were excessive, and enabled her to cope with the misfortune of being linked to a noble expletive. Her good humour was unceasing, and her countenance was as open as her heart. Fitted as she was by the sweetest of dispositions for domestic life, one can hardly wonder at her plunging into the excitements of politics when at home there was no sympathy. Hence her bitterest misfortunes originated; but one cannot, with all her indiscretions, suffer a comparison between her and the Duchesse de Longueville, which Wraxall has instituted. The Duchess of Devonshire scarcely merits the covert censure; except in beauty and talents there was no similitude.

Buoyant with health and happiness, the young duchess was introduced into the highest circles of London as a matter of course. Her husband represented one of the most influential families of the Whig aristocracy, and his name and fortune made him important.

Three West End *palaces*, as they might well be termed, Carlton House, Devonshire House, and Burlington House, were open to every parliamentary adherent of the famous *coalition*—the alliance between Lord North and Charles James Fox. Devonshire House, standing opposite to the Green Park, and placed upon an eminence, seemed to look down upon the Queen's House, as Buckingham Palace was then called. Piccadilly then, though no longer, as in Queen Anne's time, infested with highwaymen, was almost at the extremity of the West End.

In right of his descent, on his mother's side from the Boyle family, the Duke of Devonshire was also the owner of Burlington House, situated near Devonshire House, and inhabited by his brother-in-law, the Duke of Portland.

Thus a complete Whig colony existed in that part of London, the head and front of their party being no less a person than George Prince of Wales. He was at this time in the very height of his short-lived health and youth, and still more short-lived popularity, a man who possessed all the exterior qualities in which his father was deficient,—grace as well as good nature, the attribute of George III., a certain degree of cultivation, as well as of natural talent, a tall, handsome person, with a face less German in type than those of his brothers, some generosity of character—witness his kindness to Cardinal York, the brother of Prince Charles Edward, whom he pensioned—an *appearance*, at all events, of an extremely good heart, and a great capacity for social enjoyments.

Dr. Burney states that he was surprised, on meeting the prince at Lord Melbourne's, to find him, amidst the constant dissipation of his life, possessed of 'much learning, wit, knowledge of books in general, discrimination of character, and original humour.' He spoke with Dr. Charles Burney, the distinguished scholar, quoting Homer in Greek with fluency; he was a first-rate critic in music, and a capital mimic. 'Had we been in the dark,' said Dr. Burney, 'I should have sworn that Dr. Parr and Kemble were in the room.' Hence, the same judge thought 'he might be said to have as much wit as Charles II., with much more learning, for his merry majesty could spell no better than the *bourgeois gentilhomme.*' Such was the partial description of the prince by a flattered and grateful contemporary, who wrote in 1805. Twenty years later Sir Walter Scott, after dining with the then Prince Regent, paid all justice to *manners;* but pronounced his mind to be of no high order, and his taste, in so far as wit was concerned, to be condemned.

The prince was, however, just the man to be the centre of a spirited Opposition. In his heart he was Conservative; but the Whigs were his partisans against a father who strongly, and perhaps not too sternly, disapproved of his mode of life and his politics.

The circle around him was as remarkable for their talents, and, in some respects, as infamous for their vices as any Lord Rochester, or Sedley, or Etherege of the time of the second Charles. In the reign of George the Second, a Protestant Duke of Norfolk took an active part in political affairs, and formed one of the chief supporters of the Whigs. Carlton House, Devonshire House, often received in their state rooms 'Jock of Norfolk,' as he was called, whose large muscular person, more like that of a grazier or a butcher, was hailed there with delight, for his Grace commanded numerous boroughs. He was one of the most strenuous supporters of Fox, and had displayed in the House of Lords a sort of rude eloquence, characteristic of his mind and body. Nothing, however, but his rank, his wealth, his influences, his Whig opinions, could have rendered this profligate, revolting man endurable. Drunkenness is said to have been inherent in his constitution, and to have been inherited from the Plantagenets. He was known in his youth to have been found sleeping in the streets, intoxicated, on a block of wood; yet he is related to have been so capable of resisting the effects of wine, that, after laying his father, a drunkard like himself, under the table at the Thatched House, St. James's, he has been stated to have repaired to another party, there to finish the convivial rites. He was often under the influence of wine when, as Lord Surrey, he sat in the House of Commons; but was wise enough, on such occasions, to hold his tongue. He was so dirty in his person, that his servants used to take advantage of his fits of intoxication to wash him; when they stripped him as they would have done a corpse, and performed ablutions which were somewhat necessary, as he never made use of water; he was equally averse to a change of linen. One day, complaining to Dudley North that he was a prey to rheumatism, 'Pray,' cried North, 'did your Grace ever try a clean shirt?'

This uncleanly form constituted a great feature of the Whig assemblies. At that time every man wore a queue, every man had his hair powdered; yet 'Jock' renounced powder, which he never wore except at court, and cut his hair short. His appearance, therefore, must have been a strange contrast with that of the Prince of Wales, curled and powdered, with faultless ruffles, and an ample, snow-white cravat, to say nothing of the coat which looked as if it were sewn on his back. It is to the Duke of Norfolk that the suggestion of putting a tax on hair powder has been ascribed. His life was one series of profligacy. Yet, such was the perverted judgment of the day, that this unworthy descendant of the Plantagenets was as popular as any peer of his time. When sober, he was accessible, conversable, and devoid of pride. When intoxicated, he used half to confess that he was still a Catholic at heart. His conversion to the reformed faith was held not to be very sincere; and his perpetual blue coat of a peculiar shade—a dress he never varied—was said to be a penance imposed on him by his confessor. He did no credit to any Christian church; and the Church of Rome is welcome to his memory.

Richard Brinsley Sheridan, at this period in his thirty-third year, was not then wholly degraded by drinking, debt, and, as far as money was concerned, dishonesty. His countenance at this age was full of intelligence, humour, and gaiety: all these characteristics played around his mouth, and aided the effect of his oratory to the ear. His voice was singularly melodious, and a sort of fascination attended all he did and said. His face, as Milton says of the form of the fallen angel,

> 'Had not yet lost
> All her original brightness.'

Yet he lived to be known by the name of 'Bardolph'—to have every fine expression lost in traces of drunkenness. No one could have perceived, in after days, the once joyous spirit of Sheridan in a face covered with eruptions, and beaming no longer with intelligence. He resembled, says Wraxall, at sixty, one of the companions of Ulysses, who, having tasted of Circe's 'charmed cup,'

> '——— lost his upright shape,
> And downward fell into a grovelling swine.'

This extraordinary man was the husband of one of the most beautiful, and, in being his wife, one of the most unfortunate of women. Miss Linley, the daughter of a celebrated musical composer, and called, for her loveliness, the 'Maid of Bath,' had the calamity of being wooed and won by Sheridan. Never was there a more touching and instructive history than hers. Her beauty was rare, even amid the belles of a period rich in attractive women. Dark masses of hair drawn back on her brow, fell in curls on a neck of alabaster. Her features were delicate and regular; the expression of her eyes was exquisitely soft and pensive. Her charms have been transmitted to her female descendants, Mrs. Norton, the Duchess of Somerset, and Lady Dufferin, whilst they have also inherited her musical talents, and the wit and ability of their grandfather. Mrs. Sheridan, after a life of alternate splendour and privation, died at Clifton, of consumption, before middle age. Her death was saddened, if not hastened, by her carriage, as she was preparing to drive out on the Downs, being seized for her husband's debts. Whilst united to this young and lovely wife, Sheridan was one of the brightest stars in the dissolute sphere of Carlton House; but for domestic life he had neither time nor disposition. His fame was at its climax, when, during the trial of

Warren Hastings, he spoke for hours in Westminster Hall, with an eloquence never to be forgotten; then, going to the House of Commons, exhibited there powers of unrivalled oratory. Meantime the theatres were ringing with applause, and his name went from mouth to mouth whilst the 'Duenna' was acted at one house, the 'School for Scandal' at another. He was, in truth, the most highly-gifted man of his time; and he died in the fear of bailiffs taking his bed from under him—an awe-struck, forlorn, despised drunkard!

But of all the party men to whom the young Duchess of Devonshire was introduced, the most able and the most dissolute was Fox. The colouring of political friends, which concealed his vices, or rather which gave them a false hue, has long since faded away. We now know Fox as he *was*. In the latest journals of Horace Walpole, his inveterate gambling, his open profligacy, his utter want of honour, is disclosed by one of his own opinions. Corrupted ere yet he had left his home, whilst in age a boy, there is, however, the comfort of reflecting that he outlived his vices. Fox, with a green apron tied round his waist, pruning and nailing up his fruit trees at St. Ann's Hill, or amusing himself innocently with a few friends, is a pleasing object to remember, even whilst his early career recurs forcibly to the mind.

Unhappily he formed one of the most intimate of those whom Georgiana Duchess of Devonshire admitted to her home. He was soon enthralled among her votaries, yet he was by no means a pleasing object to look at as he advanced in life. He had dark saturnine features, thought by some to resemble those of Charles II., from whom he was descended in the female line: when they relaxed into a smile, they were, it is said, irresistible. Black shaggy eyebrows concealed the workings of his mind, but gave immense expression to his countenance. His figure was broad, and only graceful when his wonderful intellect threw even over that the power of genius, and produced, when in declamation, the most impassioned gestures. Having been a coxcomb in his youth, Fox was now degenerating into the sloven. The blue frock coat and buff waistcoat with which he appeared in the House of Commons were worn and shabby. Like the white rose which distinguished the Stuarts, so were the blue and buff the badge of the American insurgents and of Washington, their chief.

Having ceased to be the head of the Macaronis, as the *beau monde* were then called, Fox had devoted himself to play. Whist, quinze, and horse-racing were his passion, and he threw away a thousand pounds as if they had been a guinea; and he lost his whole fortune at the gaming-table. Before thirty he was reduced to distress, even in the common affairs of life. He could not pay the chairmen who carried him to the House. He was known to borrow money from the waiters at Brooke's, which was the rallying-point of the Opposition. There the night was spent in whist, faro, suppers, and political consultations. Dissolute as he was, there was a kindness, a generosity of disposition that made his influence over man or woman most perilous to both. Then he was one of the most accomplished of students in history and general letters; and to his studies he could even devote himself after irretrievable losses at play. Topham Beauclerk, after having passed the whole night with Fox at faro, saw him leave the club in desperation. He had lost enormously. Fearful of the consequences, Beauclerk followed him to his lodgings. Fox was in the drawing-room, intently engaged over a Greek 'Herodotus.' Beauclerk expressed his surprise. 'What would you have me do? I have lost my last shilling,' was the reply. So great was the elasticity of his disposition, sometimes, after losing all the money he could manage to borrow at faro, he used to lay his head on the table, and, instead of railing at fortune, fall fast asleep. For some years after the Duchess of Devonshire's marriage Fox had continued to represent Westminster. So long as he retained that position, Pitt's triumph could not be considered as complete, nor the Tory party as firmly established in the administration. Three candidates appeared on the hustings in April, 1784—Lord Hood, Sir Cecil Wray, and Fox. So late as the twenty-sixth of the month Wray, who had sat for some time for Westminster in Parliament, maintained a small numerical advantage over Fox. The election, which began on the first of the month, had now gone on more than three weeks; ten thousand voters had polled; and it was even expected that, since the voters were exhausted, the books would be closed, and Wray, who was second on the poll, Lord Hood being first, would carry the day.

Happily we have now no adequate notion of the terrors of such an election: it was a scene of fun and malice, spirit and baseness, alternately. Englishmen seemed hardly men: whilst they one hour blustered, the next they took the bribe, and were civil. Fox went down to Westminster in a carriage with Colonel North, Lord North's son, behind as a footman, and the well-known Colonel Hanger—one of the reprobate associates of George IV. (when Prince Regent), and long remembered on a white horse in the Park, after being deserted by the prince and out of vogue—driving, in the coat, hat, and wig of a coachman. When Queen Charlotte heard of this exploit of Colonel North's she dismissed him from his office of comptroller of her household, saying she did not covet another man's servant.

As the month drew to a close, every hour became precious, and Fox gained at this critical juncture two new and potent allies. Dressed in garter-blue and buff, in compliment to Fox and his principles, forth came the young Duchess of Devonshire and her sister, now Lady Duncannon, and solicited votes for their candidate. The mob were gratified by the aspect of so much rank, so great beauty, cringing for their support. Never, it was said, had two 'such lovely *portraits* appeared before on a *canvass*.'

It required, indeed, no ordinary courage to undertake collecting votes, for a strong disposition to rioting now manifested itself. Nevertheless, being provided with lists of the outlying voters, these two young women drove to their dwellings. In their enterprise, they had to face butchers, tailors, every craft, low or high, and to pass through the lowest, the dirtiest, and most degraded parts of London. But Fox was a hundred votes below Wray, and his fair friends were indefatigable: they forgot their dignity, their womanhood, and 'party' was their watchword. They were opposed by the Marchioness of Salisbury, whom the Tories brought forward. She was beautiful, but haughty; and her age, for she was thirty-four, whereas the Duchess of Devonshire was only twenty-six, deteriorated from the effect of her appearance.

Forgetting her rank, which Lady Salisbury always remembered, and throwing all her powers of fascination into the scale, the young duchess alighted during one of her canvassing days at a butcher's shop. The owner, in his apron and sleeves, stoutly refused his vote, except on one condition—'Would her grace give him a kiss?' The request was granted. This was one of the votes which swelled the number of two hundred and thirty-five above Sir Cecil Wray, and Fox stood second on the poll. Of course much stupid poetry was written on the occasion.

> 'Condemn not, prudes, fair Devon's plan,
>   In giving *Steel* a kiss:
> In such a cause, for such a man,
>   She could not do amiss.'

Even the Prince of Wales took an active interest in this memorable election; and George III. is said to have also interfered. Never was political rancour so high, nor conscience so low, as at that period. The hustings resembled the stand at Newmarket. 'An even bet that he comes in second,' cried one: 'five to four on this day's poll,' screamed another. Amid all these shouts, gazed at by the lowest of all human beings, the low, not only in rank but in feeling, the drunken, paid-for voters, stood the duchess and a band of fair titled friends supporting Fox, who was called the 'Man of the People.'

It was the 17th of May when Fox, over whose head a scrutiny hung on the part of Sir Cecil Wray, and who was not thought even then returned as member, was chaired. This procession took place as the poll closed. Fox was carried through the streets on a chair decorated with laurel, the ladies in blue and buff forming part of the *cortège*. Before him was displayed the prince's plume: those three ostrich feathers, the sight of which might bring back to our minds the field of Cressy, where they were won, and henceforth worn for four successive centuries. A flag, on which was inscribed, 'Sacred to Female Patriotism,' was waved by a horseman in the triumphant cavalcade. The carriages of the Duke of Devonshire and the Duke of Portland attracted even less attention than that of Fox, on the box of which were Colonel North and other friends, partizans of Lord North's, who now mingled with their former opponents. As the procession turned into Pall Mall, it was observed that the gates of Carlton House were open: it passed in, therefore, and saluted, in veering round, the Prince of Wales, who, with a number of ladies and gentlemen, stood in the balustrade in front. Fox then addressed the crowd, and attempted to disperse them; but at night the mob broke out into acts of fury, illuminated, and attacked those houses which were in sullen darkness.

The next day the Prince invited all the rank, beauty, and fashion of the Coalition party to a fête on his lawn. It was a bright day that 18th of May: and under the delicious shade of the trees the young and gay forgot perhaps, in the enchantments of the scene, politics and elections. Lord North, dressed in blue and buff—his new livery—strutted about amid those who only fifteen months before had execrated and denounced him, until, by the Coalition with Fox, he had made himself their idol. Every one, on this occasion, crowded round the minister, whose wit was as inexhaustible as his *sang-froid*, and whose conversation in its playfulness resembled that of our great premier of 1859. Blue and buff pervaded the garden. Colonel North (afterwards Lord Guildford) and George Byng, hitherto bitter enemies, were seen, dressed alike, walking together familiarly. The prince was irresistibly fascinating, and nothing could be more splendid than the fête given by royalty overwhelmed by debt.

As the party were thus enjoying themselves, by a strange coincidence the famous cream-coloured horses of George III. were beheld proceeding in solemn state down St. James's Park. His Majesty was going to Westminster to open Parliament. Nothing but a low wall separated Carlton Gardens from the park, so that the king could not forbear seeing his former minister, his son, and the successful candidate disporting themselves in all the elation of success.

In the evening Lower Grosvenor Street was blocked up with carriages, out of which gentlemen and ladies all in blue and buff descended to visit the famous Mrs. Crewe, whose husband, then member for Chester, was created, in 1806, Lord Crewe. This lady was as remarkable for her accomplishments and her worth as for her beauty; nevertheless, she permitted the admiration of Fox, who was in the rank of her admirers. The lines he wrote on her were not exaggerated. They began thus:—

> 'Where the loveliest expression to features is joined,
> By Nature's most delicate pencil design'd;
> Where blushes unbidden, and smiles without art,
> Speak the softness and feeling that dwell in the heart;
> Where in manners enchanting, no blemish we trace,
> But the soul keeps the promise we had from the face;
> Sure philosophy, reason, and coldness must prove
> Defences unequal to shield us from love.'

Nearly eight years after the famous election at Westminster, Mrs. Crewe was still in perfection, with a son of one-and-twenty, who looked like her brother. The form of her face was exquisitely lovely, her complexion radiant. 'I know not,' Miss Burney writes, 'any female in her first youth who could bear the comparison. She uglifies every one near her.'

This charming partisan of Fox had been active in his cause; and her originality of character, her good humour, her recklessness of consequences, made her a capital canvasser.

The same company that had assembled in the morning at Carlton House, now crowded into Grosvenor Street. Blue and buff were the order of the evening, the Prince of Wales wearing those colours. After supper he gave a toast—'True blue and Mrs. Crewe.' The room rang with applause. The hostess rose to return thanks. 'True blue, and all of you,' was her toast. Nor did the festivities end here. Carlton House some days afterwards received all the great world, the 'true blues' of London. The fête, which was of the most varied kind, and of the most magnificent description, began at noon, went on all night, and was not ended till the next day. Nothing could exceed its splendour. A costly banquet was prepared for the ladies, on whom his royal highness and the gentlemen waited whilst they were seated at table. Nothing could exceed the grace, the courtesy, the *tact*, of the prince on these occasions, when he forgot his two hundred thousand pounds of debts, and added to them. Louis XIV., said an eye-witness, could not have eclipsed him.

This was probably the brightest era in the life of the Duchess of Devonshire. She was the lady paramount of the aristocratic Whig circles, in which rank and literature were blended with political characters. Slanders soon coupled her name with that of Fox; and that name, though never wholly blighted, was sullied. Miss Burney meeting her at Bath, some years afterwards, describes her as no longer beautiful, but with manners exquisitely polite, and 'with a gentle quiet' of demeanour. Yet there was an expression of melancholy. 'I thought she looked oppressed within,' was Miss Burney's remark. On another occasion she found her more lively, and consequently more lovely, vivacity being so much her characteristic that her style of beauty required it. 'She was quite gay, easy, and charming; indeed that last word might have been coined for her:' and Miss Burney soon perceived that it was the sweetness of her smile, her open, ingenuous countenance, that had won her the celebrity which had attended her career of fashion.

But even then there was a canker in the duchess's felicity. Lady Elizabeth Foster, the daughter of the Earl of Bristol, and a contrast to her in person—large, dark, and handsome—had attracted the duke her husband, and the coldest of men had become deeply enamoured of this woman, whom he eventually married. Gibbon said of Lady Elizabeth, that she was the most alluring of women. Strange to say a sort of friendship existed between the duchess and Lady Elizabeth, who was with her at Bath, when Miss Burney saw them together. Even then a cloud hung over these two ladies of rank; and Mrs. Ord, Miss Burney's cautious friend, reproved her for making their acquaintance.

Three children of rare promise were given to occupy the affections which were so little reciprocated by the duke. The elder of the three, Georgiana Dorothy, afterwards married to the Earl of Carlisle, and the mother of the present Duchess of Sutherland, is described by Miss Burney, at eight years of age, as having a fine, sweet, and handsome countenance, and with the form and figure of a girl of twelve. She, as well as her sister, were at that time under the care of Miss Trimmer, the daughter of Mrs. Trimmer, one of the most admirable writers for children that has ever delighted our infancy. Miss Trimmer is described as a 'pleasing, not pretty' young lady, with great serenity of manner.

Lady Henrietta Elizabeth, married to the Earl of Granville, so long ambassador at Paris, was, 'at six years of age, by no means handsome, but had an open and pleasing countenance, and a look of the most happy disposition;' a tribute borne out by the many virtues of that admirable lady in after life. The Marquis of Hartington, afterwards Duke of Devonshire, then only fourteen months old (this was in 1791), had already a house, and a carriage to himself, almost in the style of royalty. He lived near his father, whilst the duchess was staying with her mother, Lady Spencer. To persons of domestic notions this seems a singular arrangement.

This apparently happy family party had, however, some trials to obscure their supposed felicity. Scandal not only pointed to Lady Elizabeth Foster as possessing an undue influence over the duke, but attacked the duchess in the most sacred relations of her life. The little marquis was reputed to be illegitimate; the report assumed several shapes; of course rancorous political partisans pointed to the intimacy with Fox; others to the intimacy at Carlton House. Another story also obtained credit, and never died away. This was that at the time when the duchess was confined, Lady Elizabeth gave birth to a son, the duchess to a daughter, and that the children were changed; that the late duke entered into a contract with his uncle, the late Lord George Cavendish, never to marry, in order that his lordship's children might have an undisputed succession at his Grace's death.

There was another source of disquiet to Lady Spencer and the duchess at this time, in the deep depression of Lady Duncannon. This lady, the mother of Lady Caroline Lamb, so conspicuous for her eccentricity in our own time, seems to have been affectionately beloved by her brother the Lord Spencer, the grandfather of the present earl. 'He made up to her,' says Miss Burney, 'with every mark of pitying affection, she receiving him with the most expressive pleasure, though nearly silent.' This afflicted woman lived, nevertheless, to a great age, and survived her gay, spirited sister, the Duchess of Devonshire.

Lady Spencer belonged to that class whom we now call evangelical; a class earnest in feeling, originating in a sincere desire to renovate the almost dead faith of the period; to set an example of piety and decorum; and also 'to let their light shine before men.' Miss Burney describes her as too desirous of a reputation for charity and devotion. Nevertheless, Lady Spencer could not detach her daughter from the gay world

The duchess continued to take an active part in politics, and to mingle with the tumult of elections, faro, and party triumphs, love, poetry, and the fine arts. Her son was born in the dawn of that Revolution in France which shook the foundations of all social life. At this very period a serious calamity befel their country in the first fit of insanity that attacked George III. Up to the very time when France was plunged into commotion, his Majesty, apparently in perfect health, had held his weekly levees at St. James's until the last week of October, 1788. Early in November the first paroxysms of his disordered intellect occurred at the Queen's Lodge, after dinner, her Majesty and the princesses being present. The gates of the Lodge were closed that night; no answers were given to persons making inquiries: and it was rumoured that his Majesty was dead.

The state of the public mind may readily be conceived: the capital exhibited a scene of confusion and excitement only exceeded by that displayed four years afterwards, when the decapitation of Louis XVI. was announced in London.

A regency was proposed; and six physicians were called in to act in consultation. Dr. Warren was considered to hold the first place in this learned junto. Dr. Addington, the father of the late Lord Sidmouth, Sir Lucas Pepys, and Dr. Willis, were amongst the rest. Warren was disposed to Whiggism, and thought the king's recovery doubtful; Willis was a Tory, and pronounced it possible, and indeed probable: his dictum was believed at St. James's and at Kew Palace; Warren was credited at Carlton House and Devonshire House. If the first was the oracle of White's, the second was trusted at Brookes's. The famous Duchess of Gordon, the partisan of Pitt and Dundas, supported Willis and his views, and was the whipper-in of the Tory party. The Duchess of Devonshire was the firm and powerful supporter of the prince, in his claims to the regency. The Tories were for the power, not only over the royal household, but over the council, being vested in Queen Charlotte. A caricature was circulated representing the Lord Chancellor, Pitt, and Dundas as the three 'weird sisters' gazing at the full moon. Her orb was half enlightened, half eclipsed. The part in darkness contained the king's profile; on the other side was a head, resplendent in light, graciously gazing at the weird sisters; that was the queen. In the February of the ensuing year, nevertheless, to the great joy of the nation, the king showed signs of amendment. One day, Mr. Greville, brother to the Earl of Warwick, was standing near the king's bed, and relating to Dr. Willis that Lord North had made inquiries after the king's health. 'Has he?' said the king. 'Where did he make them, at St. James's, or here?' An answer being given, 'Lord North,' said his Majesty, 'is a good man, unlike the others: he is a good man.' The party at Carlton House, amongst whom the Duchess of Devonshire must ever be ranked, were disappointed at this timely recovery, whilst the honest-hearted middle and lower classes of England were unfeignedly rejoiced; but there was too much party rancour existing for any better spirit to arise and show itself. Even in society, the venom of party was suffered to intrude. Lord Mountnorris being one evening at a ball given by the French ambassador, canvassed the whole room for a partner, but in vain. He begged Miss Vernon to interfere, and procure him a partner for a country dance. She complied, and presented him to a very elegant young lady, with whom his lordship danced, and conversed some time. Soon afterwards a gentleman said to him, 'Pray, my Lord, do you know with whom you have been dancing?' 'No,' he replied; 'pray who is she?' 'Coalitions,' said the gentleman, 'will never end; why, it is Miss Fox, the niece of Charles, and sister of Lord Holland.' The noble lord was thunderstruck. Had Pitt seen him? If so, he was undone. He ran up to reproach Miss Vernon. 'True,' was the reply; 'she *is* the niece of Fox, but since she has twenty thousand pounds to her fortune, I thought I had not acted improperly in introducing you.'

In the famous quarrel between Burke and Fox, the Duchess of Devonshire took the office of mediator. Burke thus attacked Fox in the House of Commons.

'Mr. Fox,' he said, 'has treated me with harshness and malignity. After harassing with his light troops in the skirmishes of "order," he has brought the heavy artillery of his own great abilities to bear on me. There have,' he added, 'been many differences between Mr. Fox and myself, but there has been no loss of friendship between us. There is something in this cursed French constitution which envenoms everything.'

Fox whispered, 'There is no loss of friendship between us.' Burke replied, 'There *is*. I know the price of my conduct: our friendship is at an end.'

Fox was overwhelmed with grief at these words. He rose to reply, but his feelings deprived him of utterance. Relieved by a burst of tears, whilst a deep silence pervaded the house, he at last spoke.

'However events,' he said in deep emotion, 'may have altered the mind of my honourable friend—for so I must still call him—I cannot so easily consent to relinquish and dissolve that intimate connection which has for twenty-five years subsisted between us. I hope that Mr. Burke will think on past times, and whatever conduct of mine has caused the offence, he will at least believe that I did not intend to offend.' But the quarrel was never reconciled, notwithstanding the good offices of the Duchess of Devonshire, the friend of both parties.

Soon after the commencement of the nineteenth century, this party spirit was, as it were, rebuked, first by the death of Pitt, and afterwards by that of Fox, who was long in a declining state. When he heard that Pitt had expired, he said, 'Pitt has died in January, perhaps I may go off in June. I feel my constitution dissolving.' When asked by a friend, during the month of August, to make one of a party in the country, at Christmas, he declined.

'It will be a new scene,' said his friend.

'I shall indeed be in a new scene by Christmas next,' Mr. Fox replied. On that occasion he expressed his belief in the immortality of the soul; 'but how,' he added, 'it acts as separated from the body, is beyond my capacity of judgment.' Mr. Fox took his hand and wept. 'I am happy,' he added, 'full of confidence; I may say of certainty.'

One of his greatest desires was to be removed to St. Ann's Hill, near Chertsey, the scene of his later, his reformed, his happier life. His physicians hesitated and recommended his being carried first to the Duke of Devonshire's house at Chiswick. Here, for a time, he seemed to recover health and spirits. Mrs. Fox, Lady Holland, his niece, and Lady Elizabeth Foster were around his death-bed. Many times did he take leave of those dearest to him; many times did death hover over him; yet we find no record that the Duchess of Devonshire was amongst those who received his last sigh. His last words to Mrs. Fox and Lord Holland were, 'God bless you, bless you, and you all! I die happy—I pity you!'

'Oh! my country!' were Pitt's last words; those of Fox were equally characteristic. His nature was tender and sympathetic, and had he lived in other times he would have been probably as good as he was great.

His remains were removed from Chiswick to his own apartments in St. James's, and conveyed under a splendid canopy to Westminster Abbey. As the gorgeous procession passed Carlton House, a band of music, consisting of thirty, played the 'Dead March in Saul.' The Prince of Wales had wished to follow his friend on foot to the grave, but such a tribute was forbidden by etiquette.

It is to be regretted that princes must be exempted from so many of the scenes in this sublunary life calculated to touch the heart, to chasten and elevate the spirit. As the funeral entered the Abbey, and those solemn words, 'I am the Resurrection and the Life,' were chanted, the deepest emotion affected those who had known and loved him whose pall they bore.

Among other tributes to the memory of Fox were the following lines from the pen of the Duchess of Devonshire. The visitor to Woburn Abbey will find them underneath the bust of the great statesman in a temple dedicated to Liberty by the late Duke of Bedford.

> 'Here, near the friends he lov'd, the man behold,
> In truth unshaken, and in virtue bold,
> Whose patriot zeal and uncorrupted mind
> Dared to assert the freedom of mankind;
> And, whilst extending desolation far,
> Ambition spread the hateful flames of war:
> Fearless of blame, and eloquent to save,
> 'Twas he—'twas Fox—the warning counsel gave,
> Midst jarring conflicts stemm'd the tide of blood,
> And to the menac'd world a sea-mark stood!
> Oh! had his voice in mercy's cause prevailed,
> What grateful millions had the statesman hail'd:
> Whose wisdom made the broils of nations cease,
> And taught the world humanity and peace!
> But, though he fail'd, succeeding ages here
> The vain, yet pious efforts shall revere;
> Boast in their annals his illustrious name,
> Uphold his greatness, and confirm his fame.'

The duchess only survived Fox a year: she died in 1806, beloved, charitable, penitent. Her disease was an abscess of the liver, which was detected rather suddenly, and which proved fatal some months after it was first suspected. When the Prince of Wales heard of her death, he remarked: 'Then the best-natured and best-bred woman in England is gone.' Her remains were conveyed to the family vault of the Cavendish family in All Saints' Church, Derby; and over that sepulchre one fond heart, at all events, sorrowed. Her sister, Lady Duncannon, though far inferior to the Duchess in elegance both of mind and person, had the same warm heart and strong affection for her family. During the month of July, 1811, a short time before the death of the Duke of Devonshire (the husband of the duchess), Sir Nathaniel Wraxall visited the vault of All Saints' Church. As he stood admiring the coffin in which the remains of the once lovely Georgiana lay mouldering, the woman who had accompanied him showed him the shreds of a bouquet which lay on the coffin. Like the mortal coil of that frame within, the bouquet was now reduced almost to dust. 'That nosegay,' said the woman, 'was brought here by the Countess of Bessborough, who had intended to place it herself upon the coffin of her sister; but as she approached the steps of the vault, her agony became too great to permit her to proceed. She knelt down on the stones of the church, as nearly over the place where the coffin stood in the vault below as I could direct, and there deposited the flowers, enjoining me to perform an office to which she was unequal. I fulfilled her wishes.'

By others the poor duchess was not so faithfully remembered. Her friend Lady Elizabeth Foster had long since become her rival, yet one common secret, it was believed, kept them from a rupture. Both had, it was understood, much to conceal. The story of the late Duke of Devonshire's supposed birth has been referred to: he is supposed to have been the son of the duke, but not of Georgiana Duchess of Devonshire, but of her who *afterwards* bore that title, Lady Elizabeth Foster. The inflexible determination of the late duke to remain single, according, it is said, to an agreement between him and his uncle, then Lord George Cavendish, always seemed to imply, in a man of such pure and domestic tastes, so affectionate a disposition, and so princely a fortune, some dire impediment.

In 1824, Lady Elizabeth Foster, then the second Duchess of Devonshire, expired at Rome, where she had lived many years in almost regal splendour. Amongst her most intimate friends were the Cardinal Gonsalvi and Madame Récamier, who were cognizant of the report, which was confirmed in their minds by the late duke's conduct at her death. Lady Elizabeth, as we shall still by way of distinction call her, was then so emaciated as to resemble a living spectre; but the lines of a rare and commanding beauty still remained. Her features were regular and noble, her eyes magnificent, and her attenuated figure was upright and dignified, with the step of an empress. Her complexion of marble paleness completed this portrait. Her beautiful arms and hands were still as white as ivory, though almost like a skeleton's from their thinness. She used in vain to attempt to disguise their emaciation by wearing bracelets and rings. Though surrounded by every object of art in which she delighted, by the society, both of the English, Italian, and French persons of distinction whom she preferred, there was a shade of sadness on this fascinating woman's brow, as if remembrance forbade her usual calm of life's decline.

Her stepson (so reported,) the late duke, treated her with respect and even affection, but there was an evident reserve between them. At her death he carefully excluded all friends to whom she could in her last moments confide what might perhaps, at that hour, trouble her conscience. Her friends, Madame Récamier and the Duc de Laval, were only admitted to bid her farewell when she was speechless, and a few minutes before she breathed her last.

The circumstance struck them forcibly as confirmatory of the report alluded to ; but, it must in candour be stated, that the duke's precautions may have originated in another source. His stepmother was disposed to Romanism, and he may have feared that the zeal of her Catholic friends should prompt them, if opportunity occurred, to speak to her on the subject of her faith, and to suggest the adoption of such consolations as their own notions would have thought indispensable at that awful moment. The point is one that cannot be settled. It may, however, be remarked, that in disposition, in his wide benevolence and courteous manners, the late duke greatly resembled the subject of this memoir—the beautiful, the gifted, but the worldly Georgiana Duchess of Devonshire.

LETITIA ELIZABETH LANDON. (L. E. L.)

Brompton of Yore.—The Landons.—At Hans Place.—Mrs. Rowden's Day school.—Giving out the Prizes.—Genius against Education.—Reads Walter Scott.—Mrs. Landon.—First Poem.—Bulwer on L. E. L.—Self-dependence.—Goes into Society.—'Sally Siddons.'—'The Improvisatrice.'—Never in Love.—More Imputations.—Deaths.—Miss Landon Defends Herself.—Return to Hans Place.—Her Life there.—Two Hundred Offers.—Her Society.—Literary Pursuits.—Visit to Paris.—More Calumny.—Engagement with Mr. Forster.—Broken Off.—Letter on the Subject.—Morbid Despair.—Meets Mr. Maclean.—Mr. Maclean.—His Mysterious Conduct.—Marriage.—Last Days in England.—Sails from England.—Voyage out.—Life at Cape Coast Castle.—Her Mysterious Death.—Investigations.—The Mystery Unsolved.—Suspicions.—The Widower's Tribute.—Mrs. Landon.—Remarks on L. E. L.'s Death.—Her Last Letter.—Past and Future.

IT is now more than forty years ago since an eminent writer and journalist, looking from the window of his house in Old Brompton, was attracted by the appearance of a little girl, who was trundling a hoop with one hand, and holding in the other a book of poems, of which she was catching a glimpse between the agitating course of her evolutions. It was literally 'run and read.' The gentleman was William Jerdan; the girl was Letitia Elizabeth Landon.

The scene must have been a pleasing one; the matured, successful man of letters, full of criticism and politics, Canning's last *mot*, Normanby's first novel; besieged by authors with attentions, fêted by nobles—the then prince of weekly journalists had so much still of truth in his heart, of benevolence and fatherly interest, that he paused in the intervals of his work to look at the studious yet playful child and her hoop.

She was then, in spite of adverse circumstances, a round-faced, rosy little creature, blithe as any lark, active as a butterfly, but pensive and poetic as a nightingale. Take also into your mind's picture the localities: Brompton was out of town then; haymaking went on in Brompton Crescent; monthly roses and honeysuckles flourished in Brompton Row; Michael's Grove *was* a grove, though one might count its trees; and, beyond, there were lanes that penetrated beyond Old Brompton and terminated at once in the country. Vegetation there was early and rapid, and the place had an almost village-like simplicity about it. There was no Brompton Square, no Alexander Square—neither terraces nor crescents with greater names than the mere designation, Michael's the patron saint or building sinner, wherefore one knows not, and the humble name, Brompton. Yet stay; let me look into my inestimable friend Peter Cunningham's valuable 'Handbook for London,' in which we are told how Amelia Place, now Pelham Crescent, was once a pleasant row of houses looking over a nursery garden (in L. E. L.'s time): how the churchyard, on the first grave of which she wrote one of her most beautiful poems, was in *her* childhood a blooming garden; nay more, how famed the 'hamlet,' as Cunningham calls it, of Brompton had been as the grave of authors, actors, and singers. How Beloe, the sexagenarian, and Count Rumford—strange anomaly!—had died in the same house, 45, Brompton Row; how here George Colman had succumbed to fate; then Curran; here again, Miss Pope, the lady actress *par excellence*, who taught our grandmothers how to enter a room, how to go to court, and how to contract their mouths by repeating the words 'niminy piminy,' (vide some old play in which she used to convulse the audience by these syllables). He tells us all this; so let us realize that Letitia Landon was reared amid flowers, and near the imaginative and dramatic personages in whom she ever found great interest.

She was not, however, born at Brompton, but in the adjacent parish of Chelsea, in the genteel enclosure of Hans Place, number twenty-five. Since poverty is next to a crime in some classes of English society, the lowly circumstances of her family were for some years adduced as a proof that they were of mean origin. She was descended, nevertheless, from an ancient and honourable race, the Landons of Crednell in Herefordshire, and flourished on their own estate until Sir William Landon, Knight, rashly ventured his luck in the South Sea bubble; and his estates were absorbed in the general wreck. After that time, adieu to opulence, or, indeed, to prosperity of any stable kind for that branch of the family from which Letitia was descended.

Still they were able to keep up a position in the world, and to enter those professions which hold so good a place in England. From generation to generation the Landons were beneficed clergymen: John Landon, Rector of Nursted and Ilsted in Kent, the great grandfather of Letitia, was noted for his literary abilities, which were directed against his son, the Rector of Tedstone Delamere. He was, however, encumbered with eight children, the eldest of whom was another John Landon, the father of L. E. L., who, eschewing a clerical life, quitted his home, went off to sea, made a voyage to the coast of Africa, that very south coast where his daughter afterwards perished, and came home again, quitting the service on the death of his friend and patron, Admiral Bowyer.

His younger brother, meanwhile, Whittington, had entered the church, and obtained considerable distinction at Oxford. Aided by his own scholastic knowledge, by his agreeable manners—which are said by those who remember him to have been both dignified and urbane—he became eventually Provost of Worcester College, the patronage of the Duke of Portland having been extended, in this instance, to his elevation. The Provost was also endowed with the deanery of Exeter, and his flourishing circumstances operated favourably on those of his elder brothers. Through the kindness of a mutual friend, named Churchill, John Landon became a partner in the house of Adair, then a prosperous army agent in Pall Mall.

His next piece of success was to find a wife with a good fortune—Miss Catherine Jane Bishop, of a Welsh extraction, who began life, as those who knew her formerly have asserted, when unmarried, with fourteen thousand pounds to her fortune, 'her horse, and her groom.' On the 14th of August, 1802, the eldest child of this apparently happy couple, Letitia Elizabeth, was born. They were then living in Hans Place, in a house built by Holland, the great architect of those days and those parts, and long inhabited by his son, Captain Holland. It 's situated to the west, the south-west side of the quiet little square, and is a charming house of its *genre*, with two pleasant drawing-rooms, and a third, forming a sort of conservatory boudoir, and looking into a strip of garden. Beyond, in L. E. L.'s time, were the gardens of the late Peter Denys, Esq., then residing at the Pavilion, a house also built by Holland for his own residence. The gardens were since tenanted by a market gardener, famous for his salads and asparagus.

Beyond these gardens there were only detached houses, skirting a strip of land then called Chelsea Common, but more like a large field than a common. The little garden of number twenty-five was full of roses. Umbrageous trees on the left denoted the beautiful pavilion gardens, exquisitely planted with appropriate shrubs, with a miniature lake, to which sloped a lawn, broken here and there by parterres. All this scene was familiar to L. E. L. in her infancy, and in the dawn of her childhood; and she always retained a fondness for Hans Place. A racket ground has usurped the space whereon the market gardener (the well-known Catleugh, a frequent exhibitor of geraniums) raised his salads, or gathered, for his customers the earliest strawberries with the dew still on them. The pavilion gardens are divided: land and rents have risen since the days when Letitia looked out from her nursery window on gooseberry bushes and cherry trees; yet the repose of Hans Place is still unbroken.

One beloved companion shared the small pleasures of the little Letitia, and that was her brother Whittington, some years younger than herself. They were inseparable, except when Letitia went to learn to read, taught by an invalid neighbour, who used to scatter large letters over the floor, and tell her pupil to name them, and form them into words. When she was good, the child was rewarded, and her recompense, whatever it might be, was taken home and shared with her brother. 'She must have been very quick,' M.: Landon, years afterwards, remarked, 'for she used to bring home many rewards; and I began to look eagerly for her coming back.' When unsuccessful, or inattentive, she had brought home nothing, the future poetess crept up stairs to her nurse, to whom she was much attached, to be consoled.

At five years of age, she went as a day scholar to an admirable school, at that time established at number twenty-two in Hans Place. This house, for many years in after life, was the residence of L. E. L. through sickness, in happiness, in good report and bad report: and it had other associations beside those connected with L. E. L. to arrest the attention of the passer-by. It is the next house to the pavilion gates on the east side of the square; and has a kind of off-shoot, of one story, containing a long, low room, half overshadowed with plane trees of the pavilion, half with the elms of a close, small garden in the back, in which half of L. E. L.'s life was passed.

It happened that Miss, or as she styled herself Mrs. Rowden was a lady of singular acquirements and energy: more especially she cultivated, what is now so greatly neglected, the committing to memory the English classics, and the reciting before an audience the best passages, as they do at Harrow and Eton on prize days. She was herself a poetess, and quite a character in her way; clean, lively, full of energy, kind, devoted to what she esteemed the highest of all professions, that of education. Such women are now rare. Then French was taught in Miss Rowden's school by an emigrant, the Comte St. Quentin, whose accent and idiom were very different from those of the modern French teacher, taken from a far lower class than formerly, when the noble exiles from Paris gave lessons. Hence L. E. L. acquired two things which she never lost—a love of poetry, and a pure French accent; a fair intellectual stock in trade to begin her youth with. Mary Mitford was another gifted pupil of Mrs. Rowden's, and remained for years the friend and correspondent of her instructress, who marrying the Comte St. Quentin, removed eventually to Paris. L. E. L. was not, however, very long a regular pupil of Mrs. Rowden's, but used, in after days, to attend classes there, so as to derive advantage from her plans. Amongst other celebrated persons who knew and respected Mrs. Rowden, was Lady Caroline Lamb, who was an inmate of number twenty-two for some time. Lady Caroline used to give out the prizes on breaking-up days; and for several years her graceful form was seen entering the long, low room, which has been described, leading by the hand her little boy, whom she was destined to lose. 'After the business of the day was over,' writes a former pupil of Mrs. Rowden's, 'Master Lamb used to be set on a high table to recite Shakespeare, which he did with wonderful emphasis for such a child. I well remember his giving the "Seven Ages of Man."' No wonder the poor boy died early. How little could Lady Caroline imagine that amid the smiling, eager faces then uplifted towards her, there was one for which many an eye would afterwards turn with intense eagerness as the three magic letters L. E. L. were uttered: that, in that very room, should be decided the tragical fate of that child, the youngest in the school, who could then—it was her only fault her teacher said—never walk steadily from joyousness of spirit, there suffer sickness, anxiety, and the hard unkindness from an unsparing world!

Scarcely was L. E. L. seven years old when her father removed to Trevor Park, East Barnet, and for some time her education was superintended by her excellent cousin, Miss Elizabeth Landon, who survives her intelligent little pupil. Her imagination, and more especially her memory, were now plainly apparent to her family. At night she would amuse her parents by their fireside with the wonderful castles her fancy pictured. She was perfectly happy in the garden, talking to herself, and walking with what she called her 'measuring stick' in her hand. When spoken to at such times she used to say, 'Oh! don't talk to me; I have such a delightful idea in my mind.' During all this period of her life, the education of L. E. L. was carefully attended to. It was not by an impulse of genius alone that she became a poetess, but by long mental culture of a generous kind; by reading works of sound history, travels, biography—wading through books, not skimming them, and mastering each as she went on. In music, however, although she had the advantage of being taught by Miss Bissett, a lady of first-rate powers, she never attained any proficiency, although all her life fond of vocal music. Neither could she ever be made to write a good hand. Her writing was cramped, as if she had used her left hand only, and was always a matter of difficulty to her. Her affections developed with her intellect. She was so full of faults, and yet so fond of her brother, that it was found expedient, when one was guilty of an offence, to punish the other for it. 'Nothing,' her brother said, 'could subdue her will, except it was done through her affections.' The system adopted with her was a stern one; but it prepared her for that life of work and of self-dependence which she afterwards encountered. Even at this early age the disinterested, self-denying character of her maturer years was apparent. 'I had,' writes her brother, 'petitioned my father for three shillings,' when he offered me, by way of compromise, a new eighteenpenny piece if I would learn the ballad—

> 'Gentle river, gentle river,
> Lo! thy streams are stained with gore.'

Alas! it was thirty verses long, and flesh and blood in the boy revolted. But Letitia, seeing his dilemma, offered to learn the thirty verses herself, repeated them perfectly, and got the three shillings. She then persuaded her brother to learn it, teaching him verse by verse. 'I don't,' says Mr. Landon, 'remember whether I ever said it; but I do remember that she gave me the three shillings.'

One of her early exploits was teaching her father's gardener, thirty years of age, to read: this was her first good deed. The man rose to be a milkman; and eventually, enabled by Letitia's tuition to keep his own books, he prospered so well as to settle down in a respectable public-house at Barnet.

At Trevor Park, L. E. L.'s happiest, perhaps her only *really* happy days were passed. Imagination is an infinite source of delight to children. She found in her brother a ready listener to her 'travels'—all supposititious rambles—to her 'desert island.' Happily for her, the pure, high-toned works of Walter Scott were the reading of the day. Well does every parent judge who has them in his library. It was an inestimable advantage to the young people of that time. All in *his* works has a tendency to elevate: his poetry, which is so far inferior to his prose, is devoid of the passionate gloom of Byron, free from the poisonous casuistry of Shelley. L. E. L. knew the 'Lady of the Lake' by heart, and lived on Scott's poetry, as she has said in her poem on the Great Unknown.

> 'I peopled all the walks and shades
>   With images of thine:
> This lime-tree was a lady's bower,
>   The yew-tree was a shrine;
> Almost I deem'd each sunbeam shone
> O'er bonnet, spear, and morion.'

The mental appetite of the young at that age is not *difficile;* and she forgot, in the enchanting interest of the story, the defects in Scott as a versifier: 'Marmion' was her favourite; and she sometimes in after life repeated in low, almost tremulous accents, and very impressively, those lines descriptive of Constance when brought before the conclave of monks to receive sentence. She was always touched by the recital of every valiant action; and one of her earliest pieces were stanzas on 'Sir John Doyle,' that brave old soldier (the uncle of Lady Bulwer Lytton), whom L. E. L. afterwards personally knew.

During the course of years, her character was thus formed. As it developed itself, an impressionable, hasty, honest nature appeared: tears and smiles, long after the age of infancy, came easily, and quickly succeeded each other. The sweetness of her temper in after life was remarkable. As a child, she was passionate; but she acquired afterwards one of the best sort of tempers—that which is naturally impulsive, but which is regulated by principle and firm regard for the feelings of others.

To her cousin L. E. L. owed much: from her mother she inherited much. Mrs. Landon resembled her daughter greatly. A thin, small woman, with a countenance full of animation, it was evident, from the expression of her eyes, whence the talents of L. E. L. were derived. Short as L. E. L. was, her mother was somewhat shorter; quick as were L. E. L.'s movements, those of her mother were quicker still. In voice, in native vivacity of character, they greatly resembled each other. Mrs. Landon was a person of cultivated mind, warm feelings, great penetration, considerable wit.

During the season of the prosperity of Mr. and Mrs. Landon, another daughter was born—a fragile being, who died of consumption at thirteen years of age. Mrs. Landon was devoted to this poor child, in whom, from difference of age, L. E. L. found no companionship: so that, whilst her brother was at school, she still lived, as it were, undisturbed in her own little world, and her imagination became the ascendant power of her mind.

Until the age of thirteen, L. E. L. was a healthy, blooming girl, full of spirits—a romp, as girls should be at that age; and her childhood, in spite of her melancholy account of it in several of her compositions, was a joyous one. But clouds were lowering over her home, and from henceforth the struggles, which were scarcely closed until her death, began. Mr. Landon—an amiable man, of an easy and sanguine temper—had encumbered himself with a farm, and lost large sums from the mismanagement of his bailiff. Business was not prosperous, and the failure, eventually, of Adair's house plunged him into difficulties which he never retrieved. Trevor Park was given up: and he took his wife and children to Old Brompton, where the first dawnings of L. E. L.'s genius were discovered, encouraged, and finally introduced to the world by Mr. Jerdan. It was about the year 1818 that some of L. E. L.'s poetical efforts were printed in the 'Literary Gazette,' which at that time was almost the only purely literary weekly journal, and a periodical of great influence and extended circulation.

She was only fifteen when, a year before, she had published a little volume entitled 'The Fate of Adelaide,' a poem which she dedicated to her mother's intimate friend, Mrs. Siddons. 'The Fate of Adelaide' was involved in the failure of its publisher, Mr. Warren, of Bond Street, and, though it sold well, L. E. L. never received any profit for her production. She next appeared under the shelter of her famous initials in a series of 'Poetical Sketches' in the 'Literary Gazette.' These sketches are eminently beautiful, and were deservedly successful: the initials became, as Leman Blanchard expresses it, a *name*. That was not an age of poetry; and the strong utilitarian tendencies of the times would, one might suppose, have frozen the current of a young and unknown poetical genius. Malthus and Senior flourished; Miss Martineau was not far off; Byron was 'unproper;' Scott was 'feeble;' Tennyson, a boy at college; and poetry was a thing appertaining to a long past century, not to ours. Yet passion, fancy, feeling, in all the freshness of an original mind, spoke to the heart, and had a response. When, in 1831, Sir Edward Bulwer Lytton (then Mr. Bulwer only) edited the 'New Monthly,' in his review of 'Romance and Reality'—L. E. L.'s first novel—he thus alluded to the effect produced by her poetry, and by the mystery that hung over her identity.

'We were,' he says, 'at that time more capable than we now are of poetic enthusiasm; and certainly that enthusiasm we not only felt ourselves, but we shared with every second person we then met. We were young, and at college, lavishing our golden years, not so much on the Greek verse and mystic character to which we ought, perhaps, to have been rigidly devoted, as

'"Our heart in passion and our head in rhyme."

'At that time poetry was not yet out of fashion, at least with us of the cloister, and there was always in the reading-room of the Union a rush every Saturday afternoon for the "Literary Gazette," and an impatient anxiety to hasten at once to that corner of the sheet which contained the three magical letters L. E. L. And all of us praised the verse, and all of us guessed at the author. We soon learned it was a female, and our admiration was doubled, and our conjectures tripled. Was she young? Was she pretty? And—for there were some embryo fortune-hunters among us—was she rich? We ourselves who, now staid critics and sober gentlemen, are about coldly to measure to a prose work' (what is here quoted is introductory to a review of 'Romance and Reality') 'the due quantum of laud and censure, then only thought of homage, and in verse only we condescended to use it. But the other day, in looking over some of our boyish effusions, we found a paper superscribed to L. E. L., and beginning with "Fair Spirit!"'

Whilst she was thus almost unconsciously exciting a strong curiosity about herself, the young poetess was experiencing a great calamity, which certainly overshadowed all her life with its consequences. Her father died. It was not only that she loved him—for he was a kind and proud parent—but that, just as she was entering life, her youth, her genius requiring more than ordinary protection, she lost that tie which kept together her family—that stay to which she could have looked for support when, misunderstood by some, misrepresented by others, she became the object of calumny.

The blow had another effect: it threw L. E. L. completely on her own efforts. Poverty, in that appalling form which it wears in great cities, now threatened her mother, herself, and her sister. She had always looked to her own efforts to help her family, and she joyfully became aware of her power to serve them. But from henceforth, after the first blithesome period of her songful youth, poetry became unhappily her profession. Never did any writer more wonderfully rise above the effects of task-writing than L. E. L., but that it crippled her genius there can be no doubt. And her home was happy no longer. Her mother's temper, with a warm heart as she had, clashed with hers. L. E. L. deeply regretted her father, whom she loved with that exceeding love to which is added the feeling of a more than ordinary loss. Yet she was still buoyant, hopeful, and gay as any skylark singing as it soars aloft. There is no doubt but that in the separation that afterwards ensued between her and her mother much blame was due to herself. She began to feel her powers, and to reject control. Society spoiled her, as her parents had done, not so much by over fondness, but by that pride in her talents that intoxicates. She was carried along, too, by impressions that in after life she would have repelled. Her early adversity had taught her self-dependence, and she now sometimes wished to tear herself away from constraint—to live as certain *esprits forts* did, alone; to be a Corinne, her poetry and her fame giving her a sort of brevet among girls of her own age. Yet with all this, for which she paid so dearly, her heart was as pure, her character as innocent. her taste as exalted, as that of the most irreproachable English girl who has never contemplated an emancipation from the restraints of home.

Great anxieties, too, and many coming privations, added doubtless to the irritations of that unhappy period. And there were many inconveniences in a small *ménage* to one who now had before her a career such as few women, if any, in our country could ever have contemplated as their lot. Society now found out that L. E. L., as well as her poetry, was essential to it. The first of her patronesses was the late Miss Spence, a lady known to her contemporaries as the authoress of 'Dame Rebecca Berry,' a production the credit or discredit of which was shared by Lady Bulwer Lytton, who was, at the time when it appeared, the beautiful and gifted Rosina Wheeler. Miss Spence was of Scottish origin, somehow related to Fordyce and his sermons, whom she always managed to bring out in a couplet with Lady Isabella Spence. L. E. L. was gratified by a call from Miss Spence, who in those days of leo-hunting was proud to be the first to present to a select circle in little rooms, in Little Quebec Street, Mayfair, the veritable L. E. L., fresh caught for their amusement. Here L. E. L. first met Sir Lytton Bulwer, then a fair young man, of aristrocratic elegance, full of wit and fancy, and then passionately attached to her whom he since made his wife. The *petits comités* in Little Quebec Street were often attended by Lady Caroline Lamb, who soon evinced an interest in L. E. L. which ended only with Lady Caroline's life. Miss Wheeler, to a perfect beauty of face, with her magnificent figure, united great wit, great liveliness, and a power of appreciating the genius of L. E. L. Their friendship was afterwards painfully terminated; but in Sir Bulwer Lytton L. E. L. ever found a constant, sensible, and sincere friend, whose regard for her survived her death.

Her descriptions of these social literary meetings, these *bas bleus réunions* up three pair of stairs—Miss Spence in a blue toque doing the honours—were very graphic; and Moore, who heard them sometimes, thought that the powers of Miss Austen were vested, as well as great poetical gifts, in L. E. L. But when her novels appeared it was seen that he was mistaken.

Literary and intellectual society were not, however, wholly new to L. E. L., though not in the *bas-bleu* system. Mrs. Siddons's friendship for Mrs. Landon lasted their lives, and was of an intimate character. 'Sally Siddons,' Mrs. Landon used to say, 'worked the first cap ever put on my Letitia's head when a baby.' She referred to that charming, doomed daughter of Mrs. Siddons who died of consumption whilst her mother was the star of Ireland's provincial towns. Campbell, in his 'Life of Mrs. Siddons,' has depicted the mother's agony when her darling was taken from her. Sally was engaged, it is believed, to be married to Sir Thomas Lawrence.

Accustomed also to mingle with a small number of friends of good position, whom Mrs. Landon ever retained—for her adverse circumstances never lowered her in *any way*—the manners of L. E. L. were gentle and very agreeable. She had great, very great *tact*, a natural gift, as well as the result of good early society. She was willing to be pleased, and desirous, perhaps too desirous, to please; for that, which is a virtue, sometimes induced her to say things far too flattering to be always thoroughly *meant*. She was led into it from imitation. Her nature was a sincere one; but the *bas-bleu* buttering system was then at its height.

She was at this time from eighteen to twenty-two or three, a comely girl with a blooming complexion, small, with very beautiful deep gray eyes, with dark eyelashes: her hair, never very thick, was of a deep brown, and fine as silk: her forehead and eyebrows were perfect; the one white and clear, the other arched and well defined. She was inclined rather to be fat; too healthy looking; and then her other features were defective —her nose was *retroussé*. Her mouth, however, without being particularly good, was expressive, and proportioned to her small and delicate face. Her hands and feet were perfect; and in time her figure, which had a girlish redundance of form in it, became slighter, and ended by being neat and easy, if not strictly graceful. She had a charming voice; and one could not but wonder that with that, and with so much soul, she did not sing—a sort of necessity of her nature. Few persons have had their songs set so often to music; and few persons wrote songs so adapted to society, and to the graceful performance of amateurs, as she did. Her 'I know not when I loved thee first,' and her 'Constance,' have been set by clever composers, and are deservedly popular. Her verses have always been liked by composers.

Her success brought hope to her excitable mind. Good luck, she owned, surpassed her expectations. 'I am convinced,' she wrote to her cousin, 'that a kind of curse hangs over us all.' Some lines which she composed at this time, when visiting an aunt in Gloucestershire, addressed to her mother, show a fondness that seems to render the after separation inexplicable.

In 1824, when Letitia was twenty-two years old, 'The Improvisatrice' was published. Its success was immediate. 'The stamp of originality,' as Mr. Blanchard writes, 'was on this work. There was a power in the pages that no carelessness could mar, no obscurity own—and the power was the writer's own.' 'The Improvisatrice' was identified with the writer whose soul had been for some years poured forth in songs that had all the *verve* of being improvised. Although at this period of her life it is asserted that L. E. L. had never loved, never sorrowed, her new poem, like her contributions to the 'Literary Gazette,' was full of forlorn hope and blighted affection, so given that it required some strength of reasoning not to believe them real.

> 'It was my evil star above,
>   Not my sweet lute that wrought me wrong;
> It was not song that taught me love,
>   But it was love that taught me song.'

But the instant L. E. L. was known, the circle surrounding her was disenchanted. She pleaded guilty to no sentiment; she abjured the idea of writing from her own feelings. She was so lively, so girlish; so fond of a dance, or a play, or a gay walk; so full of pleasantry, so ready with her shafts of wit, that one felt half angry with her for being so blithe and so real. Still those who knew her well did comprehend her: they knew what deep feelings lay beneath all that froth of manner which did her so much injustice. They knew that many of her sallies were drawn forth by the tiresome flattery of some, the *fade* observations of others. A successful author has much to undergo from society: the continual repetition even of the most gratifying tributes becomes wearisome beyond expression, and most of our noted authors put an embargo on it. But L. E. L.

was too good-natured to do this: she assured each admirer of her works that his or her tribute was just what she wished for. She always listened—always answered with courteous respect to the well-intended observations: it was only those conversant with the expressions of her varying face that could know what she felt.

When she said, however, that she had never been in love, she spoke, at that time, the truth; and indeed it is probable that she never experienced the passion as she described it: if she did so, the emotion was transient and produced no effect on the circumstances of her life.

She was now to be found by the numerous and fashionable visitors who were proud of her acquaintance in a small apartment in Sloane Street, where she lived under the protection of her grandmother, Mrs. Bishop, to whom she was affectionately attached. The drawing-room of these lodgings was sometimes filled with gay ladies of rank in the morning, and with men of letters and literary ladies in the evening. L. E. L. was a social being; and young as she then was—little more than twenty-three, had the gift, so perfect in France, so rare in England, of receiving well. Nothing could be more lively than these little social meetings, and nothing more unexceptionable. It is true that among men of letters, great diversities of character are to be found; but in the society of her own sex, L. E. L. was very careful how to steer her way. It was at this period that she was seized with her first severe attack of illness, inflammation of the lungs. She suffered much, and her constitution never perfectly rallied afterwards. It was about this time, also, that the first attempt to injure her character was made in the 'Sun' newspaper.

The paragraph coupled her name with that of the friend to whom she owed so much; consultations were then held by her friends as to the steps to be pursued. Mr. Jerdan advised an action being threatened if an instant contradiction did not appear; and he was *right:* a threat of that kind would probably have produced far more important consequences than the silencing an ephemeral report. It would have intimidated a host of almost invisible slanderers who found delight in bringing down to the vulgar level of their own minds one all genius and purity. Even had an action been necessary, there would have been nothing to fear. Every action of L. E. L.'s life was open as daylight. From first to last she was always in the sight of friends, many of them married; her mornings were passed in incessant writing; her evenings in society; whilst her grandmother never left the house.

Well might she write these exquisite lines at the close of her second poem, 'The Troubadour,' to her father's memory:

> ' My heart said, no name but thine
> Should be on this last page of mine.
> My father! though no more thine ear
> Censure or praise of mine can hear,
> It soothes me to embalm thy name
> With all my hope, my pride, my fame!
>
> * * * *
>
> My own dear father, time may bring
> Chance, change, upon his rainbow wing,
> But never will thy name depart—
> The household god of thy child's heart—
> Until thy orphan child may share
> The grave where her best feelings are.
> Never, dear father, love can be
> Like the dear love I had for thee.'

It was during the height of her fame also, raised to its climax by the publication of 'The Troubadour,' that her young sister sank away, happy in being taken from the adversity which she had never had physical strength to bear. L. E. L. was not aware of her danger till all hope was gone; then she hastened to her mother's. Never can her description be forgotten of her feelings on gazing on the living skeleton before her. At this period, and ever afterwards, she began to contribute regularly to her mother's means of subsistence. This was one of the greatest sources of satisfaction in her independence; and the generous-hearted girl felt it to be so.

She was plunged into the full career of London society when her grandmother died, and her plans were again unsettled. Perhaps in not returning to her mother, L. E. L., as an authoress, was right; as a member of society she was wrong. As an authoress she required quiet; entire freedom from irritation; absence from small worries incidental to a home of privation. Advice that she could not always follow, yet dared not, lest altercation should arise, dispute. After a lapse of years these considerations seem valid, and constitute a plea for that which was constantly urged against her—her absence from her mother's protection. It was, in point of fact, all that could be urged to her detriment. In referring to the reports against her, she thus wrote in the bitterness of her soul :—

'I have not written so soon as I intended, first because I wished to be able to tell you I had taken some steps towards change; and I also wished, if possible, to subdue the bitterness and irritation of feelings not to be expressed to one so kind as yourself. I have succeeded better in the first than the last. I think of the treatment I have received until my soul writhes under the powerlessness of its anger. It is only because I am poor, unprotected, and dependent on popularity that I am a mark for all the gratuitous insolence and malice of idleness and ill-nature. And I cannot but feel deeply that had I been possessed of rank and opulence, either these remarks had never been made, or, if they had, how trivial would their consequence have been to me! I must begin with the only subject—the only thing in the world I really feel an interest in—my writings.' * * * 'When my "Improvisatrice" came out, nobody discovered what is alleged against it. I did not take up a review, a magazine, a newspaper, but if it named my book it was to praise "the delicacy," "the grace," "the purity of feminine feeling" it displayed.' * * * 'With regard to the immoral and improper tendency of my productions, I can only say it is not my fault if there are minds, which, like negroes, cast a dark shadow on a mirror, however clear and pure in itself.' * * * 'As to the report you named, I know not which is greatest—the absurdity or the malice. Circumstances have made me very much indebted to the gentleman [whose name was coupled with hers] for much of kindness. I have not a friend in the world but himself to manage anything of business, whether literary or pecuniary.' * * * 'Place yourself in my situation. Could you have hunted London for a publisher; endured all the alternate hot and cold water thrown on your exertions; bargained for what sum they might be pleased to give; and after all canvassed, examined, nay quarrelled over accounts the most intricate in the world? And again, after success had procured money, what was I to do with it? Though ignorant of business, I must know I could not lock it up in a box.' * * * 'Who was to undertake this—I can only call it drudgery—but some one to whom my literary exertions could in return be as valuable as theirs to me? But it is not on this ground that I express my surprise at so cruel a calumny, but actually on that of our slight intercourse. He is in the habit of calling on his way into town, and unless it is on a Sunday afternoon, which is almost his only leisure time for looking over letters, manuscripts, &c., five or ten minutes is the usual time of his visit. We visit in such different circles, that if I except the evening he took Agnes and myself to Miss B——'s, I cannot recall our ever meeting in any one of the round of winter parties. The more I think of my past life and of my future prospects, the more dreary do they seem. I have known little else than privation, disappointment, unkindness and harassment. From the time I was fifteen, my life has been one continual struggle in some shape or another against absolute poverty, and I must say not a tithe of my profits have I ever expended on myself.' 'No one knows but myself what I have had to contend with.'

She might well exclaim, as she did: 'Oh for oblivion and five hundred a year!'

She had now removed into Hans Place, to the very number twenty-two, where her childish gaiety had put the whole propriety of a range of girls out. Mrs. Rowden had now left, and the school was under the guidance of three ladies, named Lance, whose aged father lived with them. No residence could be more unobjectionable. Hans Place was, and it still is, the quietest nook in London. The school not being large, the Misses Lance received two or three ladies of strict respectability as inmates; and gladly retained L. E. L. from the great consideration she ever showed them, from the absence of all self-indulgence in her nature, and from a general esteem and regard for her, on far lower terms than the rest. It was, indeed, requisite, for the labour of the pen is precarious, and may be suspended at any time by ill-health, or blasted altogether by the failure of a publisher.

L. E. L. established herself in a small attic looking out into the square, with its small, well-guarded circles of shrubs and turf, and there slept and wrote, often till the depth of winter, without a fire. She dined with the school, drank tea in the parlour with old Mr. Lance and his daughters, and received her visitors in the long, low room in which in her careless infancy she had seen Lady Caroline Lamb deliver the prizes. The chief trouble she gave was in the continual opening of the door to coroneted carriages, or loungers from the clubs, or those killers of one's morning, intimate friends, who think they are privileged to look in early, and ruin their hosts with the interruption. Then, at night, some lady would often call and take the poetess to some gay fête; L. E. L. all this time retaining the freshness of her clear, fair complexion, and improving in form, in manner, and in *style*, that all-important ingredient for success; yet, as she once bitterly said, when comments were made on her dress (which was somewhat fanciful), 'It is very easy for those whose only trouble on that head is to change, to find fault with one who never knew in her life what it was to have two new dresses at a time.' Yet those were precisely the critics who gave no quarter to the poor and hardworked writer.

Visits to her two uncles, the Dean of Exeter, and the Rev. James Landon, the Rector of Aberford in Yorkshire, varied her brilliant, toilsome life. She spoke of Oxford with rapture. One may, indeed, well conceive how gladly she would ramble in the delicious gardens of Worcester College, with its glassy water, its ancestral trees, and the cloistral looking old portion of the college over which her uncle presided.

Poetry was not at that time so fashionable among the young Oxonians as now, when every undergraduate has a Tennyson, so that she never achieved the exploit of captivating a fellow nor of breaking the heart of any student.

At Aberford she spent the Christmas of 1825, where it was properly disseminated that she was the 'London author.' The consequence, she said in one of her letters, was, that 'seated by the only young man I had beheld, I acted upon him like an air-pump, suspending his very breath and motion; and my asking him for a mince pie, a dish of which I had for some time been surveying with longing eyes, acted like an electric shock, and his start not a little discomposed a no-age-at-all, silk-vested spinster, whose plate was thereby deposited in her lap; and last not least in the hurry he forgot to help me!'

'I grant,' she adds, 'that in the country, nothing seems easier than to become the golden calf of a circle; but I never envied Miss Seward.'

Meantime, whilst slanders lay dormant, other reports were circulated. It was said that she had had two hundred offers; but it was, she said, very unfortunate that her offers should be so much like the passage to the North Pole and Wordsworth's cuckoo—talked of but never seen. It is undoubted that she had a proposal from a rich American, and that several young men were her votaries, though without, perhaps, much hope of success; but still she had then met no one to whom she could give her whole affections. She was rather unimpressionable in that particular, as the favourites of society usually are. Whatsoever the reports against her, they never affected her reception in the gay, and indeed in the great world. From Sir Edward and Lady Bulwer, and Mrs. Windham Lewis (Mrs. Disraeli), she found a constant welcome; and the friends formed in these somewhat similar coteries were not lost. The late Lady Emmeline Stuart Wortley sought her out, and introduced her to the Marchioness of Londonderry, at whose splendid assemblies the youthful poetess was the star of the evening.

Lady Caroline Lamb was dead, but many of the individuals whom L. E. L. had met under her roof were still delighted to lionize her: the late Lord Munster was one of her kindest and most partial friends.

It is invidious to mention a host of great names, as if high-sounding titles could add to the lustre of true genius. But, in treating of L. E. L. as a social being, whilst she may hardly be deemed in strict parlance a Queen of Society, it must be allowed that brilliant and exciting scenes were for many years **her** appointed spher

In her own little home, however, she had her votaries and her throne. It is now long since forgotten, how in the long, 'ow room, papered as it was with one of those dim papers of the last forty years, which makes 'darkness visible,' L. E. L. gave a fancy ball, which was attended in fancy dresses by Sir E. and Lady Bulwer, and other friends—some proportion of whom were editors and publishers, for L. E. L. never forgot that she had to depend on the press for support. Sometimes she received a small *réunion* of all her regiment of authors and journalists, the Misses Lance her chaperons, or some lady of consequence and often of rank. Lady Stepney was one of her most indulgent friends; Mr. and Mrs. Hall also gave her their support. Not even Hannah More brought to life could have found anything to challenge censure in these agreeable and irreproachable evenings; but whilst this may be called the sunshiny day of her brief and unquiet maturity, she was often sad at heart. 'Let any one,' she wrote to a friend, 'look their own past experience steadily in the face, and what a dark and discouraging aspect it will present! How many enjoyments have passed away for ever! how much warmth and kindliness of feeling! how many generous beliefs! * * * As to love—does it dare to treasure its deepest feelings in the presence of what we call the world? As to friendship—how many would weigh your dearest interests for one instant against the very lightest of their own? And as to fame, of what avail is it in the grave?—and during life it will be denied or dealt forth grudgingly. No, no; to be as indifferent as you can possibly contrive, to aim only at present amusement and passing popularity, is the best system for a steam-coach along the railroad of life; let who will break the stones and keep up the fire!'

This is the language of a mind and body overworked; for all L. E. L.'s efforts of the muse were not always spontaneous. Mr. Jerdan, who arranged her affairs with publishers, gives a statement of all that she accomplished, and all that she received for her writings during the whole of her literary career. He puts it thus:—

			£
For 'The Easter Offering' she received		. .	50
'The Improvisatrice'	,,	. .	300
'The Troubadour'	,,	. .	600
'The Golden Violet'	,,	. .	200
'The Venetian Bracelet'	,,	. .	150
'Romance and Reality'	,,	. .	300
'Heath's Book of Beauty'	,,	. .	300
'Francesca Carrara'	,,	. .	300
And certainly for Annuals, Magazines, and Periodicals, not less in ten or twelve years than		. . . .	200
			£2480

Mr. Jerdan has not, however, mentioned 'Ethel Churchill,' the best of L. E. L.'s three novels. Those who are not in the habit of writing cannot conceive the exhaustion, the effort, the dejection of mind and lassitude of body which exertions of this nature, when continual, produce. Often has L. E. L. started from her bed, after spending an evening in society, and in the morning, when the printer's boy was waiting, written on her knees a sonnet, or the remaining lines of a poem. She wrote with wonderful facility; but the mental excitement was unceasing, and much of her now constant ill-health was ascribed to that incessant wear and tear of every faculty. She was also disappointed about this time in the property which she expected to receive from her grandmother, who had, as some ladies are obliged to do, sunk the greater part in an annuity. She bequeathed, however, the rest to L. E. L., and this sum, three hundred and fifty pounds, was every farthing she ever received after the age of seventeen, independently of her own exertions. This fact proves what women *can* do, with industry and ability: it ought to be an incentive to parents to educate the intellect, not merely to promote mechanical accomplishments.

Her annual income may, therefore, be estimated at two hundred and fifty pounds. Out of this sum she reserved for her own use one hundred and twenty pounds: the rest she devoted to her mother, and to the aid of her brother, who had passed through Oxford, and had taken holy orders. She never owed a sixpence; but she never had a farthing to spend over the necessaries of life. 'In truth,' she was, as Mr. Jerdan remarks, 'the most unselfish of human beings.' In 1834, L. E. L. visited Paris. She was happy in finding a most desirable escort in Miss Turin, a lady some years older than herself. Her letters from France are charming—so natural, at times so poetical, so *young*, and so fresh.

Everything delighted her—the caps of the women, the Tuileries, the shops, and the civil people in them; and even the exquisite dinners. But she was disappointed in finding all the *beau monde* out of Paris; and perceived, as most foreigners do, that being in that gay city in June is not seeing Paris. Mr. and Mrs. Gore, however, welcomed her, and several French and German *littérateurs*. Amable Tastu and his wife :—Odillon Barrot, Heine, and others, called upon her, and commiserated her for being in that enchanting city when every one was out of town. Not even the charms of the Boulevards, where her hotel was situated, could prevent L. E. L. from feeling that her visit, as far as seeing Parisian society was concerned, was a failure. She was not aware that it is only the *demi-monde* who are seen in Paris in the summer, for if not absent, the French are then invisible. L. E. L. was essentially, with all her poetic genius, a lover of society. 'Excepting the visits that are paid me,' she writes, ' I can see nothing of the people; as to sights, you know me too well to suppose that I care about them two straws. I would sooner have a morning visit from an amusing person than see the Tuileries or the Louvre ten times over.' Like most English people, she fell into the error of supposing it necessary to have a gentleman to accompany a lady to sights; not being aware that a young lady, accompanied by another lady of *un âge décent*, may go to any *respectable* public place in Paris. She had, however, some alleviations to her disappointment; Madame Tastu presented her to Madame Récamier, at whose house she met Chateaubriand, and Prosper Mérimée paid her much attention. But L. E. L. did not enjoy herself in what it requires almost an apprenticeship to enjoy— French society.

We have referred to the calumny which followed L. E. L. through life. It was about this time that its shafts, which had affected first her peace of mind, now influenced her destiny.

She was in the zenith of her fame when Mr. Forster, then a young barrister, and, at the same time, the editor of the 'Examiner,' made her an offer of marriage. Mr. Forster's personal character was unexceptionable—an honourable, warmhearted, and highly talented man. He was sincerely attached to L. E. L.; but no sooner was he accepted, than *friends* stepped forward to tell him a thousand tales of her supposed imprudencies and even criminalities. Mr. Forster did not believe these imputations; but, desiring that they should be cleared away, he mentioned them to L. E. L. as statements that ought to be refuted. Her answer was: 'Go to my female friends, the married, the respectable, the trustworthy friends whom I see almost daily. Make every enquiry in your power.' Her injunctions were followed: all were unanimous in expressing their horror at the slanders against one whom they both loved and respected. Mr. Forster was satisfied. He urged L. E. L. to give him a right to protect her by instantly consenting to a marriage. 'No,' she answered firmly; 'I will never marry a man who has distrusted me.' The marriage was definitively broken off, and L. E. L. lost a prospect of being domesticated with a man whose abilities she almost reverenced, and of living in that scene and that society which she always preferred to any other—the literary society of London.

It is possible that if L. E. L. had been devoutly attached to Mr. Forster she would not have suffered this painful occurrence to have separated her for ever from him. *But she was not.* Mr. Blanchard, wishing to spare the feelings that were, on one side, most genuine, has represented the rupture of the engagement as a high-minded act of self-sacrifice, from a principle of wounded honour, on the part of L. E. L. A friend, a gentleman, who knew her well, probed the matter to the quick. He urged her for her own happiness not to persist in this, as he thought, needless separation. She promptly assured him that her affections were *not* interested in the brief engagement, and she spoke in a tone that convinced him that she meant what she said. Yet, that the act cost her much, no one who reads the letters here inserted (taken from Mr. Blanchard's Memoir) can entertain a doubt. She did ample justice to the generous heart that had never really doubted her; and the struggle produced a severe, and at one time dangerous illness, which long left its traces on her delicate frame. If those who calumniated her be still living, no monitions are needful to touch the conscience of the false witness. Here is the reproof. Here is L. E. L.'s fate read to you: the chance of protection, of home happiness, of an existence of comparative ease, is before her; here she flings it from her, and the close of her life's brief tragedy soon follows.

After the deed was done, as is almost always the case, her sentiments somewhat changed—a state of exasperation came on. Alas! was it not augmented by the wanton hints of the careless or the mischievous? She became irritated against him who, of all that ever paid her the attentions of a lover, perhaps most truly loved her. Upon being told that the late Allan Cunningham, whom she appreciated, as all who knew him must have done, as a noble specimen of mankind, stated to a friend of hers the circumstances here related, adding that the engagement was likely to be renewed, she repelled the idea with great vehemence, and, in a tone and manner very unusual to one of so gentle a nature, begged that the subject might never be mentioned to her again.

Let the letter, accompanied with this explanation, now interpret her feelings at the moment when it was written. It is expressed with all the kindliness, the impulsiveness, and the true sincerity of her noble nature. Nor can those who knew her peruse it without a pang.

'I have already written to you two notes which I fear you could scarcely read or understand. I am to-day sitting up for an hour, and though strictly forbidden to write, it will be the least evil. I wish I could send you my inmost soul to read, for I feel at this moment the utter powerlessness of words. I have suffered for the last three days a degree of torture that made Dr. Thomson say, "You have an idea of what the rack is now." It was nothing to what I suffered from my own feelings.

* * * * * *

'Again I repeat that I will not allow you to consider yourself bound to me by any possible tie. To any friend to whom you may have stated our engagement, I cannot object to your stating the truth. Do every justice to your own kind and generous conduct. I am placed in a most cruel and difficult position. Give me the satisfaction of, as far as rests with myself, having nothing to reproach myself with. The more I think, the more I feel I ought not—I cannot—allow you to unite yourself with one accused of—I cannot write it. The mere suspicion is dreadful as death. Were it stated as a fact, that might be disproved. Were it a difficulty of any other kind, I might say, Look back at every action of my life, ask every friend I have. But what answer can I give, or what security have I against the assertion of a man's vanity, or the slander of a vulgar woman's tongue? I feel that to give up all idea of a near and dear connection is as much my duty to myself as to you. Why should you be exposed to the annoyance, the mortification, of having the name of the woman you honour with your regard coupled with insolent insinuations? You never would bear it.

'I have just received your notes. God bless you!—but—After Monday I shall, I hope, be visible; at present it is impossible. My complaint is inflammation of the liver, and I am ordered complete repose—as if it were possible! Can you read this?—Under any circumstances, the

'Most grateful and affectionate of your friends,
'L. E. LANDON.'

Let the poison rest: nothing now can harm her whom it so sharply pained, so deeply injured then.

'She hath no need of tears.'

It is, however, remarkable that the slander could never be traced. It was circulated in drawing-rooms, breathing into the atmosphere, tainting with its foul current the minds of those even who hung over L. E. L.'s chair with seeming pleasure, or who gazed on her from some remote corner, wondering at the gaiety of her spirits, the gentle sweetness of her deportment.

A whisper went round: those who knew her best caught it as it went, but never could the first whisperer be detected. The report always stopped short somewhere, and was angrily disclaimed by some one just as one believed that the source was ascertained. It is fruitless, perhaps foolish, to dwell on these remembrances now; for she is long since at rest in heaven, and justified by universal assent here.

She now often talked of marrying any one, and of wishing to get away, far away from England, and from those who thus misunderstood her. Formerly she had been too indifferent to these reports; now she became too sensitive. To be captious was not in her nature, yet she was becoming morbid, depressed, hopeless: yet never did a revengeful or bitter sentiment pain those who most loved her, and who watched over her with sorrowing care; for her health was now almost constantly variable. Happily her friend, her first friend, Mr. Jerdan and his daughters, did not forsake her on account of the coarse and cruel manner in which the name of L. E. L. had been traduced on his account. They were devoted to her to the last.

To all ordinary observers L. E. L.'s spirits seemed quite to recover the shock just described. She was more sought after in the society of the great than ever; and, to do them justice, the ladies of rank who welcomed her to their houses never lent an ear to the rumours against her: they were, and they still are, in that class, too well accustomed to *on dits* of a calumnious nature to conceive those which were levelled against an unprotected young woman of any moment. Besides, with all their defects as a class, there is a loftiness of feeling in the English aristocracy, and an independence of action which are not to be found in the middle ranks of society.

It was before her wounded spirit had been perfectly soothed that L. E. L. met one evening, at the house of a mutual friend at Hampstead, the late George Maclean, then governor of Cape Coast Castle. Mr. Maclean had just then distinguished himself by great judgment, and some considerable amount of personal valour, in quelling an insurrection of Ashantees, during which General Turner had perished.

L. E. L. was greatly touched by anything that approached

to heroism. Her fine lines on Sir Walter Manny show her sentiment for the old chivalric gallantry. She heard much of Mr. Maclean from her friend Miss Emma Roberts, who had introduced her to Mr. and Mrs. Matthew Forster, Mr. Maclean's intimate associates. There was to be a party to welcome the hero, and L. E. L. was invited. In her enthusiasm she wore a Scotch Tartan scarf over her shoulders. She had a ribbon in her hair, and a sash also, of the Maclean Tartan; and she set out for the *soirée* in great spirits, resolved on thus complimenting the hero.

Mr. Maclean was much struck by her appearance. In looks L. E. L. was improved, by being more delicate than ever in form and complexion. The rich hues of the Tartan over her white muslin dress became her neck. She had at this time every advantage of a comfortable home. The Miss Lances had given up 22, Hans Place; then she lived some time with a friend of theirs (an excellent woman), Mrs. Sheldon; *she* also changed her plans of life; but after the cruel rupture of her engagement with Mr. Forster, a lady of large fortune, living with every luxury in Hyde Park Street, insisted on L. E. L.'s making her house her home, received and treated her as a daughter, and gave her what she could not otherwise have expected, the protection of herself and her husband, persons of the highest respectability and character.

Under these favourable and happy auspices did L. E. L. begin her fatal acquaintance with Mr. Maclean. Never had she been before so serene, so protected, so happy. She had an elegant drawing-room allotted her to receive separately her own friends: a carriage was always ready for her to make visits. Nothing could exceed the almost maternal care that watched over her still frequent illnesses.

Those who so loved, so cared for her, lived to mourn her, but they are now at rest. Honoured be their memory—good, pious, generous as they were.

Still L. E. L. felt that she was not independent, and hers was an independent mind. All these circumstances combined made her wish to have a claim, a home somewhere; **and Mr.**

Maclean soon offered to her these sighed-for objects of her heart.

He was accepted, and introduced to her friends as her betrothed. Many approved her choice. Mr. Maclean was of an ancient Scottish family, the son of the Rev. James Maclean of Urquhart, Elgin, and the nephew of General Sir John Maclean. In early youth he had been sent out to Africa as Colonial Secretary at Cape Coast Castle: he was scarcely of age when he was made governor of the colony. He was a grave, spare man, between thirty and forty when he became engaged to L. E. L., but he looked very much older. His face, without being very plain, was not agreeable. It was pallid: and his dark hair fell upon a brow by no means of an elevated or intellectual cast. His dark-gray eyes were seldom raised to meet those of another. He was very taciturn, and still spoke his native Scotch, when he did speak, which was seldom: never, if he could help it. A practical man, he seemed to look upon all sentiment as folly, wit as superfluous, taste and fancy as weakness of mind, the softer passions as a waste of time. Still he was L. E. L.'s choice—her mature choice. His position was good; and, except the necessity of going to Africa, there was nothing to be said against the marriage.

Most mysteriously, the engagement was suddenly interrupted by Mr. Maclean's leaving London, and ceasing all correspondence. L. E. L. hoped for the best: wrote to him—no answer; wrote again—no answer again. Then her health became affected: she had an attack of nervous fever. She explained all: the calumnies had reached him also. Her depression was extreme; and her attachment for Mr. Maclean appeared to be deeper than it had ever before been to any of her many suitors. After some time, during which Mr. Maclean maintained a rigid silence, he reappeared; entered into no explanations; vouchsafed no apology. But it seems L. E. L. was satisfied, and the engagement went on. She was not, at first, aware that Mr. Maclean was obliged to return to Cape Coast, and probably expected that after so long a service in so dreadful a climate he would have been promoted to some other post. But it was not to be so; and she heard of his resolution to resume his duties at the colony without changing her determination to marry him.

This all took place in the summer of 1837. Mr. Blanchard states, in his 'Memoirs of L. E. L.,' that the impediment to their union had been on prudential accounts only, and that never did Mr. Maclean for an instant give credit to the reports against her. Still, another obstacle arose. L. E. L. was informed by a friend that Mr. Maclean was already privately married to a woman of colour at Cape Coast. The assertion was distinctly denied, however, by Mr. Maclean: no connection of the kind, he said, existed; nor had any connection of *any* kind existed for a considerable time. There existed, nevertheless, a certain degree of anxiety in the mind of L. E. L. A marriage is legal in England if it has been celebrated according to the rites of the colony in which it has taken place. Mr. Maclean, however, explained himself wholly to the satisfaction of Miss Landon; and she never communicated what had passed between them, nor her annoyance on the subject to her brother until *after* her marriage.

Preparations were then in progress for their immediate union, and L. E. L. felt a perfect confidence in the truth and honour of Mr. Maclean. She believed him to be free: and her convictions may have been correct.

A brief period of happiness was now her lot. Her health was still precarious, but improving. 'Perhaps one reason that I am so recovered is,' she wrote to Lady Stepney, 'that I am so much happier. All the misery I have suffered for the last few months is past like a dream—one which, I trust in God, I shall never know again. Now my own inward feelings are what they used to be. You would not now have to complain of my despondency.' And at this time her admirable novel of 'Ethel Churchill' having been most successful, her happiness seemed complete.

On the 7th of June, 1838, she was married to Mr. Maclean, the ceremonial taking place in St. Mary's, Bryanston Square. It was, by Mr. Maclean's wish, so strictly private that even the family with whom L. E. L. resided did not know that it had taken place until a fortnight afterwards. Mr. Landon, the bride's brother, performed the ceremony: Sir Edward Bulwer Lytton gave the bride away. After the service, all who were present at the church, except the bride and bridegroom, made their congratulations and went away. Mr. and Mrs. Maclean went to the Sackville Street Hotel; but on the following day L. E. L. returned to her friend's house, and entered into society, as usual, under her maiden name. It is impossible to avoid suspecting that this arrangement was the result of some fear in Mr. Maclean's mind lest the event should be known too soon at Cape Coast; but the reason he alleged was his dislike to congratulations and festivities, and the great amount of business which he still had to transact at the Colonial Office before his return.

It was on the day of the coronation of Queen Victoria, June 28th, 1838, that L. E. L. was last seen on any public occasion in this country. Invitations had been sent to her from most of the best clubs in London to occupy a place at their windows. She chose Crockford's, as being nearest to Piccadilly: she wished to leave as soon as the procession had passed to the Abbey. Some who knew her glanced from their carriage as the unparalleled *cortège* passed down St. James's Street. She wore a white bridal bonnet and a simple muslin dress, and with a party of friends stood in a balcony, waving her handkerchief in the enthusiasm of the moment as the troops appeared. As the last regiment of the gorgeous Lancers rode down the street she suddenly withdrew, and those who were watching her from the opposite window saw her no more.

That evening many friends called on her in Hyde Park Street to bid her farewell. The town was blazing with illuminations, the bells were ringing, the populace was hurrying here and there as L. E. L. received for the last time those she had loved so well. In the morning before, hurried to death, she had nevertheless found time to see Dr. Schloss, the publisher of the 'Bijou Almanack,' to which she had for some years given her name and poems gratuitously. The simple German shed tears as he thanked her for her liberality, her endeavours to serve him, her sympathy for a poor stranger. L. E. L. was truly charitable. She could not give money, but she gave her time, her toil, wherever there was distress.

In the evening the scene was changed. The gay, the literary friends, the lovely daughters of the house—now, alas! gone, save two—the early friend of her girlhood, Sir Edward Lytton Bulwer, Mrs. Disraeli, and many others, lingered long to wish her happiness and a safe return. It was understood that she was only to remain three years at Cape Coast, and the delicacy of her lungs rendered it, on that account, even desirable for her to go to a warm climate, as she had been threatened with asthma. At supper Sir E. L. Bulwer, in a graceful speech, proposed the health of 'his daughter,' alluding to his having acted as a father at her marriage. The vessel did not sail from Portsmouth until the 5th of July, but on the morning of the 28th of June, L. E. L. quitted London for ever. So painful and protracted was the parting that she and her companions were too late for the first train. She was much excited by this her first journey by a railroad, and said to Mr. Maclean, 'Why don't you have them in Africa?' but towards evening she became much depressed, and a sort of terror seemed to possess her mind at the separation from her brother. Poor L. E. L.! When her brother, during their stay at the inn at Portsmouth, said to her, 'What shall you do without your friends to talk to?' 'Oh!' she replied, 'I shall talk to them through my books.' She had already planned work which would require just three years to finish. 'Every one,' her brother wrote, 'was full of hopes, and though, perhaps, they sounded more like doubts, there was no want of cheerfulness at dinner, especially on her part. But the brig was all this time getting away from Spithead, and the captain of the cutter which followed, to take Mr. Hugh Maclean and myself back, came below and said we could not stay any longer. All our spirits, real or not, dropped at once. The others went out, and I remained some time with my sister. At last they came down, and took her upon deck. I then perceived that Mrs. Bailey, who had not been before observed by us, was in the adjoining cabin, and I took the opportunity of speaking to her, as the only European female who would be near my sister; and the impression which at the time she made on my mind was that of a woman both kind-hearted and trustworthy. We parted again on leaving the vessel, but nothing more was said. My sister continued standing on the deck and looking towards us as long as I could trace her figure against the sky.'

The brig 'Maclean,' in which Mr. Maclean and L. E. L. sailed, had been fitted up, as far as the accommodation for L. E. L. was concerned, with every attention to her comfort. The weather was fair, and the voyage prosperous. There was nothing more than the ordinary discomforts of a sea voyage; but in so saying, a volume of small miseries is implied. Mrs. Bailey, the wife of the steward of the ship, acted as L. E. L.'s maid: no English servant was permitted to accompany her as a permanent attendant, an arrangement which L. E. L. most bitterly regretted, and which must be for ever lamented by her surviving friends. After a time, L. E. L. was sufficiently recovered from sea sickness to write two of the most exquisite poems that she ever composed—'The Polar Star,' and the 'Night at Sea.' They were transmitted to her friends: the last legacy from the warm heart that, when the poems were read, with tears, in England, had ceased to beat. She still affixed to them her initials, L. E. L. On the 15th of August she thus wrote to her brother: 'Cape Coast Castle. Thank goodness I am on land again. Last night we arrived; the lighthouse became visible, and from that time, gun after gun was fired to attract attention, to say nothing of most ingenious fireworks invented on the spur of the moment. A fishing boat put off, and in that, about two o'clock at night, Mr. Maclean left the ship, taking them all by surprise, no one supposing he would go through the surf on such a foggy and dark night. I cannot tell you my anxiety, but he returned safe, though wet to the skin. We found the secretary dead, poor young man! so that everything was in utter confusion.' This was, indeed, an inauspicious beginning; but it was not until long afterwards that the friends of L. E. L. attached any importance to this strange conduct on the part of Mr. Maclean; when his thus going ashore in the dead of the night was a source of some suspicions that he had deemed it necessary to send away from the fort, in which his bride was so soon to take up her abode, some persons probably long established there. But no *fact* of the kind has transpired.

When she landed, L. E. L. was in good health. For some time she wrote cheerfully, and favourably of her new home. The next letter to Mr. Blanchard describes the castle and her mode of life. That mode of life was changed, it is true, from the half-sorrowful, half-pleasurable existence of London; but L. E. L. was one who could readily adapt herself to everything Her own health continued good, but a severe illness of Mr. Maclean's seemed to cause her much anxiety and fatigue. For four nights she scarcely took any rest; still, and with all the in conveniences of having no competent servant, the amiable, unselfish L. E. L. wrote to her dearest friend, 'I cannot tell you how much better the place is than we supposed. If I had been allowed to bring a good English servant with me, to which there is not one single objection, I could be as comfortable as possible.'

She spoke more highly, too, in that letter, of Mr. Maclean's public character, and the reputation he had for strict justice. Allegations had certainly been made against him in England for cruelty, by a Captain Burgoyne, who married a daughter of Lady Elizabeth and Sir Murray Macgregor, and who, with his wife, passed two years at Cape Coast; but these had been silenced, if not refuted.

In subsequent letters, Mrs. Maclean's tone regarding her husband changed considerably. Mr. Maclean left her the whole day alone, until seven in the evening, and also entrenched himself in a quarter of the huge fort or castle, where he forbade her to follow him. She confessed that she thought him strange, inert beyond description, very reserved, and never speaking a word more than he could avoid. Still her spirits were good. She spoke of no unkindness. He seemed to leave her to write, or to think, or to wander about the fort just as she pleased.

The total solitude, the absence from loved friends, would have tried the courage of one less elastic than herself, but hers stood the shock.

At the close of the year 1838, the brig 'Maclean,' in which

L. E. L. had sailed for Africa, returned, bringing the tidings of her death. She was well and cheerful on the evening of Sunday, the 14th of October, and had occupied herself in writing to her English friends for several days. On the 15th of the month, Emily Bailey, the stewardess, and her only English attendant, was to return in the 'Maclean.' Between the hours of eight and nine, Mrs. Bailey went to Mrs. Maclean's room in order to give her a note addressed to her by an official in the colony. She attempted to open the door, but was unable to do so for several minutes, owing to some heavy weight on the inside. When she at last succeeded, she perceived Mrs. Maclean lying on the floor with her face against the door, and with a bottle—an empty bottle—in her hand. There was a slight bruise on the cheek of the dead, or dying, L. E. L. Mrs. Bailey fancied she heard a faint sigh as she leant over her. She went, however, instantly for her husband, to call Mr. Maclean, who came immediately, and sent directly for advice. The surgeon to the fort, Mr. Cobbold, who came promptly, and Mr. Maclean, carried the body to a bed in the room, and efforts were made to resuscitate life, but wholly in vain.

The bottle was then examined: it had evidently contained prussic acid, and was labelled, 'Hydrocyanicum Delatum. Pharm. Lond. 1836.' The awe-struck persons in that chamber of death then looked around. A letter was on the table, which she, who lay before them unconscious, had been writing. The ink was scarcely dry with which she had penned those last words to her friend, Mrs. Fagan: '*Write about yourself; nothing else half so much interests your affectionate* L. E. Maclean.'

She had even dated her letters, so composed had been her thoughts, 'Cape Coast Castle, Oct. 15.' These were the last lines she ever traced.

Mr. Maclean had risen from a bed of sickness to rush to his wife's apartment. He was the last person, except Mrs. Bailey, who had seen her alive. She had gone to his room—which seems, at all events during his illness, not to have been *hers*—to give him some arrowroot; and complaining of weariness, had said she would go to bed again for an hour and a half. What he felt, what he said, how he stood the shock of seeing her, whose last act had been one of kindness to him, a corpse, is not recorded, and no one ever read his countenance.

An inquest was summoned, and depositions taken; and everything seemed more and more mysterious in proportion to what was disclosed. She had been seen in health the night before: yet Mrs. Bailey stated that she had had spasms, and was in the habit of taking prussic acid for spasms; and he concluded that she must have taken an over-dose that day. Nevertheless, no odour of prussic acid was emitted from the mouth: and the learned—among the rest, the late Robert Liston, then in London—on being applied to, declared that had she died from prussic acid, 'she could not have retained the bottle in her hand; that the muscles would have been relaxed.' Mr. Cobbold, the surgeon, merely deposed that the pupils were dilated, the heart still weakly beating, and that he had given ammonia, but in vain. He does not say that the ammonia was swallowed; he does not say that it was rejected.

Then the question arose, where could she have got the prussic acid which, according to Mrs. Bailey, she used so freely? Mr. Maclean stated—' in her medicine chest:' and the assertion went down well at Cape Coast; but when the matter transpired in England, Mr. Squires, of Oxford Street, the chemist who had prepared and supplied the medicine chest, affirmed that no prussic acid had been supplied in it; and on hunting up all the prescriptions written for L. E. L. by Dr. Thomson, who had alone attended her for fourteen years, it was discovered that prussic acid had never been ordered for L. E. L. either for spasms or for any other disorder.

No post-mortem examination was proposed, or made: the inquest and the funeral were all ended in six hours after the lamented L. E. L. had ceased to exist. The verdict of the coroner's inquest was that the death of Letitia Elizabeth Maclean was 'caused by her having incautiously taken an over-dose of prussic acid, which, from evidence, it appears she had been in the habit of taking as a remedy for spasmodic affections, to which she was liable.'

The names of the coroner and jury are given in Mr. Blanchard's Memoir. All that is put down accurately; but one important fact was omitted, that after her leaving Mr. Maclean's room, a cup of coffee had been handed in to L. E. L. by a little native boy, whose office it was to attend in the gallery or corridor in which her room was situated. Why was this boy not called in evidence? Why was not the cup found, and any portion of its contents, if still in it, analyzed? That cup must have been in the room in which this fatal mishap, or secret poisoning, took place; yet no mention was made of it on the inquest. Whichever it may be set down to—whether to accident or to a dark designing act—can never now be known, till we stand *there*, where all things are known. The truth has never transpired. Reports even prevailed that the cause of death was suicide; but there was the undried letter—that effusion of affection, to Mrs. Fagan, to give that—the *last* reproach to one so calumniated—the lie. By some, and especially by Mrs. Maclean's afflicted mother, who long survived the blow, it was believed to be an accident. By others it has been suspected that the repudiated wife, or mistress, whose claims so nearly prevented this ill-omened marriage, was in some remote corner of the fortress still; and, as the natives of that coast are wonderful adepts in the art of poisoning, it has been thought that L. E. L. fell a victim to jealousy: and that Mr. Maclean was anxious, by the hurried and irregular proceedings adopted, to screen her from the consequences, and to prevent disclosures ruinous to himself.

Some years afterwards the govenor of Cape Coast came to England. He must then have been made fully aware of all that the press had published—the public had said about his wife's mysterious death. Yet he was wise enough never to enter into any justification. The secretary of the colonies, at the time of L. E. L.'s death, was equally forbearing. Lord Normanby and Lord John Russell, successively in office in that department, found, as they wrote to the afflicted brother, 'so many difficulties in the way, that they were obliged, with great regret, to abandon their original intention of inquiry.' The 'difficulties' arose, it is suspected, in the strenuous exertions and promised vote of an active M.P. who had interposed to save his absent friend the annoyance of an inquiry; but the people of England, who look upon L. E. L. as a child of genius all their own, will ever regret that some measures were not taken in spite of 'difficulties,' to clear up this dark story.

After Mr. Maclean's death, which happened about six years after that of L. E. L., two young English officers visited Cape Coast: they landed, indeed, chiefly for the purpose of learning all they could about the young poetess, whose name was still remembered, when they were at Cape Coast, as of one to whom all felt respect during her brief sojourn. They tried to gain particulars of Mr. Maclean's last illness. It was long: but never, during that weary journey through the valley of the shadow of death, except once, did he breathe *her* name—never did he refer to what must have pained him, the reports about the manner of that death! He requested his secretary to take especial care of a box of papers which he always kept under his bed, and to destroy them after his death, of the certainty of which he was aware.

Mr. Blanchard, in 1841, wrote: 'A handsome marblet is on its way, it appears, to Cape Coast Castle, to be erected in the castle, bearing the following inscription:—

'Hic jacet sepultum
Omne quod mortale fuit
LETITIÆ ELIZABETHÆ MACLEAN.
Quam egregia ornatam indole
Musis præcipue amatam
Omniumque amores secum trahentem
In ipso ætatis flore
Die Octobris XV. A.D. M.D.CCC.XXXVIII.,
Ætat. XXXVI.
Quod spectas, viator, marmor,
Vanum heu doloris monumentum
Conjux mœrens erexit.'

'Here lies interred
All that was mortal
Of LETITIA ELIZABETH MACLEAN.
Adorned with a lofty mind,
Singularly favoured of the Muses,
And dearly beloved by all,
She was prematurely snatched away
By death in the flower of her age,
On the 15th of October, 1838,
Aged 36 years.

The marble which you behold, O traveller,
A sorrowing husband has erected:
Vain emblem of his grief!'

Mr. Maclean's body was interred, by his own direction, by that of his wife: and that was the only reference made to L. E. L. by her husband. It was proposed to erect a tablet to the memory of L. E. L., by subscription, in that church at Brompton, on which she wrote her poem—'The First Grave.' But Mrs. Landon's circumstances after her gifted child's death were found to be so indigent, that it was thought better to raise a subscription to support her than to erect a tablet. The late Mrs. Bulwer Lytton, and Sir Edward Bulwer Lytton came forward to aid in this last act of respect to L. E. L.'s memory: and Sir E. B. Lytton continued a handsome annual subscription till the death of Mrs. Landon in 1854. Sir Robert Peel assigned to her a small pension of fifteen pounds, all that he had then to bestow out of a fund at the disposal of the Prime Minister's wife: and these resources, with the aid of her son, who, then a curate only, could only assist, not wholly maintain his poor mother, made her tolerably comfortable during her life. It had been a life of trial; and long before it was the will of God that her spirit should be at rest, she had 'longed to be dissolved, and be with God.' At length she sank to rest, full of faith, and hope, and piously nursed by the niece who had educated L. E. L., and who had sustained her in her many sorrows. Mrs. Landon survived her daughter nearly twenty years: during that wearisome period she was never known either to touch upon the subject of her differences with L. E. L., nor, latterly, to refer to her death.

It will naturally be asked why Mr. Maclean left the mother of his wife to the generosity of friends, to support her after she, who had ever cared for her mother's wants first, was gone.

Mrs. Landon was a woman of an independent spirit. She could not be insensible to the convictions in the mind of others, that her gifted child had not had justice done her, *after* death. The hurried inquest, the careless garbled evidence, the pretext of the bottle—all raised suspicions which may have been wholly groundless, but which cannot be condemned as unlikely or unnatural. By the brig 'Maclean,' Mr. Maclean wrote to her, and referring to the allowance of fifty pounds a year, which Mrs. Maclean always made her (though adding to it often considerable sums), he engaged to double that provision and to give her a hundred pounds a year for her life. Mrs. Landon, in reply, said that 'could she be assured her daughter was *happy* with him, she would thankfully accept that annuity.' No answer was returned, nor did Mr. Maclean ever communicate with Mrs. Landon again. When he came to England, he did not attempt to see her: nothing that had belonged to L. E. L. was even sent, as is usual in such cases, to her mother or to any friend or relative.

Such are the unsatisfactory facts appertaining to the sudden close of a life so cherished. Time has not contributed one gleam of light upon an event which is still deplored, for surviving friends: and which, even now and then seems to recur to the memory of the public like a painful but half-forgotten dream. We shall never be more enlightened than we are now; but of this, let those who delight in L. E. L.'s exquisite verses be assured, that it was not *suicide* that took her, not, we trust, unprepared from a world she loved well, with all its thorny cares. Had such an idea as that of self-destruction crossed her mind, she would have written to her brother, whom she so fondly loved, in explanation, in extenuation—a farewell, a plea, would have been found in her writing somewhere. But, to show the state of her mind, calm, though pensive, as that of an exile might incline to be, she penned this last letter to a beautiful and intelligent friend, long since, as well as her husband, Colonel Fagan, also deceased.

'MY DEAREST MARIA,

'I cannot but write you a brief account, how I enact the part of a feminine Robinson Crusoe. I must say, it itself, the place is infinitely superior to all I have ever dreamed of. The castle is a fine building; the rooms excellent. I do not suffer from heat; insects there are few or none; and I am in excellent health. The solitude, except an occasional dinner, is absolute; from seven in the morning till seven, when we dine, I never see Mr. Maclean, and rarely any one else. We were welcomed by a series of dinners which I am glad are over, for it is very awkward to be the only lady; still the great kindness with which I have been treated, and the very pleasant manners of many of the gentlemen, make me feel it as little as possible. Last week we had a visit from Captain Castle, of the 'Pylades.' His story is very melancholy. He married, six months before he left England, one of the Miss Hills, Sir John Hill's daughter, and she died just as he received orders to return home. We had also a visit from Colonel Bosch, the Dutch governor, a most gentlemanlike man. But fancy how awkward the next morning: I cannot induce Mr. Maclean to rise, and I have to make breakfast, and do the honours of adieu to him and his officers; white plumes, mustachios, and all. I think I never felt more embarrassed. I have not yet felt the want of society in the least. I do not wish to form new friends, and never does a day pass without thinking most affectionately of my old ones. On three sides we are surrounded by the sea. I like the perpetual dash upon the rocks; one wave comes up after another, and is for ever dashed to pieces, like human hopes that only swell to be disappointed. We advance—up springs the shining froth of love or hope, a moment white, and gone for ever! The land view, with its cocoa and palm trees, is very striking; it is like a scene in the "Arabian Nights." Of a night the beauty is very remarkable; the sea is of a silvery purple, and the moon deserves all that has been said in her favour. I have only once been out of the fort by daylight, and then was delighted. The salt lakes were first dyed a deep crimson by the setting sun, and as we returned they seemed a faint violet in the twilight, just broken by a thousand stars, while before us was the red beacon-light. The chance of sending this letter is a very sudden one, or I should have ventured to write to General Fagan, to whom I beg the very kindest regards. Dearest, do not forget me. Pray write to me, "Mrs. George Maclean, Cape Coast Castle, care of Messrs. Foster and Smith, 5, New City Chambers, Bishopsgate Street." Write about yourself—nothing else half so much interests

'Your affectionate

'*Cape Coast Castle, Oct.* 15.   L. E. MACLEAN.'

THE POET'S EXILE--L. E. L. AT CAPE COAST CASTLE.

Past and Future.

No one who reads this letter can doubt the collected mind, the clear memory, the reasonable emotion, with which it was written. There is not a single exaggerated expression in the whole composition. She even gives her direction to her friend as if she contemplated the certainty of a continued correspondence.

To conclude with her own exquisite lines:—

> ' The future never renders to the past
>   The young beliefs intrusted to its keeping;
> Inscribe one sentence—life's first truth and last—
>   On the pale marble where our dust is sleeping:
>   We might have been.'

MADAME DE SÉVIGNÉ.

At the Age of Fifteen.—The Saint—Her Grandmother.—Her Marriage.—The Cardinal de Retz.—Society under Louis XIV.—The Hôtel de Rambouillet. —The Précieuses Ridicules.—Madame de Sévigné among them.—The Reward of Virtue.—Temp. Louis XIV.—Madame de Sévigné in Love.—The Outbreak of the 'Fronde.'—Ninon de l'Enclos.—De Sévigné Killed in a Duel.—The Court of Louis XIV.—Anecdote of Racine.—The Arnaulds.— Religion of the Day.—The Bandits of La Trappe.—The Ascetics of Port-Royal.—Madame de Sévigné's Idolatry.—Anecdote of Boileau.—Anecdote of Fénélon.—The Knox of the French Court.—La Rochefoucauld.—Fouquet the Swindler.—Madame de Sévigné at Paris.—Madame de Sévigné Introduced.—A French Marriage.—Madame de Grignan.—Classics and Vice.—An Indulgent Mother.—Young de Sévigné.—Madame de Sévigné's Letters.—Madame de Sévigné's Affection.—Letter-writing.—Death.—Death of Madame de Grignan.

A FRENCHWOMAN with none of the vices and little of the frivolity of Frenchwomen, a true Louis-Quatorzienne without the prejudices of that reign, a woman of society and one of its leaders, yet a prodigy of domestic affections, a frequenter of the court but a lover of the fields, a wit without attempting it, and a great writer without knowing it, Marie de Sévigné has justly won the admiration of every great man who appreciates wit and honours virtue. Even the satirical Saint-Simon can find nothing to say against her, but praises her ease, her natural graces, her goodness, and her knowledge. Horace Walpole, himself the prince of letter-writers, made an idol of her, and tried to copy her style, which he considered as his finest model. Of her very portrait he says, enthusiastically: 'I am going to build an altar for it, under the title of Notre Dame des Rochers,' in allusion to her country-house in Brittany, Les Rochers. Mackintosh is loud in her praises. He read her letters while in India, and his journal has frequent notices of them 'She has so filled my heart,' he says, ' with affectionate interest in her, as a living friend, that I can scarcely bring myself to think of her as being a writer, or having a style; but she has become a celebrated, probably an immortal writer without expecting it.' Of her easy yet forcible style, he says, in speaking of a passage in one of her letters, ' Tacitus and Machiavel could have said nothing better.' But Lamartine, one of her latest biographers, is perhaps her greatest admirer. He views her with a poet's eyes, and calls her ' almost a poetess,' and 'the Petrarch of French prose.' He sees in her the one great instance, that has come down to us in literature, of maternal devotion, and, as an embodiment of this idea, has not hesitated to count her among the great civilizers of the world, and to place her name side by side with those of Socrates, Homer, Milton, Bossuet, and Fénelon. To a less romantic vision this excessive devotion to a daughter, ' *qui ne la méritait que médiocrement*,' says Saint-Simon, may appear like a weakness, still more so when contrasted with her indifference to her son; and it is perhaps rather as a woman of the world, standing out virtuous and sensible in an age of universal vice and extravagance of opinions, that the English reader will prefer to contemplate Madame de Sévigné.

Her life has indeed two sides, the romantic and the practical. Her early life, her devotion to her husband, and her absorbing passion for her daughter, belong to the former. The rest is so sober, that some have called her cold, and even her greatest admirers confessed her lukewarm.

In the old abbey-house of Livry in the forest of Bondi near Paris, there lived, about the year 1642, an old man and a young girl, like a dusty, black-lettered folio lit up by a stray sunbeam, when the bookcase is opened. Christophe de Coulanges is the abbé of Livry, a worthy old man, visited from time to time by men of learning, and, though of severe piety, not quite separated from the outer world. His niece, Marie de Rabutin, is an orphan of fifteen, his charge and his pupil. This young girl is indeed a joy in his quiet house. Her face alone is beautiful. The fresh delicate complexion, the oval form, the features regular if not classical, the rich abundance of fair hair, are all of themselves enough for beauty. La Fontaine wrote of her—

> 'With bandaged eyes you seem the God of Love;
> His mother, when those eyes illume the face.'

But those large blue eyes, dreamy one moment, with falling lids, and the next lit up with thought and mirth, are the centre fires of the whole, and in them the expression is for ever changing. Add to this a slight and graceful figure, and it is easy to understand that even her beauty dazzled the world of Paris at her first appearance. And this girl, beautiful and gay as she is, is now studying Greek and Latin with her old uncle, now receiving learned lessons from Ménage and Chapelain, and collecting a stock of erudition which was to fit her in after life for the companionship of men whose names are classical.

It is remarkable that a woman, who, if she had nothing further to distinguish her, would remain to the world as the type of a mother's devotion, should not only have been left motherless when six years old, but have had a grandmother so little aware of maternal duty, that she could abandon her young children to enter a convent, though her son threw himself across the threshold of her house to prevent her departure, for which act, and the building eighty convents, the Church of Rome thought fit to canonize her. The husband of this infatuated woman was Christophe de Rabutin, Baron de Chantal and Seigneur de Bourbily, which lies near Semur in the department of the Côte d'Or, and between thirty and forty miles from Dijon. The family was old and respectable, but not one of the great families of France. The son of this Christophe married a Mademoiselle de Coulanges, daughter of an influential house. Their only child was Marie, afterwards Madame de Sévigné. She was born at Paris on the 5th of February, 1626, and brought up at the Château de Bourbily. In 1628, her father died in the defence of the Ile de Rhé againgst the English; and not long after his widow followed him, leaving the little child of six years old with no nearer relative, on her father's side, than her grandmother, who, as indifferent to her grandchild as she had been to her own children, left her to the care of a maternal uncle, the Abbé de Coulanges. At Livry, of which she so often speaks in her letters, she passed the next nine years of her life under the protection of this uncle, thus escaping that education of the convent to which young girls were then subjected, and of which she afterwards herself expressed her disapproval.

At fifteen the beautiful Mademoiselle de Rabutin-Chantal, sole heiress to an estate of three hundred thousand francs, was introduced by the De Colanges to the court and court-circles of Paris, and was at once pronounced fascinating. She had indeed qualities which made such a verdict universal. It was not only the gay and light who were charmed with her mirth and beauty: the more serious found in her a fund of solid learning after the fashion of those times, and a power and taste for reflection. And these qualities were set in the yet more valuable attributes of a rare modesty free from all prudery, and a good heart ready for the cultivation of friendship.

The young girl was beset with candidates for her hand, among whom were members of the noblest families in France. Her choice was unfettered. She was an orphan, an only child, and an heiress; and there is therefore every reason to believe that the choice she made was that of her own heart. It does but add one instance more to the hundreds that might be quoted of women actuated in this most solemn matter purely by fancy. Young as she was, for she was married at seventeen, Marie de Rabutin had sufficient perception of character already not to be misled by mere appearances, or dazzled by external extractions. Yet the Marquis de Sévigné was a man who had little but these to offer. Handsome, dashing, and courageous, he was at the same time selfish, sensual, and incapable of a sincere attachment. He accepted the devotion she offered him with careless indifference; and, insensible alike to her superiority of mind and integrity of character, threw her over for acquaintances utterly unworthy of comparison with his young wife. He was of an old Breton family, and a *maréchal de camp*, and held a good position at court. To add to this, he was a relation and favourite of the Cardinal de Retz, then coadjuteur to the Archbishop of Paris; and the Abbé de Coulanges, influenced by these considerations, favoured rather than opposed the match.

The Cardinal de Retz was at that time the rising star in France. Richelieu had been dead about two years: his mantle had descended on the shoulders of Mazarin; but there was already a party formed against the crafty Italian, and Paul de Gondy, then about thirty years old, was on the look-out for an opportunity of putting himself forward. Richelieu had already pronounced him 'a dangerous spirit,' on reading his book 'La Conjuration de Fiesque,' which De Gondy had written when eighteen years of age. On the death of his uncle, in 1643, he was made Archbishop of Paris. Like his predecessors, he had been destined for a courtier or a soldier, rather than a priest. Richelieu was educated for the army, Mazarin served in it: De Gondy was forced to take orders against his will, and had passed his early days in duels and gallantries. Like his predecessors, again, he was a man of ambition, but, unlike them, he had no definite purpose in view. He caballed and plotted more for the pleasure of being in the opposition than to gain a step towards an end. The power he obtained was immense, but he trifled with it. Wavering and hotheaded, he rushed into new intrigues while the old ones were yet incomplete; and while for a time he was more popular than either Richelieu or Mazarin had ever been, he failed to make use of the advantages, and wasted his energies in petty enterprises. Yet he seems to have been a loveable character, and in after years Madame de Sévigné, who saw more of him than any one else, was much attached to her 'dear cardinal.' Her intimacy with him was afterwards fatal to her favour at court. Louis XIV. hated nothing so much as the recollection of the *Fronde*, in which De Retz had taken so prominent a part, and this dislike he extended even to the cardinal's friends.

Monsieur de Sévigné then might be considered certain of promotion from his connection with the cardinal, and the marriage was therefore looked upon as a good one. It was destined to prove very different.

THE HOTEL DE RAMBOUILLET.

The life of a Frenchwoman then, as much as in the present day, began with marriage; and Madame de Sévigné entered upon hers in an age of great promise, the forerunner of the Augustan age of France. The turbulent ministry of Richelieu was followed by a reaction in favour of letters, learning, and the measures of peace. Anne of Austria was guided by the wily but conciliating Mazarin; and the factions which had disturbed France so long were reduced for a time to mere intrigues of court. The society of Paris had at length breathing space from stormy politics, and turned to the softer allurements of wit and letters. This society, circling round the court, influenced and controlled by it, yet possessed a freedom of thought which has been little known in France since those days. The great men of the age of Louis Quatorze were still young, but the Cid of Corneille and the Maxims of La Rochefoucauld were already in the mouths of all readers. On the other hand, vice was rampant, encouraged by the example of the court, and religion was reduced to bigotry or asceticism. Priests ruled the court, and were foremost in its luxurious sensuality. When repentance came, as it often did with the decline of power or the decay of beauty, the penitent rushed from a world where all was so hollow, and where their attraction was no longer felt, and hid their heads in convents or monasteries, which rivalled one another in the severity of their asceticism. Port-Royal and La Trappe were living sepulchres where elegant courtiers and gallant reprobates mortified the flesh they had spared nothing to indulge, and thought to pacify heaven by the torture of their long-pampered bodies. It was an age of extravagance in feeling, and prejudice in thought. The people were despised, 'the country' identified with the king. France was the court, Paris the small circle of courtiers who hovered round it.

The chief centre of this circle at this period was the Hôtel de Rambouillet: Madame de Rambouillet, a Florentine by birth, and connected with the Medici, had brought with her to Paris a love of Italian poetry and a pardon for Italian licentiousness. She gathered round her all the lovers of literature, and admitted, at the same time, the lovers of life who crowded in from the court. They talked of the virtues of Greece and Rome, and exemplified in themselves the vices of France. Hither came Mazarin to play cards and talk bad French; De Retz and a whole host of love-making abbés in his wake. Here La Rochefoucauld observed human nature in the narrow sphere which is the 'world' in his maxims, and made love to *les beaux yeux* of the Duchesse de Longueville, politician and authoress. Here came the great magistrates and dignitaries of state, headed by the magnificent swindler Fouquet, the financier, whose acquaintance Madame de Sévigné probably made in these salons. The 'dignity of wit,' which was then as high, if not higher, a title than office to the popularity of these circles, was represented by all the talkers of the day, among them being conspicuous two near relations of Madame de Sévigné. Monsieur de Coulanges, a cousin on her mother's side, was a merry little man, celebrated for telling, or rather acting, a good story, which always set the company in a roar of laughter. De Bussy-Rabutin, a connection on her father's side, was almost as popular a letter-writer as Madame de Sévigné herself. He was a gallant of the first water, always pushing intrigues, always repulsed, and always visiting his repellers with the lash of satire, and the yet more cowardly weapon of calumny. Vain to excess, he was also contemptibly servile, and when sent into exile by Louis Quatorze, he could not endure his fate with noble resignation, but attacked the monarch with slavish entreaties and nauseous flattery.

But the cream of the society at the Hôtel de Rambouillet was that knot of absurd blue-stockings, whom Molière annihilated in his 'Précieuses Ridicules,' a name derived from a habit which these classical ladies had of addressing one another as '*ma précieuse.*' Of these female pedants Mademoiselle Scudéry, the authoress of terrible romances in ten or twelve volumes, in which Cyrus or Ibrahim was the hero, and warriors of the ancient world talked and acted much in the same strain as the ornaments of the Regency, was *facile princeps*. Around the 'incomparable Sappho,' as this lady was called in her set, were gathered a number of learned individuals of the same cast: Julie, the daughter of Madame de

Rambouillet, christened by the '*Précieuses*,' 'the incomparable Artemis,' and Pélisson, the ugliest man of his day, of whom Boileau wrote

'L'or même a Pélisson donne un teint de beauté;'

and who, after having tamed spiders in the Bastille for five years, was rewarded by Mademoiselle de Scudéry with the character of Acante in her novels, were among the most celebrated. The '*Précieuses*' and their male admirers talked classics, composed and (cruel torture!) read sonnets and epigrams, exchanged compliments with elaborate allusions to Augustus, Alcibiades, Artaxerxes, or any other hero of antiquity, and believed themselves to be the only really educated and truly gifted people in France. In later days Mademoiselle de Scudéry transferred the same society to her own house; but at this time the '*Précieuses*' thronged the Hôtel de Rambouillet in great numbers, where Madame de Rambouillet, to save herself the trouble of accompanying every visitor through the antechamber, often received them in bed, as Mazarin afterwards did his own guests. This troublesome custom of going a certain length with your guest, according to his or her rank, was at that time imperative, and is still kept up in some old-fashioned circles in Paris. Saint-Simon relates an anecdote of some nobleman who was very precise on this point, and annoyed his visitors with it so much, that at last one of them locked the door upon him as he went out; but the polite host was not to be so eluded, and positively got out of the window in order to make his guest the proper farewell bow at the front door.

Into this mixed côterie of pedants and prudes on the one hand, and unprincipled pleasure-seekers on the other, the young Marquise de Sévigné was introduced, with wit enough to make her an object with the one, and beauty enough to render her a victim of the other set. Sense and modesty contrived to triumph over the temptations of both. Though she is sometimes included in the lists of '*les Précieuses*,' she had quite good taste enough to laugh at their rhapsodical absurdities; and on the other hand her strong principle, which her enemies designated coldness, enabled her to overcome the allurements of the other extreme.

Nor was she exempt from trials. Already her worthless husband had proved his indifference to her in a series of intrigues for which there was no excuse. She was left very much alone in her domestic life; and yet in an age when vice was the rule, virtue the exception, she maintained the high purity of her reputation. It is a curious proof of the feeling of that age, that Madame de Sévigné could accept as friends the very men whom she rejected as lovers. Among these the principal were the magnificent Fouquet, of whom Boileau wrote—

'Jamais surintendant ne trouva de cruelles;'

Madame de Sévigné making an exception to his successes; the Prince de Conti, the Comte du Lude, a noted lady-killer, and Bussy-Rabutin, of whom we have spoken, and who, when his fair cousin rejected his vile suit, revenged himself by calumnies which no one, fortunately for her, would believe.

Yet, in after years, Madame de Sévigné was a devoted friend to Fouquet, and corresponded on easy terms with Bussy-Rabutin. What a story does this tell of the depravity of that age! Nay, she even went further, and appears to have herself agreed in the verdict of her age which pronounced her virtue to be mere insensibility. Far from being proud of having rejected these suitors, she seems sorry that she was compelled to offend them in so doing, and excuses rather than glories in their rejection. Certainly her correctness, from whatever cause it arose, is much to her honour. Temptation, encouragement, and example surrounded her on every side. Propriety of conduct was not only an exception in those circles, but an odious exception. The woman who would not be as bad as her neighbours drew upon herself their envy and hatred. She was denounced as a prude, a prig, one who set herself up to be superior, and so forth. Such humours, so they were regarded, were fit, not for society, but for the cloister. Thither let her carry her virtue, if she chose, but not intrude it where it could only suggest disagreeable comparisons. Such was the feeling of the day, and for such judgments it was but poor consolation to be compared by '*les Précieuses*' of the Hôtel Rambouillet to some high-featured Lucretia of classical history.

Then, again, Madame de Sévigné's admirers were not men of ordinary stamp. Fouquet's ill-gotten wealth, De Conti's rank, Du Lude's handsome face, and Bussy's insolence, were such high recommendations among the ladies of the court, that it was an honour rather than a disgrace, to be singled out by them, and Madame de Sévigné's rejection of these lady-killers was set down to pride or obstinacy.

No one could imagine all the time—for it was too strange an idea to enter into anybody's head—that Madame de Sévigné, gay, charming, and beautiful as she was, was still in love with her husband; and had any one supposed it, for a moment, the cruel conduct of this man would have made such a devotion appear extravagant in their eyes. Madame de Sévigné did not reproach him, but secretly mourned over his inconstancy, and hoped for an ultimate improvement. To effect this, she, with much difficulty, persuaded him about two years after their marriage to quit the temptations of Paris and retire with her to their château at 'Les Rochers,' in Brittany, in the neighbourhood of Vitré. We can well understand that this step was dictated by nothing but the desire of recalling to herself her estranged husband. To quit Paris at nineteen, in the zenith of her success, when her beauty was fresher and fuller than it could ever be again, would have been to any Frenchwoman like a voluntary entrance of purgatory; but to quit it for a lonely château, in a dark, foggy, ungenial country; to leave all the wit, mind, and spirit of the Place Royale for the heavy platitudes of half-drunken hunters, or the tittle tattle of rustics who had never emerged from their narrow district, and, Chinese-like, recognized no world beyond it, must have been trying to any woman of mind. Yet Madame de Sévigné seems to have been quite happy in here enjoying for a time the careless affection of a man to whom she was passionately attached. The young wife was satisfied if she could only have him to herself; she did not ask for much love, knowing that he could not and would not give it her.

Here, then, the young couple, he twenty-four and she only

twenty, passed the succeeding three years with just so much society as the neighbourhood afforded, which, if any comparison can be made between Brittany of the present day and Brittany of two centuries ago, was very little. In March, 1647, her first child was born, that only son, of whom, in after days, she wrote so amusingly, and who seems to have mingled a very small share of his mother's good sense with the extravagant love of dissipation which he inherited from his father. But the following year was yet more blessed by the birth of that daughter, afterwards Madame de Grignan, to whom she addressed her famous letters, and for whom she felt—if indeed there is no affectation in her style—an affection which has been extolled as the *ne plus ultra* of maternal tenderness.

Her happiness, however, was not to be long-lived. In 1648, not long after the birth of this second child, there broke out in France that incomprehensible and apparently most useless revolt, which goes by the name of 'La Fronde.' At the head of the movement was Madame de Sévigné's friend and her husband's relative, the Cardinal de Retz. The rise of De Gondy, the cardinal, had been rapid. Vincent de Paul had been his tutor, yet how little had he profited by the lessons of that great man—if we may not say, great saint? Little more, indeed, than to acquire the art of conversion. De Gondy used it to turn a Huguenot into a Romanist; and Louis XIII., delighted with his success, appointed him the coadjuteur of the Archbishop of Paris. In 1643, at the age of twenty-nine, the young schemer was raised to the archiepiscopal chair. No longer able with dignity to indulge in the extravagances of vice, he had recourse to those of political intrigue. Mazarin was his main point of attack. He courted and gained the affections of the people; and unable openly, from his position, to wage war against his rival, he encouraged the popular discontent, seized the opportunity of an *émeute* in 1648, and using the Duc de Beaufort as his lay instrument, to carry out his own machinations, developed it speedily into a civil war.

This was now raging, and the Marquis de Sévigné as a soldier in the royal service was recalled from his retirement in Brittany to his duties in the capital. This was unfortunate for his poor wife. At his request she returned to Paris with her children, but only to experience fresh slights, and endure new insults from her inconstant husband. Among the famous women of Paris—famous for beauty, wit, and want of modesty—Ninon de l'Enclos was at that time the most notorious. Though openly depraved she was not entirely excluded from the higher ranks of society: Madame de Maintenon, herself irreproachable, was not ashamed to be her intimate friend and companion; and it is curious to find Madame de Sévigné speaking of her familiarly as 'Ninon.' With this person Monsieur de Sévigné fell, or affected to fall in love, and dissipated his fortune for her worthless smiles. It was in vain that his neglected wife sought to recall him; and at last she yielded to the advice of her former guardian, the Abbé de Coulanges, and after making an arrangement for a separate maintenance, retired with her children to Les Rochers, leaving her husband to his profligate life in Paris. We have no means of ascertaining what efforts the wife did really make to save her wretched husband; but if these seem to have been slight, insufficient, and unworthy of the deep attachment she felt for him, we must remember in palliation, how much the ideas of that age differed from our own on these subjects. As we shall afterwards see, in speaking of her son, Madame de Sévigné, like the rest of the then world, looked on such attachments as follies rather than vices, and perhaps the danger of her husband's *soul* was the last thought that entered her mind. As to her attachment, there can be little doubt that, constant only in inconstancy, the Marquis de Sévigné had at last chilled it by his conduct. But whatever she may have felt, the punishment that followed to her and to him disarms us of all reproaches.

She had not been long in retirement at Les Rochers when she received a letter which felled her to the ground. Her husband, she was told, was desperately wounded. In the course of a scandalous intrigue he had run athwart the ambition of the young Chevalier d'Albret, another dissolute courtier; a quarrel had arisen; a duel had followed, and this was the result. Madame de Sévigné wrote to her husband a letter of tender reproaches and woman-like forgiveness. The news was false The quarrel had indeed taken place—the duel had been arranged—but it had not yet come off. The letter of his wife may have brought some remorse into the profligate's heart, but could not avert the catastrophe. The misnamed 'honour' of the age demanded the blood of one or other of the foes. They met and fought, and De Sévigné fell. He was in his twenty-seventh year, and left behind him a wife of twenty-three and two young children.

Thus closed the first romance of Marie de Rabutin's life. She had loved and chosen this man from her heart. She had forgiven his inconstancy, and endured his neglect. He was now taken from her and slain in a quarrel for a woman unfit to be her rival. So completely had he neglected her, that she had nothing of his to cherish as a relic; and in her grief and love was fain to demand from the very woman for whom he had abandoned her his portrait and a lock of his hair. Her grief, indeed, was so intense that we are told that in after years she could never meet his antagonist (if we may not say his murderer) without falling into a swoon. He had absorbed all her love, and she was one of those women whose passion has but one centre. When that was gone, and grief after long years had calmed down, the passion still survived in a maturer form, and the deep love of the wife passed into a calmer yet as powerful attachment for her—and his—child; and it is only thus that we can account for her devotion to her daughter, Madame de Grignan.

The reckless Marquis de Sévigné had squandered his own fortune and his wife's on worthless objects, and Madame de Sévigné found it necessary to retrench for several years. She now devoted herself to the education of her children, and passed her time chiefly at the house of the old Abbé de Coulanges, her first protector. But she well knew that her son would require that personal interest at the court through which alone came fortune and promotion, and she resolved to return to Paris. Some four or five years after her husband's death she again entered the salons of Paris, a young widow of seven and twenty, as beautiful as ever, and celebrated for her wit and *abandon*.

The court of Louis Quatorze was now in its highest glory

The great men of every tone and taste who had been young ten years before were now risen into eminence; and Madame de Sévigné could soon count the best of them among her friends and correspondents. Corneille, Racine, Moliere, La Fontaine, and Boileau were the poets and satirists with whom she talked and laughed. Her more serious thoughts were imparted to or drawn out by the two Arnaulds, the founders of Port-Royal and fathers of Jansenism, with their pupil, the suffering, patient, and delicate Pascal; and by the grandest preachers of the century, Bourdaloue, Mascaron, and Bossuet. Among her heroes were the restless De Retz; the heroic Scotchman Montrose, then an exile; La Rochefoucauld, the author of the 'Maxims;' Marshal Turenne; Le Grand Colbert; Condé; and more of the great and pseudo-great men of the Augustan age of France. The ladies with whom she mixed have names scarcely less historic. There were the Duchess de Longueville, the political intriguante of the Fronde; the penitent La Valliere; the heartless but respectable Madame de Maintenon; Madame de Montespan; the Countess d'Olonne, daughter of Madame de Rambouillet; and another star of the *Précieuses*, Madame de La Fayette, the authoress of 'Zaide' and other novels, but more celebrated as the devoted friend of La Rochefoucauld, of whom she said, ' Il m'a donné son esprit, mais j'ai réformé son cœur,' which, if a true boast, was not an insignificant one. As Madame de Sévigné was a woman of no little perception, her opinions of some of these contemporaries, as we find them in her letters, will not be without interest.

With regard to the poets, the French have found fault with her for setting Corneille so far above Racine. This was undoubtedly the fashion of the day, as she herself tells us, and Madame de Sévigné may have been influenced by it; but, whatever the common taste in France, there are eminent judges in England who find more nature and truer passion in the older tragedian. She admired Racine extremely, especially his 'Bajazet' and 'Esther.' Of the former she says: 'The character of Bajazet is frigid; the customs of the Turks are not correctly observed; they don't make so much fuss about marrying; the crisis is not well prepared, and one cannot enter into the causes of this great butchery; however, there are some good things in it, but nothing perfectly good, nothing to elevate, none of those bursts which make us shudder in Corneille's pieces.' Again she says of Racine, 'he composes plays for La Champmêlé' (an actress with whom he was in love, and to whom he taught her parts), 'but not for future ages. Long life, then, to our old friend Corneille; let us forgive him a few bad verses in consideration of the divine bursts which carry us away; they are master-strokes which cannot be imitated. Boileau says even more of him than I do.'

As an instance of the flattery to which even genius stooped, in speaking to a monarch who loved adulation more than anything, she relates an answer made by Racine to Louis Quatorze, when the sovereign expressed his regret that the poet had not accompanied the army in its last campaign. 'Sire,' said Racine, 'we had none but town clothes, and had ordered others to be made, but the places you attacked were all taken before they could be finished.' 'This,' adds Madame de Sévigné, 'was pleasantly received.'

Boileau and La Fontaine were both great favourites with Madame de Sévigné. The fables of the latter were even then learnt by heart and recited in society, as they still are among old-fashioned people in France. Of the famous satirist Boileau she said to his face that 'he was tender in prose but cruel in verse;' a very true verdict, for he was as amiable in private life as he was bitter on paper.

All the Arnaulds were friends of Madame de Sévigné, but she was most intimate with Arnauld d'Andilly and his son the Marquis de Pomponne. This family of Arnaulds—the most respectable, most learned, and most religious in France of that period—has been identified with the famous Society of Port-Royal, and this, again, with the anti-Jesuit doctrines of Jansenism. The progress of that society was, in fact, owing to them. In 1625, the nuns of a convent called Port-Royal des Champs, near Paris, found that the site, owing to the marshes, was too pestilential to remain in, and were forced to quit their establishment. Madame Arnauld, a rich widow, and the mother of the commissary-general, Arnauld d'Andilly, and of the famous Bishop of Angers, bought for them the Hôtel de Clugny in Paris, and with her daughter as abbess, gave to the new establishment the name of Port-Royal of Paris. She herself and six of her daughters, besides her granddaughter, La Mère Angélique, who was the abbess of Port-Royal, were all inmates of this convent, and were noted for their austere virtues and unparalleled learning. Richelieu said of them that they were as pure as angels, but as proud as demons.

In 1637, the two young men, M. Lemaitre, a lawyer, and M. de Serricourt, an officer in the army, agreed that the world was all vanity, and that happiness was only to be found in pious solitude. Such was, indeed, the religion of the day, and such it often is when society reaches that point of civilization where vice and luxury take the place of manly exertion. It was the spirit of the early Christians, who saw with disgust the profligacy and effeminacy of Greece and Rome: and it was almost the spirit of our own Puritans who recoiled from the license of the courts of James and Charles. Asceticism is a feature peculiar to civilization. It is a reaction in favour of manliness. Unknown to rude ages of stirring life, and unnecessary to ages of purer and really higher civilization, it seems to mark those which are distinguished for their extravagance, luxury, and profligacy. It is an indignant rebound from effeminate vices into a simplicity of life which, whatever else may be said of it, appears to be manly from the very courage and self-denial which it exacts. But it is no less extravagant than that which it flees; it is no less an unnatural and even diseased condition, and it is only such an age as those in which it occurs that can mistake it for religion. 'The greater the sinner, the greater,' indeed, ' the saint.' The ascetics of all ages have been generally the worst of men before their change; they only exchange one luxury for another, and in the intensity of self-torture they find a comfort, almost, one may say, an ease (for habit makes it so), which exempts them from the far more trying exercise of true religion. It requires little discernment to perceive that it is far easier to live on bread and water in an obscure cell, tearing one's flesh with knotted cords, than to meet temptation in an open field and there resist it.

But an extravagant age naturally confounds an extravagance with religion, and the ascetics of the days of Louis Quatorze were admired by the court, whose members probably intended, when youth, beauty, and fashion had left them, to follow in their steps, and pacify an evil conscience by almost childish severities. At the time that Madame de Sévigné wrote, a noted instance of sudden conversion had taken place. The young and handsome De Rancé was the most dissipated of all the dissipated abbés of that priest-haunted court. His excesses were the talk even of people who were too accustomed to excesses to notice them. In 1657 the small-pox was raging in Paris, and about the same time the abbé was desperately in love with Madame de Montbazon, a celebrated beauty. Calling on her one day, he found the servants away and the doors open, and walked up to her room without waiting to be announced. He opened the door, and in a leaden coffin beheld the headless form of the lady he had loved so passionately. On the ground by its side was the once beautiful head itself, now a hideous mask. The small-pox had attacked her in its most violent form and in a few hours she was dead. Her servants, dreading the contagion, had sent for the first coffin that could be found. It was too short, and they had resorted to the horrid expedient of decapitation to meet the difficulty. Her lover had come in at the very moment that they were gone to fetch a hearse to carry the body away. He staggered back from the awful sight, and escaping from the house, vowed to bury himself alive for the rest of his days. And he did so.

In the centre of a dense huge forest near Evreux, in Normandy, is a close, narrow valley, still as a grave and dark as a pit. Around it the jealous cliffs rise high and steep, and the forest itself penetrates into the abyss, as if to add to its gloomy darkness. In the bottom of it eleven foul and stagnant pools load the heavy air with sickness, and in the middle of these there stood the once famous monastery of La Trappe. It was a den of thieves. The monks, secure in their foul pit, far from the world, and protected by the pathless forest, issued in lawless bands at night, armed to the teeth, and concealing themselves along the highway, rushed out to plunder the unsuspecting traveller. They were known in the province as 'The bandits of La Trappe.'

Among these men De Rancé went alone, unarmed, and little by little gained an ascendancy over their minds, till he brought them one after another to quit their lawless life, and return to one of asceticism. But the rules he enjoined could not but be severe, and he made them more and more so, Bread, water, vegetables, was all their food. The furniture of their cells was replaced by a truckle bed of rope, a rug, and a human skull. The silence of the gloomy valley was doubled by the terrible silence imposed for the sake of security on its half-dead inhabitants. The stalwart but now wasting figures of the once lawless monks passed one another without a word. Their sealed tongues were loosed only for one hour on Sunday, and then it was to speak of matters of faith and doctrine. The world was, or seemed to be forgotten; shut out, foregone for ever. None knew his fellow's name, except the abbot himself. Each new-comer took a new name when he renounced the world; and once a father and son lived there together unknown to each other, till the latter died. It was then that on his tombstone the father read the young man's name, and recognised his son. Pain and self-torture were courted as redemptives, and De Rancé turned away a novice because he noticed that while weeding he pushed aside the nettles, to prevent being stung!

In such a grave did De Rancé bury himself, and the Trappists were the wonder and admiration of the age.

It is not therefore surprising that the example of Lemaitre and Serricourt should have been eagerly followed by the courtiers and gallants whose consciences were pricked. In a short time they had a large band of companions, renouncing the world, and bent on learning and good works, and these men called themselves the Society of Port-Royal. They differed from monks in being bound by no vows, and wearing no peculiar dress. Their clothing was plain; their lives simple and penitential; their time given to study and the care of the poor. They soon increased in such numbers that, finding their house in Paris too small, they retired to the convent of Port-Royal des Champs, which had been abandoned by its nuns. Here they set to work to drain and cultivate the valley, and the once gay courtiers were transformed to labourers and mechanics, gardeners and carpenters, and had to wield spade and mattock in the delicate white hands which had hitherto handled only the sword or played with a lady's fan. They soon became fashionable saints. The court ladies poured out their sorrows and sins to them, and received very blunt wholesome advice in return; and parents of all ranks sent their children to be educated by them. Their system of tuition, and the grammars they prepared, are still upheld and even employed n France and Switzerland. Madame de Sévigné, who visited Port-Royal des Champs in 1674, when the nuns had returned there once more, calls it a paradise, and says that 'holiness extends for a league all round it.' 'The nuns are angels on earth,' she adds, with a touch of her usual levity; 'it is a hideous valley, just fitted to inspire a taste for working out one's salvation:' a truly Louis-Quatorzian idea.

Arnauld d'Andilly entered the *confrèrie* at the age of fifty-five, after passing his life in court and camp, holding the appointment of Commissary General. When Madame de Sévigné knew him, in 1671, he was a very old man. She relates an interview which she had with him at Pomponne, his son's house. Her '*bon homme*,' as she affectionately calls him, proved his good sense in the serious conversation that followed. 'He said that I was a pretty heathen; that I made an idol of you in my heart; that this kind of idolatry was as dangerous as any other, although it might seem to me less heinous; and that, in short, I should look to myself.' He talked to her for six hours, but does not seem to have cured her, though what he said is precisely what any modern reader must think when he reads her extravagant phrases of affection for her indifferent daughter. Arnauld d'Andilly had two sons and five nephews, all members of the Society of Port-Royal.

Among these the chief friend of Madame de Sévigné was the Marquis de Pomponne, one of his sons. He was a man of great capabilities, and an honourable, dignified character. He held the post of Secretary of State for Foreign Affairs from 1671 to 1679, when he was dismissed, and retired to Pomponne, where Madame de Sévigné and his friends constantly visited him. Pascal, the disciple of the Arnaulds, the mathematician, philosopher, and saint, was another of Madame de Sévigné's heroes. A paralytic stroke at eighteen deprived him of the use of his limbs, and from that time he was never free from suffering: yet not contented with this, he became a recluse, and to complete his torments wore a belt of pointed iron. His 'Pensées' were the admiration of every reader, and Boileau thought them better than anything ancient or modern. Madame de Sévigné gives an anecdote on this subject. Boileau was dining with a Jesuit, and the Jesuits, as is known, detested the Jansenists, among whom Pascal was counted. The conversation turned on ancient authors, when Boileau exclaimed that he knew of a modern one superior to them all. The Jesuit asked who it was. Boileau did not like to say. 'You have read his book, I am sure,' said he. The Jesuit pressed him to reveal the name, and the company joining with them, Boileau at last exclaimed—'M. Pascal.' 'Pascal!' cried the Jesuit, red with rage; 'oh! Pascal is as good as anything false can be.' 'False!' cried Boileau; 'false, *mon père!* he is as true as inimitable. He has been translated into three languages.' 'That does not make him true.' Boileau grew warm. 'What!' he cried; 'do you talk of the false? Dare you deny that one of your own writers has said, that a Christian is not obliged to love God?' 'Sir,' said the Jesuit, trying to calm him, 'we must make distinctions.' 'Distinctions! *Morbleu!* Distinctions about loving God!' And so saying, Boileau jumped up, ran to the other end of the room, and refused to speak to the Jesuit for the rest of the evening.

The influence of the Arnaulds on Madame de Sévigné was perceptible in after years; but it is remarkable that the powerful sermons of men who were not such enthusiasts, but viewed religion in a truer light—men like Bossuet, Bourdaloue, Mascaron, and Fléchier, the greatest preachers of their day, and among the greatest ever heard in France—should not have moved her so much as the private conversations of a family of ascetics. The fact was, that to hear sermons, and comment on them, was then, as now, a fashion; and then, as now, the style was admired or criticised: the words were declared powerful, searching, and so forth, but the matter was not taken to the heart. The warnings, the entreaties, the thunders of men who were sincere in their condemnation of the vices of the court were listened to as a piece of well-studied oratory to be talked of in their salons, in the same tone as one talked of the eloquence of Demosthenes and Cicero; and because they were regarded in this light, because the power of a sermon led only to a calculation how soon the preacher would be raised to a bishopric, or what reception he would get at court after it, the most solemn warnings took no effect. Courtiers looked forward to redeeming the present by an old age of penance: but in the mean time the king's commands must be attended to, the king's vices imitated, and there was no time to think of the King of all kings.

It is somewhat in this spirit that Madame de Sévigné speaks of the celebrated sermons, or rather discourses, of her day. Of Bossuet, indeed, she speaks little, but about Bourdaloue, the court preacher, and an intrepid thunderer against the court vices, she is always enthusiastic. Bourdaloue was the Knox of the French court, and spared neither king nor courtiers. Madame de Sévigné tells us that he even described people in his sermons, though reserving their names. Such a licence was permitted and even defended by Louis XIV. As an instance of it, we have the anecdote of Fénelon, who once being asleep during a sermon in the chapel at Versailles—what must laymen have done, if even Fénelon could sleep in church? —was suddenly awakened by the voice of the preacher, dropping from its lofty tone to a very practical one, and exclaiming —'Awaken that sleeping abbé, who comes to church only to pay court to his Majesty!' Such apostrophes remind us of Baptist Noel pointing out to his congregation the ladies who wore flowers in their bonnets. But even in Madame de Sévigné's highest praise of Bourdaloue, we see the feeling of the age with respect to sermons. 'He preached divinely.' 'You would have been enchanted.' 'How can one love God when one hears none but bad sermons?' and so forth. The religion of the day was a purely formal one, and the sermon was admired but rarely felt. Madame de Sévigné passes with ease from extolling the finest tirades of Bourdaloue or Mascaron to an easy smile about the depravity of her own son. That Bourdaloue, however, was no ordinary preacher, we can understand, from the fact that she and Boileau, who both cordially hated the Jesuits, could not help admiring him, Jesuit though he was.

Among the other great men of the day, those she most admired were the Cardinal de Retz and La Rochefoucauld. She was intimate with the former for thirty years. She says of him at one time: 'His soul is of so superior an order that one cannot expect for him a mere common end, as for others.' At another, she anticipates that he will yet effect something remarkable, and even be made pope. 'He lives,' she writes in 1675, 'after his retirement, a very pious life, goes to all the services, and dines at the refectory on fast days:' not a very great stretch of religion for a cardinal forsooth, but for a courtier in surplice, such as De Retz really was, a great change for the better. At this period, however, he was employed, not on pious reflections, but rather worldly recollections, for he was writing his Memoirs, as everybody of any mind did in those days. At another time she says: 'I love and honour his eminence in a manner which makes the thought' (of his illness) 'a torment to me; time cannot diminish my feelings for him.' There is no doubt that with all his faults, De Retz was a loveable man and Madame de Sévigné would doubtless have been louder in her praises of him had she not been writing to a daughter who detested him. One thing the cardinal did which, considering his age, claims our esteem for him—he paid his debts. They amounted to more than a million francs (forty thousand pounds), which would be equal to fully seventy thousand in the present day. Madame de Sévigné says: 'He copied no one in this, and no one will copy him.' No courtier, still more no cardinal, ever thought of such an act of honesty in those days; and De Retz stood alone in this respect.

It is pleasant to read her account of La Rochefoucauld's warm domestic affections; and we may ask whether the man who reduced vice and virtue alike to the principle of self-love, did not prove something higher in his own case. Madame de Sévigné says: 'As for M. de la Rochefoucauld, he was going, like a child, to revisit Verteuil, and the spots where he has shot and hunted with so much pleasure. I do not say "where he has fallen in love," for I do not believe that he has ever been in love.' He appears to have profited himself by his maxims, and to have endured the terrible attacks of gout, under which he at last succumbed, with a firmness worthy of the author of the 'Maxims.' Of those reflections, Madame de Sévigné says, what we probably all feel on reading them: 'There are some of them which are divine, and to my shame, some, too, which I cannot understand;' with this difference, that we are not ashamed of our impossibility to comprehend them.

Both De Retz and La Rochefoucauld were of the Fronde party, and Madame de Sévigné, though she took no active share in it, as the Duchesses de Longueville and De Chevreuse did, had to bear the ill-will of Louis on account of her friendship for these two men. To add to this, when the papers of the Finance Minister, Fouquet, were examined, some letters from her were found among those of his particular friends, and the dislike of the monarch was assured. In days when a sovereign's frown was the prelude to total disgrace, this was no slight danger; but every one agrees in acquitting this worthy woman of any of that servility to which even the most independent descended before Louis XIV., and she remained true to her friend, who had also aspired to be her lover. That Fouquet embezzled the funds of the state to an extent unparalleled in the annals of swindling, there can be little doubt, and that he even plotted against the crown itself appears no less certain; but whether Madame de Sévigné believed these accusations or not, she continued true in her friendship, and always spoke of the financier as unfortunate rather than criminal. Her letters were perfectly innocent in every respect; but their discovery seems to have caused some suspicions among her acquaintance, and to have drawn forth an exculpation of herself in writing to M. de Pomponne. 'I assure you,' she says, 'no matter how much credit I may gain from those who do me the justice of believing that I had no other intercourse with him than this, I cannot help feeling deeply distressed at being compelled to justify myself, and very probably without success, in the estimation of a thousand people who will never believe the simple truth.' Fouquet had fortified the island of Belle-Isle as a place of refuge, and in the last moment, when warned of the king's suspicions by the Duchess de Chevreuse, had set out to Nantes with a view to retiring to his fortress. Louis, for his own reasons, allowed him to depart; but the moment he had done so he summoned an officer of his guard and commissioned him to arrest the fugitive. It is said that he had only delayed this measure as a prudential precaution; but that when Fouquet's guest at an entertainment of unusual magnificence, given by the minister at his Château de Vaux, the king had seen in his cabinet a portrait of Mdlle. de la Valliére, with whom he was then in love, and incensed at finding a rival as well as a thief in his *surintendant*, had wished to have him arrested in the middle of the fête, but was deterred from doing so by Anne of Austria. Fouquet was, at any rate, brought back to Paris, underwent a long trial before the Parliament, where Madame de Sévigné, disguised by a mask, watched the bearing of her friend on his defence, and was eventually condemned to imprisonment for life at Pignerol, where he lingered for nineteen years, and died in 1680. Madame de Sévigné's letters, during the period of his trial are full of the most tender anxiety for her friend, and are sufficient proof that her virtue cannot be ascribed, as it has been, to mere insensibility. Her friendship for Fouquet partakes, indeed, of the character of attachment, and we need not be surprised that by this time the widow had forgotten a husband so completely unworthy of her. Fouquet was a man who inspired attachment; and the many friends who shared his disgrace, La Fontaine and the two Arnaulds among them, seem to have been moved by a sincere affection. Madame de Sévigné, at least, never forgot the prisoner at Pignerol, as his other friends did; but if she had any sentiment for Fouquet, it was the only one she felt after the death of her husband.

During the fourteen or fifteen years that followed that event she was occupied partly with the education of her children and partly with the society of Paris. In the prime of her life, her wit, and her beauty, she was everywhere sought for and enthusiastically welcomed. She was suited to all the kinds of society that then circled round the court. Her learning made her a fit companion for *les Précieuses*, though she did not go along with their absurdities. Her wit and still pretty face gave her the power of shining among the gayer sets, and her good sense and womanlike hero-worship recommended her to the political intriguers, of whom so many were her intimate friends; while her strict propriety of conduct did not exclude her from the society of the more serious men of the age. She was everywhere a favourite, and when she left Paris, Paris unanimously implored her to return.

Meanwhile she was devoted to her children, especially to her daughter. She gave them the education which was then thought a good one, prepared them for this world rather than the next, taught them classics more than Christianity, and gave them polish rather than principle. Her beloved daughter was in due time introduced, and excited the most marked sensation. The Comte de Treville, then an oracle at court, said of her, 'This beauty will set the world on fire.' Ménage called her 'The miracle of our days,' and De Bussy-Rabutin, who had been in love with her mother, named her '*La plus jolie fille de France*,' a name which stuck to her for years. It is difficult to understand all this admiration when we look at the portraits that have come down to us of Madame de Grignan. We are at once inclined to give the preference to her mother. The daughter's features were neither very regular nor very pleasing, as far as we can judge. The complexion appears to have been brilliant and delicate, and the rich hair, though a shade darker than Madame de Sévigné's, was even more luxuriant and beautiful. But the expression is cold and uninteresting. The dark eyes want that life and changefulness which was such a charm in her mother's face, and the general air is one of languor. She wanted, in fact, that cheerfulness which had made Madame de Sévigné so universal a favourite. She herself wrote to her mother: 'At first sight people think me adorable, but on further acquaintance they love me no longer;' and if we can judge from letters, her character was not one to elicit sympathy or affection. Her beauty was not sufficient to make up for the smallness of her fortune and her mother's ill-favour at court; and much as she was admired, the adored daughter was not sought by any of those desirable young men on whom Madame de Sévigné, with a mother's ambition, fixed her desiring eyes.

Angry at this, mother and daughter both agreed to quit Paris, and spend a whole winter at Les Rochers. When they returned to Paris, the beauty of Mdlle. de Sévigné is said to have made some impression on the king; but her coldness still repelled the young men of great families. She had already arrived at, and almost passed the age at which a '*jeune fille*' was expected in those days to 'form an alliance.' She was nineteen, and that was a terrible age. A year passed, and she was still Mdlle. de Sévigné; another, and then both mother and daughter gave up the hope of a brilliant marriage, and arranged one which was positively bad.

The Comte de Grignan was a lieutenant-general in Languedoc; of good descent and excellent reputation. On the other hand, he was forty years old, had been twice married already, was a heavy, stolid, uninteresting man, and was not, apparently, very deeply devoted to Mdlle. de Sévigné. Nevertheless, when he proposed he was readily accepted. An extract from a letter of Madame de Sévigné shows what could be thought of the sacred tie of matrimony in those days. 'His former wives,' she writes, 'have died in order to make room for my daughter, and destiny, in a moment of unwonted kindness, had also removed his father and his son; so that, possessing greater riches than ever, and uniting by birth, connection, and excellent qualities, all that we could desire, we made no hesitating terms, as it is usually the custom to do, and we feel much indebted to the two families which have passed away before us. The world seems satisfied, which is much. * * * He has fortune, rank, office, esteem, and consideration in society. What more should we expect? I think we come well out of the scrape.' A scrape it was, in those days, to be single at twenty!

This indifferent pair was united on the 29th of January, 1669, and for a short time Madame de Sévigné's desire of keeping her daughter by her was granted. But the separation she dreaded came at last. M. de Grignan was appointed Vice-Governor of Provence, and was compelled to leave Paris for the south of France. Madame de Sévigné induced him to leave his wife behind for her confinement. She gave birth to a daughter, Marie, who was called Mdlle. d'Adhemar, and who some years afterwards was sent, according to a custom of the day, which sacrificed the daughters to make up the fortune of the sons, to a convent, from which she never emerged. Her other daughter, Pauline, '*cette jeune Pauline*,' afterwards became Madame de Simiane, the friend of Massillon and a letter-writer, like her grandmother, but of inferior merit.

The separation of Madame de Sévigné and her beloved daughter, which took place in 1670, was a terrible blow to the former; but we are indebted to it for a collection of the most curious and interesting letters ever written, which have the advantage of having been penned in perfect simplicity, with no thought of publication, and no desire, as those of Walpole evince, of being read with admiration in a circle of clever acquaintance. From this period Madame de Sévigné seems to have lived only for her daughter. Madame de Grignan returned this devotion with something like indifference. Her letters to her mother have been lost. It is said that her daughter Madame de Simiane destroyed them on religious grounds. Madame de Grignan was a devoted admirer of Descartes, whom she called her *père;* and she not only studied his works with assiduity, but seems to have enlarged on philosophy in her letters. It is said, too, that in some of them she turned into ridicule the absurd religious, or rather superstitious processions of La Provence, processions at which Massillon was afterwards so much disgusted that he put an end to them. But this ridicule was enough to shock the prejudices of her daughter. From the few letters that remain, the character of Madame de Grignan appears to have been frigid and reasonable, rather than warm and joyous like that of her mother. Even from Madame de Sévigné's letters we gather that she wearied of the extravagant devotion of her parent, who seems at times almost to make excuses for her affection. On the other hand, Madame de Grignan's moral character was irreproachable. Wedded to a husband to whom she was indifferent, she espoused philosophy rather than court admiration; and however cold her letters may have been, we may gather, from Madame de Sévigné's remarks, that they contained matter worthy of the consideration of thinkers. On the whole, it may be well regretted that they are lost to us.

While thus devoted to her daughter, Madame de Sévigné cared too little for her son.

This young man was of a weak character, vacillating between the best and the worst impulses. He had received an excellent education, but not sufficient principle to enable him to meet the temptations of Parisian life, in days when the monarch himself set the example of depravity. He was devoted to classical literature, and great in Homer, Virgil, and Horace, and even printed a dissertation on a passage of the last, about which he and Dacier had a dispute. He was educated for the army, and at the age of twenty took part in an expedition to Crete. The Turks had been besieging Candia for twenty-four years. France was their ally, but her sympathies naturally went with the Venetians who held the capital of the island. Louis could not therefore send a regular expedition to their relief, but he authorised the Comte de la Feuillade to raise a corps of gentlemen-volunteers to aid the Venetians, and among them the sons of all the greatest French families enrolled themselves. The young Comte de St. Paul, the son of the Duchesse de Longueville, raised a squadron of one hundred and fifty young cavaliers, all eager to fight in the cause of Christianity. By the advice of Turenne, who was a friend of Madame de Sévigné's, her son joined this corps, and set out for Crete. The French volunteers did, however, more harm than good by their rashness and folly, making repeated sorties against the Turks, in which their numbers were soon terribly reduced. The survivors quarrelled with the Venetian defenders of the town, and set sail before it was taken, returning to France with little glory, though they made the most of it.

M. de Sévigné returned to Paris, and while waiting for promotion followed in the common stream and wasted his fortune upon actresses. He was at one time the rival of Racine in his

admiration of La Champmêlé, at another he was devoted to
Ninon de l'Enclos, who had before ruined his father, and was now
no less than fifty-four years of age, yet still lovely and attractive.
She is said to have preserved her beauty and appearance of youth
to the last. The part played by Madame de Sévigné on this occasion is very remarkable. Her son, who had a great affection
for her and great confidence in her good sense, actually confided
these amours to his mother. Madame de Sévigné was too
much imbued with the spirit of her age to be very much
shocked, but had too much sense not to wish to reform him.
Not only was he dissipating his fortune—'his hand is a crucible
in which money melts away,' she writes—but he was, she feared
following in the steps of his unfortunate father, and might come
to as bad an end. Like him he was very handsome and a great
favourite, but he had inherited from his mother an inclination
to better things, which showed itself from time to time in fits
of deep contrition. Madame de Sévigné did not, as some
mothers would have done, thrust him away from her and leave
him to sink deeper in the mire. She listened to his confidence,
and even laughed at his amusing adventures, but attempted to
show him reasonably the folly of his conduct; and when she
saw that a change had come over him, seized the moment and
drew him back gently to the contemplation of a better life.
Yet, strange to say, she talks lightly of all this to her daughter,
narrates his gallantries and adventures, his successes and re-
pulses, with a light pen, and passes in the next sentence to
praises of the divine eloquence of Bourdaloue or Mascaron!
Nothing could more completely show the feeling of her age.
Fortunately, perhaps, for her son, he had a strong satiric vein:
he was a warm admirer of Boileau. His letters, some of
which remain, are written in an amusing, clever style. He saw
the absurdity of his own conduct. Madame de Sévigné tells
us that he even read to her some of his letters to the actress
La Champmêlé. They were full of the most extravagant passion, she says, and M. de Sévigné laughed at them as merrily
as she did herself. This consciousness of his own absurdity,
mingled with his mother's reproaches, had the effect of curing
him for a time. Madame de Sévigné took him down to

Brittany; and the country, that panacea for all the diseases, mental and bodily, of the city, worked a salutary effect on him. In 1677 he bought the post of second lieutenant of the Gendarmes-Dauphins; and from his account of himself to his sister, he was now very steady and living under his mother's roof. In the following year he distinguished himself at the siege of Mons: and his squadron, in covering a battery, endured a fire of nine guns for two hours with such pertinacity as to draw forth the admiration even of the enemy. In 1683, Madame de Sévigné succeeded in finding a wife for him, Mdlle. de Bréhan, the daughter of a rich *Conseiller du Parlement*, of excellent family, and, having a fortune of two hundred thousand francs; 'a great marriage in these days,' says Madame de Sévigné. His marriage saved him. He became a respectable member of society, occupied himself with literature, and showed a tendency to become *dévot*, which after his mother's death he developed very strongly. His wife had a like propensity, and they bought a house in the Rue St. Jacques, at Paris, in order to be near their religious counsellors.

The last ties of Madame de Sévigné's life were broken at the marriage of her daughter, as the first had been at the death of her husband. From that period, 1669, to her death in 1696, a space of twenty-seven years, she seems to have lived for letter writing. If we except Corbinelli, an Italian who had come with Mazarin to France, and been employed diplomatically by him in Italy, and who, says Lamartine, 'was an Italian Saint-Evremond, able to compete with the greatest minds, but shrinking from an encounter with the difficulties which lie in the path of fame, and assuming, as much through idleness as want of ambition, the character of an amateur'—with the exception of this man, who was devoted to her as a friend, called on her every day when she was in Paris, and even followed her to Livry and Les Rochers, we do not find that she felt any attachment to man or woman, except her daughter, up to the time of her death. Her friendships for De Retz, for La Rochefoucauld, and others, had more of admiration than sentiment in them. Thus her life became wrapt up in her daughter, to whom she wrote three or four times a week, and even oftener, sometimes even twice a day. At the same time, the necessity of getting promotion for her son, and perhaps a natural love for society, kept her, whenever in Paris, in the circles of the gay and intellectual. In 1679 she took a long lease of the Hôtel de Carnavalet, a fine old house in the Rue Culture Sainte-Catherine; and here she received those celebrated friends of whom an account has already been given. Though now far past her fiftieth year, and no longer a beauty, her wit and the friendship which the leading men and women felt for her, kept her still a popular favourite in the court society, though to the court itself she went rarely, owing to the coldness with which Louis XIV. treated her as a former friend of Fouquet and La Fronde. With the gossip of this society her letters are full: but we cannot accuse her of being a mere gossip, as some letter-writers have been. She is less so, for instance, than Horace Walpole. Her letters contain just as much talk on books, religion, philosophy, and general politics, as on the frowns and smiles of the great monarch, the favour accorded to this courtier, the disgrace of another, the marriages contracted, the *bons mots* pronounced and circulated, and so forth; and the oddity of it is, that she passes without a second's hesitation from the slightest to the gravest subject, and back again.

But though it is in society that she shines most, and is most interesting in her judgments of men and measures and her anecdotes of the court, there is a soft and romantic touch, a touch almost of poetry, throughout her letters, that redeems the worldliness of the rest. She was a thorough Frenchwoman, but not a thorough Parisian. When she went to see the old '*bien bon*' (her uncle the abbé) at Livry, or when she was far away in the inaccessible solitudes of Brittany, she does not repine, nor regret the metropolis as a more vulgar mind would. She rejoices in the song of the nightingale, in the change of the leaf, in the glad freshness of the air, and in her own simple way becomes a poet without meaning it.

Madame de Sévigné was not ambitious. Unlike most of her lady friends, she could admire her heroes without joining in their political schemes. Thus it is, that those twenty-seven years of her life, during which she wrote her letters, are full,

not of her own doings, or cares, or hopes, or projects, but of
the private history of the court of Louis XIV., and, what in its
way is as interesting and certainly more sunny to look upon, the
private history of a mother's heart. We, the calm readers of
to-day, fret and are half indignant when she breaks away from a
narration that throws or seems to throw a new light on the
character of one of the great men or women of the day, or
even to illustrate history in a valuable manner, to cover her
cold philosophizing daughter with tender phrases: but to a
poetical mind this very fault is a beauty. It shows how profound was the mother's pride she felt, and proves that these
expressions of affection to which, perhaps, the French of to-day
would apply the epithet *banale*—hackneyed—were not neatly
turned for admiration, but positively sprang from a heart absorbed with a single interest. Even her gossip is intended to
give pleasure to her daughter; and when she speaks of her
own friends, she is careful not to say too much of those whom
she knows her child dislikes.

The charm of her letters is, that they were written only to
be read by that one centre of all her affections. When she
writes to Bussy, or to Madame La Fayette, there is indeed the
same glowing wit and neatness, the same mark of a clever observer of all that goes on around her; but there is less of that
peculiar natural grace which is the real secret of her artless
style. She is again and again an instance of the old truth, that
nature and the heart are the best masters of composition, and
that if men and women would write as they feel and think,
they would always write readably, if not absolutely well.

To write letters was indeed the great accomplishment of
women of that day, for they had nothing to do with music,
and very little with any other art. All the lady-wits, wrote
letters by the hundred. Madame de Coulanges, Madame La
Fayette, Madame de Grignan, Madame de Simiane, and others,
have left more or less of their epistolary productions; and certainly for ease, elegance, and refinement they surpass anything
of the kind that has appeared in any other day or country. The
letters of Madame de Sévigné may not have that distinct interest which we find in those of Lady Mary Wortley Montagu

and others of our own country; but they are far superior to them in taste and refinement. There is little coarseness in her letters. There is certainly a little now and then, but such as the open expression of the age warranted. In Lady Mary's there is a downright disregard of all decency at times, and such as the custom of no age could warrant.

For thirty years after her death Madame de Sévigné's letters were unknown to any but Madame de Grignan and a few friends. A selection was made from them in 1724, and published. They are said to have been rapidly written, with little respect for caligraphy, in a thin, careless hand. Like all the letters of the time they were tied round with a string of floss silk and sealed on either side.

The letter-writing years of Madame de Sévigné's life passed calmly and pleasantly. She had few or no real anxieties, and few events in her life, beyond the trifling ones with which her letters are replete. She lived at her Hôtel du Carnavalet in Paris, or at Livry, or at Les Rochers, and everywhere she recalled her daughter's presence. As Arnauld told her, she made an idol of that daughter, but that was all. In her latter years she too, like all the rest, became *dévote*, a word to be translated by 'pious' rather than 'religious.' A *dévote* went to mass twice a day, and made an intimate friend of her confessor. Madame de Sévigné gives a good reason for the love that ladies have of frequent confession. They like, she tells us, to talk of themselves, and would rather talk ill of themselves than not at all. The *dévotes* did much good in a systematic way, and as a salve for a poor conscience, but they did not necessarily give up society, or even bad society. 'Bless the man!' said one of them at a dinner party, when a servant filled her glass with wine, 'does he not know that I am *dévote*?' The servant's mistake was very excusable.

Madame de Sévigné died, as she had lived, for her daughter. While at Les Rochers she learned that Madame de Grignan was attacked by an internal disease, lingering but not dangerous. She set off, though it was winter, on the long and at that time hazardous journey to Provence, and there she tended her daughter day and night for three months. She was nearly seventy years of age, and this exertion was too much for her. Madame de Grignan recovered, but her mother succumbed to the fatigues of nursing her. She was seized with malignant small-pox, and died on the 16th of April, 1696, in her seventieth year. She was buried in the chapel of the Château de Grignan. Her daughter survived her only nine years, dying in 1705, from grief for the loss of her only son, the young Marquis de Grignan.

Her letters, as Lamartine says, are her real tomb. In them her soul is to be found. They are worth reading for many reasons. They are a truer history of the reign of Louis XIV. than any that has been written. They are the purest outburst of an excellent heart. They are free from any spiteful or evil spirit; they breathe a calm, which in this world of worry is most refreshing; they are a monument of motherly affection. Madame de Sévigné is not entitled to the name of a 'great woman;' she has worked or helped to work no great change in the human race. She was a *woman* in every sense, and did not emerge from a woman's natural sphere. She was a Frenchwoman in every sense, yet she is perhaps the very best instance we can find of a Frenchwoman. In short, we cannot read her letters without admiring her for her mind, and loving her for her heart.

SYDNEY LADY MORGAN.

Lady Morgan of What?—Her Ladyship's Eyes.—The Old Irish Girl.—The Pet of the Green-room.—Her First Literary Attempts.—Attacked by Croker.—Party Lies.—Lady Morgan as an Irish Apostle.—Family Ties.—Sir Charles.—Lady Morgan's Religious Opinions.—Sets Out for Italy.—At Paris.—The False Miladi Morgan.—Arrives at La Grange.—La Fayette.—At La Grange.—Society in Paris.—The City of Calvin.—Meets Lord Byron.—Byron's Miniature.—Lady Cork and the Watches.—Lady Charleville in her Chair.—Pink and Blue Nights.—Lady Morgan's Drawing-room.—The Princess.—Winnows her Society.—Last Years and Death.—Her Geniality and Benevolence.

SYDNEY LADY MORGAN, as she latterly styled herself; but I remember her first as Lady Morgan merely, with a respectable-looking husband, a large, light, heavy man, in spectacles, who at once worshipped and admonished her as we do a child.

It was in what she used to call the out-of-the-way regions of North Marylebone that I had stood near a piano the whole evening, endeavouring to make out who could be that short personage who sat behind a small table (though in the circle), on which was set one of those dark-green circular shades which spring up out of a stand; yet even this protection to her poor eyes was not thought enough, for the lady held before her face a green fan, so that a deep shade was cast upon the diminutive figure behind; and even in a well-lighted room she was as much in retreat as if she had been taking her pleasure on a sunless day in an arbour.

I soon perceived that she was a centre of attraction even in that room where Agnes Strickland at one time, Campbell at another, Rogers, and, in the course of the evening, numberless scientific celebrities had come and gone. Sheil, even then partially bald, sat down near her, and relapsed into his beloved brogue, and there was such a play of wit between them, such brilliant attacks on his part, such pungent yet good-natured retorts on hers, that I felt sure she was from the dear Emerald Isle; one of a race that has always its joke and its reply, even at death's door.

I said to a grim-looking gentleman near, 'I am a stranger, sir; pray who is that?'

I turned my eyes towards the green fan.

'That lady? do you mean that very nice-looking person near the screen? A fair, comely lady, with light hair? Well, you remember hearing of Miss O'Neil—before you were born, it must have been; that is she: she is now Lady Becher.'

'O yes, I know; I did not mean her. There is a lady—see, Lady Becher is bending now to talk to her; she holds a fan.'

'Oh! don't you know? Lady Morgan, of course.'

'Lady Morgan! but—'

'I don't mean Lady Morgan of Tredegar, but the authoress of "The Princess," of "Florence Macarthy;" don't you remember?'

'Certainly.'

'Every one knows her,' pursued my informant, who, I found afterwards, was a well-known reviewer; 'you will find her agreeable: she makes herself pleasant.'

And, indeed, so I thought: for it was some time before I could get a cool post of observation. Having at last entrenched myself near a folding door, behind a fat dowager, I took a calm survey of Sydney Lady Morgan. She appeared to me then on the wrong side of the half-century; no one, however, even now, knows the year of her birth, for she had the tact to keep it to herself, but it is conjectured to have been 1777, or thereabouts; but no one could have supposed it possible who knew her, even at the last, that she could be eighty. She was then a very small and very slight woman, with an easy drooping figure, that looked as if Nature had been careless when she put it together; and then she was somewhat crooked, though not strikingly so, nor was it very obvious even when, as she used to say, she 'circulated' through the room at her own soirées; and this defect, good woman as she was, as a plea she used to attribute to having practised the harp too much in her youth. But I believe that there were few women of the period in which Lady Morgan figured as a girl, that were straight, thanks to stiff stays and backboards.

Her face, though never more than agreeable, had a great charm in its feminine contour. She wore at that time her own hair. I will not swear that it was *all* her own, for there were suspicious-looking curls dripping down upon the slight throat; but it was evidently partly natural, for it was thin, and drawn across her wide forehead with a sort of tasteful negligence. It was, however, of a lighter hue than the bands with which, in her last days, she attempted to restore the venerable ruin of Sydney Lady Morgan.

Her eyes were large, and of a bluish grey, in early life probably blue. One of them had a slight cast, and went off at a tangent to the right; but this did not spoil the expression, which was very sweet and very thoughtful, without, at any time that I knew her, being brilliant or searching. She always looked like a person who saw imperfectly; and she always spoke of herself as half blind, and talked of visits from Alexander and dark rooms, leeches and shades; and I never saw her without that green fan in her hand. It became an antiquity like herself. Yet I believe she saw more than any one else did; nothing escaped her. She knew every *nuance* of feeling that passed in the minds of others; she remarked dress, and she never *un*intentionally forgot or mistook a person.

Her other features were neither prominent nor beautiful; yet peculiar—Lady Morgan's own mouth and nose. I never saw any one that resembled her; and if our grandmothers were here to say it, they would declare that Lady Morgan had been a pretty woman.

She had the manner of a woman who has been attractive, and that supplies the want of a chronicle. Besides the face was soft, agreeable, kindly—somewhat wrinkled even then, but harmoniously tinted with a *soupçon* of rouge. I remember her dress perfectly. It was juvenile to a fault—white muslin, short sleeves, and a broad green sash tied behind; something dropping and light about her head; and a lace scarf over her shoulders. She was still the Wild Irish Girl in fancy, though rather an old Irish girl.

She soon, however, changed this style; and though I never saw her what is called well dressed, if one were to take her and measure her by the yard, yet she had an intuitive notion of the becoming, combined, at that period of her life, with a close attention to economy.

This remarkable woman was born, then (let us concede it), in the year 1777, on ship-board, between Ireland and England. Her father, Mr. Macowen, was an actor, a singer, the manager of a theatre, and a man of talent and local celebrity. It is said that he was handsome and dashing, and had the reputation of being more successful with the ladies than with the public as an actor. His good looks he transmitted partially only to Sydney, but in full splendour to her sister the late Lady Clarke, who was extremely handsome.

Abjuring the Mac, as there was then a strong prejudice against the sons of Erin, this lady-slayer came over to London, and appeared in Rowe's heavy play as Tamerlane. Theatrical critics were in those days as much guided by party views as the House of Commons: there were persons who could not tolerate Kemble, but who idolized Young; and Garrick, in whose wake Mr. Owenson must have followed, had his detractors, who adored Betterton. And so, whilst some praised, others decried Mr. Owenson's Tamerlane; and the unsuccessful player was obliged to leave London and start for the provinces. Whilst 'starring' at Shrewsbury, the handsome Irishman captivated a certain Miss Hill; a 'single woman of a certain age,' just old enough, happily for him, to be foolish on matrimonial points. She eloped with him, and they were married; and their first child was a daughter, the gifted, charming Sydney, so called, as well as many of her female contemporaries in the west country of Ireland, in grateful remembrance to Sir Henry Sydney, who was Lord Deputy of Ireland in the time of Elizabeth.

Such was the origin of one whose life presents an instance of what unassisted women can do, to raise themselves in the scale of society, upon even a slender stock of education, with energy and talent. Who would have predicted that the small, fragile child, bred up amid actors, learning first her letters, probably, upon a playbill—conversant with properties—the pet of the green-room—whose loud merry laugh might be heard before the drop-scene was drawn up, behind the foot-lights,—who would suppose that she would have lived to eighty-two, to figure in the most polite neighbourhood of London, among the most lettered, the most famous, and the most aristocratic society in the world?

Her father had all the qualities which were afterwards developed, under more favourable circumstances, in her. He was fond of the arts, to which she always professed devotion, though no judge of art. He was immensely convivial—hence her hereditary taste for society, and her aptitude at conversation. His companionship in his own way was delightful; so was hers in a more refined and genial form. He sang excellently: she also sang and played on the harp. He was a man who delighted to bring forward young poets: here was a grand point of resemblance. Nothing delighted Lady Morgan more than to have a pet poet, whose fame she wished to nurture: whose work, sent bound, and with a copy of verses to *her* specially, she used to lay on her table—that little table near her; and to show, only to *show*, to her visitors, saying, 'The gentleman you met on the stairs with that wild-looking hair is an enthusiastic young poet; see, this is his last. I don't offer to lend it to you, you can get it for seven and sixpence at Pickering's.'

Upon scraps of education Sydney throve mentally, as girls do upon an unsystematic bringing up. It is Miss Austen, I think, who says that reading to oneself *is* an education to girls. I dare say it was the only one Miss Austen had; but then her reading would be solid works—Bowdler, Hannah More, who flourished in Bath in her time, Russell's 'Modern Europe,' and a few proper novels. But Sydney's studies were, as she grew up, at once more desultory and ambitious. She learned Italian, and read the 'Natural History' of Lord Bacon. More especially she devoured the history of her native land, which Ireland undoubtedly was; and she mixed up all these pursuits with music and poetry, sang to her harp, wrote a volume of poems, and published them by subscription, dedicated to Lady

Moira, whose lord was then Lord Lieutenant. She wrote, too, in periodicals. She used to relate how enchanted she was when for some tale the editor sent her two guineas, her first-earned money, and those two guineas, she said, were the source of all her scribbling: the encouragement was worth hundreds. It seems almost like a lesson to editors not *too* sternly to crush young hopes, lest, with the chaff often first put out, good seed is destroyed. It is well known that Mrs. Gaskell, whose novels are classics in their way, vainly tried many years ago to get a volume of poems published, though they had much of the fancy and grandeur of thought observable in 'Ruth;' and it is also true that Charlotte Brontë's first work was sent to every publisher in London, until it excited, by its veteran exterior, the curiosity of Mr. Williams, the able literary adviser of Smith and Elder, who read it and refused it, but suggested that the authoress should try a fresh subject; and 'Jane Eyre' was produced.

Armed with her two guineas, a large sum for the little harpist, Sydney wrote her 'Wild Irish Girl,' original, romantic, and absurd. Far better was her 'Novice of St. Dominick,' the effort of her maturer years, of which the story is interesting, although the incidents are improbable, and there is in it a tone of truer feeling than her later novels display. All these avocations were interspersed with poetic flights. Lady Morgan was the writer of 'Kate Kearney.' She published, also, a collection of Irish melodies antecedent to Moore's: she played and sang to her harp in every society into which her precocious talents brought her; yet still she was but 'Miss Owenson,' the 'Wild Irish Girl.' Single women can do little to form a circle; they can but adorn one when formed: Lady Morgan, as 'Miss Owenson,' was a delightful and a popular member of society, but a member only; young, without influence, devoid of aristocratic connection, and poor.

There was one feature in her destinies: she was early appropriated by the Liberal party as their own. She was of that day when Irish wrongs were rife, and the wounds inflicted on an oppressed country during the Rebellion were unhealed. She grew up in the politics of the Emmetts and of Lord Edward Fitzgerald; and though her large amount of common sense modified, in after life, the convictions of her youth, she was consistent to the last, and perfectly aware of the errors of her countrymen. When she had fully emerged into literary eminence, and her works were popular in England, Mr. Wilson Croker, the last of the exploded race of political bigots, attacked her personally and cruelly. He pretended to start a commission of enquiry on her age, her parentage, her early position. 'Have we not seen this lady on stages and at fairs?' he asked in the pages of the 'Quarterly Review.' He turned upon her that which a gentlewoman can least stand—the laugh. We may dispute facts, but no one can deprecate a laugh. And his taunts, his stinging criticisms, his private influence, his party importance as the great organ of the spiteful, amused the world for a time, and alarmed the steady-going aristocrats of Grosvenor Square, who drew back in haste from what they believed to be a mingled mass of false pretentions, bad singing, reprehensible politics, and questionable religious convictions. In those days the passions even of good men predisposed them to credit that which assimilated to their own prejudices. A man used to be thought, as in the days of the 'Spectator,' of no principles who did not believe a certain amount of falsehoods. 'Party lies' were at their acme. In the words of Addison: 'The coffee-houses were supported by them; the press was choked by them: eminent authors lived upon them.' 'Our bottle-conversation,' he says, 'is so infected by them, that a party lie is grown as fashionable an entertainment as a lively catch or a merry story.' And, in the same way, the exaggerations of 'John Bull,' in the days of Theodore Hook, of the 'Satirist,' the 'Age,' and, I am sorry to add, of the 'Quarterly Review,' furnished all the great talkers of the time with subjects for after dinner discourse. Nor were those the days in which 'lies were discharged in the air, and began to hurt nobody.'* The West End of London was then all Tory, and small people thought it fashionable to belong to that *clique* which ate with silver forks and abhorred Russell Square. Whiggism and *mau-*

* See Addison on Party Lying; a capital paper. No. 507, Saturday, October 10.

vais ton were thought to go together: as in France, the old Legitimists despise the Liberal party not so much for their opinions as for their alleged vulgarity; and these convictions had their influence in crushing Lady Morgan at first, and for some time. Her gaiety, her real kindness of heart, and her talents, won, however, the heart of Dr. Morgan, a physician of good family, and a widower, of moderate but comfortable income: and being eventually knighted (it is said, partly from compliment to *her*), at Dublin, she assumed, as his wife, a position at once eminently respectable and agreeable. Meantime, her pen had been in active requisition. 'Ida of Athens' and 'The Missionary,' though popular at the time of their appearance, are now forgotten: they are manifestly the work of a young and orinal author. As a writer, Lady Morgan gained much by her marriage. The poetry of her life was perhaps gone; but the cultivated taste and logical mind of her husband rectified her exuberant fancies; and, as a married woman, her best novels were produced: 'O'Donnel' was considered by herself to be her masterpiece: it placed her on a literary eminence, as the first novelist that advocated the Irish cause, and fearlessly she wrote. It is true that Miss Edgeworth's 'Castle Rack-rent' had then appeared; (her delightful tale 'The Absentee' was of later date;) but whilst she assailed the defective habits and principles of the people, pointing out also the effects of the false and ancient system that England had pursued towards Ireland, Lady Morgan took up the more romantic features of the cause. The works of Miss Edgeworth tend to reform, to instruct: her story is subservient to her purpose. The novels of Lady Morgan excite the passions and enlist the sympathies. The one is the disciple of reason and truth—the other, the organ of fancy, political convictions, and romance.

It was in 1818, when the sprightly authoress must have been forty-one years of age, that Lady Morgan engaged to write her book on France. She had by that time seen enough of society in this country and in Ireland, to prepare her for the task: for it is of little avail to send out individuals to judge of foreign circles who have seen no good companies in their own nation; and although with the brand of the 'Quarterly' upon her, **Lady**

Morgan had even then tasted largely of the pleasures afforded by those aristocratic circles which she ever loved 'not wisely, but too well.' Her 'Book of the Boudoir' gives an animated picture of Irish noblesse and their provincial life: in depicting that in England she is less fortunate. As L. E. L. said of Mr. Galt: 'He is like Antæus, never strong, except when he touches his native land;' so may it be said of Lady Morgan, that she was never so humorous in thought, so felicitous in expression, so brilliant in fancy, as when her conversation or her writings turned on her country, and the 'Paddies,' as she irreverently styled them, formed her theme.

Her journeys to France, to Italy, and to Spain constituted the different epochs of her uneventful life. Let us, before we start with her on those tours, look for an instant into her interior life at home, and see how in her mature age she shone as a domestic companion, sister, wife.

People who assert that Lady Morgan was a mere woman of society, 'pleasant but wrong,' caring for no one, devoid of genuine feeling, content with all that the world offers, knew her but little. It is too much the custom to assign that description of character to persons of a lively, social nature. Lady Morgan was a woman of the warmest affections; devoted to her family ties. Her sister, Lady Clarke, had married an eminent surgeon in Dublin, and was the mother of several daughters when Lady Morgan meditated her first continental journey. These children were the objects of a tenderness perfectly maternal. In one of her letters to Lady Clarke, Lady Morgan thus refers to them:—

'Dear little toddles! I am sure that nepotism is an organic affection in single and childless women. It is a maternal instinct gone astray. In popes and princes it is a frustrated ambition:—a substitute for paternity. It is a dangerous tendency; aunts and uncles never love "wisely, but too well;" besides, it brings with it responsibilities without authority, and imposes duties without giving rights: and so bye-bye babies.'

There was not a word of exaggeration in all this. These 'babies' grew up to be elegant, handsome, and accomplished women, in whose dawn of life their Aunt Sydney found a deep interest: they were the delight of her middle life, and one of them the solace of her age. In the fulness of her success as a 'Queen of Society,' Lady Morgan was rarely to be seen without one of her nieces, whose musical powers, whose love of art, reminded her of the days when she was, as she used to say, a sort of show-girl, with her harp and her Irish melodies. Upon the death of one of her nieces, the first Mrs. Marmion Savage, Lady Morgan sorrowed as a mother would have done. Every tie she had was dear to her: the warm Irish heart was never choked by the cares and deceitfulness of life. In her 'nepotism' she reminded one of a Frenchwoman, to whom the ties of relationship, which we English are too prone to cast away from us, are stronger in our continental neighbours than in any other European country.

As a wife she was pre-eminently happy from similarity of tastes. Sir Charles soon participated in her literary objects, and became the writer of the grave articles in the 'Monthly Magazine,' published by Colburn, and at one time edited by Thomas Campbell, and later by Sir Edward Bulwer Lytton. Sir Charles had a dignified, calm manner, which well supported the gay, though always gentle Sydney in society. He was still and ever devoted to that profession which, above all others, settles itself in the mind of man, forms that mind, applies itself to almost every circumstance in life, and is reverenced by the mature intellect because it is useful, enlarged, and true. Sir Charles Morgan was a physician of that period when the *gentleman* was necessary to the profession. He ceased, with his marriage, to practise, but devoted himself to philosophy and literature. As a writer his works have not lived: as a philosopher, there was one vital canker in his code. He was sceptical: there have been those who have declared that he was even an unbeliever: but it is generally thought that his notions were those of Cuvier: those that Lawrence once advocated, but which he has long since nobly recanted—of Materialism and Deism, not of bold Atheism. And the fact, that even the opinions of Sir Charles Morgan went to this extent is dubious. But, unhappily, it is but too true that his influence had a serious effect on the mind of his wife.

That ' party lie' which, diffused amongst thousands, is 'as a drop of the blackest tincture, wears away and vanishes when mixed and confused in a considerable body of water.' Yet 'the blot is still in it, but is not able to discover itself:'* that falsehood represented her as scoffing at every form of faith. Yet such was not the case: unfortunately, the term *liberal* had in her mind been confounded with incredulity. Her faith was not that of the Church of England, but had its own form, independent of creeds. How far her heterodoxy went, whether to the very confines of unbelief or merely to externals, was obvious to those who intimately knew her. In her later years, she was dazzled by the cleverness of the book styled 'Vestiges of Creation,' and adopted many of its arguments. Yet an eminent scientific man who conversed with her, expressed an opinion that her convictions were unsound, though not wholly sceptical. Her house was the resort of many clergymen: her favourite niece was married to a clergyman of great worth and piety, who was on the happiest terms with her: no one ever went to her large parties without seeing there the Dean of St. Paul's, Dr. Milman, and many others, who would have turned away with horror from a female Atheist, even in all the radiance of talent and success. She belonged, indeed, in her youth to that period when all faith, all observances, had been but recently overthrown, and were slowly reasserting themselves after the shock of the French Revolution. In her first work on France, Lady Morgan has described the reorganization of society under the Bourbons, after the Restoration in 1816. It is still thought, in some circles of Parisian *littérateurs*, that to be incredulous, or, as they term it, philosophic, is a proof of the *esprit fort*, to which distinction some women make the fatal mistake of aspiring. But in Lady Morgan's days the notion was in full force. She thirsted for that society in which she could meet with responsive liberalism of all kinds, and received with delight an offer from the late Henry Colburn, that enterprising and liberal publisher, to set off for Italy, and to write a work upon it of the same description as her (still un-

* Addison.

equalled) book on France. Her own words must impart the offer, and its reception :—

'This morning as I was on my knees, all dust and dowdiness, comes the English post—old Colburn—no, not old Colburn, but young, enthusiastic Colburn, in love with "Florence Macarthy," and a little *épris* with the author! "Italy, by Lady Morgan!" He is not touched, but rapt, and makes a dashing offer of two thousand pounds, to be printed in quarto, like "France:" but we are to start off immediately, and I have immediately answered him in the words of Sileno in "Midas:"

'" Done! Strike hands!
I take your offer:
Further on I may fare worse."'

Lady Morgan set off instantly *viâ* London for France. Over that country the mistaken policy of Lous XVIII. had even then cast a gloom; but the lively Sydney was happy in the Society of La Fayette, of Humboldt, then in Paris, of Dénon, Lacroix, and last, not least, of the Princess Jablonsky. Her portraits are wonderfully graphic, and, though true, not ill-natured. Witness, in her diary, an admirable description of Louis XVIII. :—
'A fine gentleman, an elegant scholar; graceful (if not grateful), as the Bourbons always are; gracious, as the French princes have been, though their courtesies meant nothing.

Whilst Lady Morgan had much to allege against those whom she styles 'the Tory detractors of England,' at the head of them 'The Quarterly,' she owed to her success as a partisan the introduction to Château la Grange. Her 'France,' which had gone through three editions in one year, was proscribed by *Louis aux Huitres*, as Louis XVIII. was then styled. A sort of interdict to her entering France had also been placed by the government of that country: nevertheless, tempted by La Fayette, who had assured her that it was chiefly a matter of form, she resolved to go, and the result was one of the most delightful visits that she had ever enjoyed.

In the month of August, 1818, Lady Morgan quitted the 'darling dusty old Fabrique,' as she calls it, the *Hôtel d' Espagne*, in the Faubourg St. Germain, for the Château la Grange, situated in the Department de la Brie. During the whole of her stay in Paris this indefatigable woman had been 'cramming for her journey to Italy, and reading all that she could collect on the subject at the Bibliothèque Royale.

She now prepared to set off on her journey with all the spirits of eighteen; bought herself a '*chapeau de soleil*' in the *Marché des Innocents*, with a bunch of corn-flowers stuck in the midst of it; made a tour of calls and sights; dined in a little public-house under the heights of Montmorenci, on the door of which was inscribed '*Ici on danse tous les jours;*' admired the practice, and remarked what misery and murder it would spare if such prevailed in England instead of drinking gin and porter; passed the evening at Baron Dénon's, where she met Ségur and Humboldt. The separation between Bonaparte and Josephine was still the theme of Parisian soirées, and Humboldt told some pleasing anecdotes in mitigation of the supposed hardness of Napoleon's character. Then Lady Morgan departed for La Grange; on her journey to which a curious incident showed her the conspicuous place which she then occupied in the minds of the French; for her liberal principles had met with a responsive voice among a certain class in France as far removed from the doctrines of the Rouge Republican as from the absolutism of the despot: these were the '*Industriels*,' a class to be distinguished from the '*Ouvriers*,' of whom they are the aristocracy, the higher order of mechanics.

Delighted with France, she always declared that there was then twenty times more liberality and public spirit than in Ireland, and that pamphlets were published there which would have been prosecuted in England. Perhaps her opinion was warped by the favourable manner in which her work on France had been received. As she was proceeding to visit General La Fayette—whose part in the first French Revolution is familiar to every one—she met with a curious compliment to herself. Waiting at Grandville for La Fayette's carriage, which was to meet her there, she and Sir Charles joined a group who were standing outside the inn watching some one at the window. 'What is it?' asked the unconscious Sydney. 'What does it mean?' 'Oh!' cried the man, 'c'est Miladi Morgan, who has spoken so well of us workmen in her book about France. She is

THE COUNTERFEIT LADY MORGAN.

waiting for General La Fayette's carriage.' 'At that moment,' writes the heroine of the story, '" the Lady Morgan" came to the window. It is impossible to describe anything so grotesque, though such figures are still seen in France. A head, powdered and *crêpée*, two feet high; several *couches* of rouge on her cheek, and more than one on her chin; black patches *à discrétion*: a dress of damask silk with scarlet flowers.' This venerable lady, above seventy, received the homage of the assembled admirers with the utmost complaisance, and coming out, entered her vehicle; it was called a *désobligeante*, corresponding probably to our antique *vis-à-vis* of the days of 'old Q' and Queen Charlotte: a coachman in a 'livery as ancient and dusty as if he had served in the Fronde,' drove this grand *dame de province* away from the *real* Lady Morgan and her husband, who were enchanted to see the gracious bows and smiles with which the old lady received the homage intended elsewhere. Lady Morgan, nevertheless, was dying to come out with the secret.

'Hitherto,' she writes to her sister, 'Morgan had kept me quiet, but my vanity at last broke bounds: my charming *chapeau de paille*, with its poppy flowers; my French cashmere; and my coquetry, which, young or old, will go with me to my grave, would stand it no longer.

'"Odious! in woollen! 'twould a saint provoke!"
Were the last words that poor Narcissa spoke.

'As I was stepping into the La Grange carriage, I bowed to the nice "young man" who handed me in: "*Je suis, moi, la véritable Lady Morgan.*" He said he guessed as much.'

Lady Morgan and her husband arrived at La Grange on a fine September evening. The old castle tower, with the mantling ivy over it planted by Charles James Fox, the glowing sunset and the dark woods beyond, formed a scene not to be forgotten. At the castle gate stood the noble and venerable La Fayette, the 'Cromwell-Grandison' to whom poor Maria Antoinette had turned for help, and whom she had innocently admired. He was surrounded by his grand-children, then twelve in number; and conducting with all the grace of his country the welcome strangers to the *salon*, presented them to

Ary Scheffer, since famed in art, and to Auguste Thierry. Carbonel the composer, who set Beranger's songs to music, and two Americans, formed the party, with the exception of two English gentlemen, one of whom told Lady Morgan that he had expected to find La Fayette eighty years old. 'Where have you picked up such a notion?' was the reply. 'Why, in your ladyship's work on France, reviewed by the "Quarterly." The "Quarterly" said that the general was a dotard.' Lady Morgan's own description of this truly hospitable household is a true but somewhat sad picture of what a French château afforded before the insane law of partition cut up everything like substantial prosperity in France. Few of the nobles of that country can now afford to live as La Fayette did, with twenty or thirty guests dining daily under the groined roof of the old stone hall, at a table where each dropped into his place without ceremony; where all ostentation was banished; no plate allowed for ornament; an excellent plain French dinner and delightful conversation forming the entertainment. Yet among those who sat round that board were the descendants of some of the most renowned families of France. 'I never,' Lady Morgan wrote to her sister, her beloved Olivia, 'saw such a beautiful picture of domestic happiness, virtue, and talent.' What increased the enjoyment of the warm-hearted little Irishwoman was, that 'Morgan was happy.' Seated under the towers of La Grange by the side of a pond, fishing, or listening to Carbonel singing Beranger's vaudeville, '*Il est passé le bon vieux temps,*' the ci-devant physician forgot the delights of the Paris hospitals, in which he took a deep interest.

As the host and his guests strolled through the woods of La Grange, Lady Morgan ventured to ask the general whether it was true that he had gone with Marie Antoinette to a masked ball in Paris, the queen leaning on his arm. 'I am afraid,' he answered, in that low emphatic voice peculiar to him, 'that it was so. She was,' he added, 'so indiscreet, and I can conscientiously say, so innocent.'

Poor Marie Antoinette! Years after her doom, thus was her fame justified by one whose good opinion she valued: and when Lady Morgan, with some hesitation, resumed: 'The world said, general, that she favoured the young champion, "*le héros des deux mondes.*"'

'*Cancan de salon !*' he briefly answered, and the subject was dropped.

Sunday was a day of rest as well as a festival at La Grange.

At eight the great hall, perforated by Turenne's bullets during the war of the Fronde, was filled with peasantry, the servants, one or two *gendarmes* who looked in, and all the company; peers of France, artists, writers, the general and his twelve grandchildren; the concierge being the musician. As he struck up a *ronde*, the whole company formed themselves into that popular dance, at which Louis Philippe, when at Eu, often delighted to look on, especially when words were sung, as the dance went round. It is the national country dance of France. Whilst the guests were footing it, a party consisting of a young man in deep mourning, followed by his servants and portmanteau, passed behind the dancers into the interior of the castle. This proved to be Auguste de Staël, the favourite and only surviving son of the celebrated authoress.

After 'charming days, more charming evenings,' listening alternately to Carbonel's compositions and to Thierry's anecdotes, sitting to Scheffer for her portrait, walking *sur la pelouse* till sunset, and talking to the general about Bonaparte till bedtime, Lady Morgan returned to Paris. She left La Grange with deep regret. 'All the clever men from Paris come here constantly,' she wrote to her sister. 'My little harp (which some Frenchwoman had mistaken for a dead child in its coffin) has the greatest success.'

At the Château la Grange, Lady Morgan enjoyed those rich delights which society such as she met there, afford, when coupled with the contemplation of virtue and domestic happiness. La Fayette, after a stirring life, was closing his days in peace among his family; Lady Morgan fully appreciated the unanimity of a French home *de province*. The perfect system that pervades families; the obedience of the young; the rapt devotion of the old to the younger members; the art and part the old servants take in everything; the unaffected freedom which never dispenses with politeness, but abhors ostentation;—this she could fully comprehend. But there was one want ungratified—she desired to see Béranger. Why was the lyric satirist not there?

'Because,' said La Fayette, 'he won't come. I have asked him and he has refused, on the same principle that he declined to dine with Talleyrand and the Rochefoucaulds; because I am "*trop grand seigneur.*"' His answer to La Fayette was: 'My instinct leads me to the *caveau*, and not to the *château*.' Béranger was not tempted to the drawing-rooms of the great, and thus escaped a distinction which might have fettered his verses, and which certainly would have diluted the strength of his genius.

In the midst of all her felicity, she never forgot the absent. To her sister she wrote: 'I am quite delighted you have a boy: he will be easily provided for. We will educate him amongst us, and he will be a protection to his sisters. What I would give to have you all here!'

She spent some time in Paris after her visit to La Grange; and in that gay capital learned that art of society which she never lost. Great names crowded to her Wednesday evenings in the Rue St. Augustin, in which central situation she had fixed herself, Talma reciting 'coldly but finely' Shakspeare in French (Ducie's translation). Jouy, the '*Erémite de la Chaussée d'Antin*,' complaining that his new play was prohibited by the censor of the press; the beautiful Comtesse de la Rochefoucauld; the Princess de Beauveau, and her daughters; and the Duchesse de Broglie, were amongst the French notabilities who adorned her *salon*. Lady Morgan had always her degrees of welcome. Some she received 'with acclamation;' any one who, as she pronounced of Thierry and Ary Scheffer, 'bade fair for posterity,' was always well received. About others she had her caprices: no one could sooner throw people just at the distance she liked than Lady Morgan. Though she professed, after the French fashion, that people were always to be let in, those who came without invitation on nights when the party had been invited, were sure to find out their mistake. 'I saw your windows lighted up, and, dear Lady Morgan, I came in, and here I am,' said a lady to her, under this predicament, one evening.

'So I see,' was the dry answer, and Sydney turned from her. This was in London.

Lady Morgan, during the winter of 1818, was still preparing for Italy, at that time a journey of some risk. She must have been in her true element in Paris. Christmas came, and with it the dismissal of De Cazes, and the establishment of an Ultra ministry. Benjamin Constant was her frequent visitor, and read with real or feigned delight her 'Florence Macarthy.' She was beginning to find her popularity a burden; yet she undertook the journey to Geneva with 'fear, if not with misgivings.' Even Colburn's two thousand pounds could not make her think it otherwise than awful. Nevertheless, at last, with a sort of ecstacy, she wrote 'Geneva' on the top of her letters. At that striking city, she was received with great cordiality both by Dumont and Sismondi; but she had, she avowed, no antecedents or impressions about the 'City of Calvin.' It contrasted strangely with the fantastic and historical Paris, that city of pleasant memories, which she had left. By a sort of instinct, as it seemed, she selected the Hôtel de la Balance as her abode, and inhabited the very rooms in which Madame de Staël held her famous literary receptions when she visited Geneva from Coppet. At the Baron de Bonstetten's Lady Morgan met De Candolle, M. Betanist, and Pictet; but Dumont, who had been tutor to the late Lord Lansdowne, and spoke English perfectly, was her favourite *littérateur*. The conversation in such society she describes as the perfection of enjoyment; light though literary; desultory, but interspersed with personal anecdote, and therefore piquant. 'It was at Geneva,' adds this indomitable partisan, 'that we first breathed the air of a republic.' She must have had enough of republics since that time, after the failure in France, and its result.

In the spring of April, 1819, Lady Morgan announced to her sister that she was 'all Italy's.' It could not have been easy to return to task-work after all the holiday time in Paris and Geneva. In the former capital Lady Morgan had avoided her countrywomen, who played at hazard, and were not respectable. She now begged Lady Clarke, her 'dear Livy,' not to send any of the 'Crawleys,' *trespassing* after her; 'not to give any one her Italian address except the O'Connor Don.' She went, feeling that she had a great vocation, but very little confidence in being able to do anything in the regeneration of Italy. This was 'sixty years ago;' alas! what has been done since?

In Italy she formed the acquaintance of Lord Byron, of whom her reminiscences were vivid even to her latest days. Lady Morgan was a lenient judge of those errors which the world, properly, visits severely. Bitter, like all the Irish when offended, her moral decisions were, nevertheless, generally fair. When she knew Byron, he was under a deserved cloud of reprobation, even by that exalted society which overlooked the example of George IV. and ignored his connection with Lady Conyngham. Byron was just then finally separated from his wife. That story which got abroad, that Dr. Lushington, who was the great adviser of the separation, knew of circumstances too dreadful to be disclosed, which fully justified that step—a step which, as usual, drove the husband to desperation, without insuring the wife's peace—was generally circulated. Those exquisite lines—

'Fare thee well, and if for ever,
Still for ever fare thee well,'

were in every one's mouth, in every one's heart, when Lady Morgan saw Lord Byron. She always espoused his cause. An exquisite miniature of the ill-starred poet remained till her death in her drawing-room, bequeathed to her by Lady Caroline Lamb. The noble brow; the blue, clear, speaking eyes; the fine classic nose; and, above all, the beautiful mouth, full of sweetness, yet firm and sensible, are evidence of the likeness being faithful. It is just such a head as one would wish a poet to be endowed with: it does not give the impression of an 'imagination of fire playing round a heart of ice,' as Southey would have us think of Byron, but of a genial, thoughtful nature—of a man born to be loved, though forced into evil by an adverse destiny. This was, above all, the picture in her possession to which Lady Morgan always drew the attention of strangers, and it hung near the sofa on which she usually sat.

The ignorance and indolence of the Italian ladies struck this active woman forcibly. Yet she defends them in her work on Italy from the general charge of pervading immorality, and contends that there are families as pure, as well-principled, and as domestic as in England.

She returned to England to form that circle in which she lived, and in which she delighted ever after. The fierceness of parties was subsiding when she took up her temporary abode in James Street, Buckingham Gate, in a house belonging to Sir Henry Bulwer, with whom, as with his celebrated brother, Lady Morgan was intimate. Her 'Florence Macarthy,' appeared, and her fame as a novelist was high: she ventured, also, into the paths which even she was glad to illumine by her imagination. Full of Italy, she wrote a very interesting life, or rather sketch of the life of Salvator Rosa. She published, also, her 'O'Briens and O'Flahertys;' but the greatest of her works of fiction, 'The Princess,' was yet to come.

Lady Morgan after a time removed to William Street, Knightsbridge, where in the immediate proximity of all the *beau monde* of London, she established her quarters. Having been much abroad, Lady Morgan did not deem it necessary to give large expensive dinners in order to 'keep her world' together. She seldom received dinner company; and when she did so, her table was never thronged, six or eight formed its fullest complement of guests; and, indeed, her means did not permit the extravagance of a proper London dinner. During Lord Melbourne's administration she received a pension of three hundred pounds a year for her services as the supporter of the liberal party in Ireland. Sir Charles Morgan had also a tolerable income; so that, to the end of her days, Lady Morgan could not have known pecuniary anxiety. She was by nature hospitable, though not extravagant, and assembled some of the best company in London upon Lady Cork's principle of 'plenty of tea and wax lights.' 'The world,' she used to say, 'is a very good world, but you must seek it; it will not do to neglect it.'

Early in life Lady Morgan had been intimate with the Abercorn family. The Dowager Lady Cork—the Miss Monkton of Miss Burney's days—was one of her friends. Lady Cork was eccentric, and had an absent way of putting into her pocket anything that lay before her. It is related of her that being one day at the house of a noble earl in ——— Square, some very ancient and valuable watches belonging to the family of her host were shown. 'I tremble,' whispered a fashionable divine, to whose extemporary sermons half the west end of London thronged, 'to see those watches in Lady Cork's hands.'

'They are as safe, sir, with me, as with you,' was her reply (having overheard him), and time proved that she was right. The earl, by no means a type of 'absolute wisdom,' was gathered to his fathers. His countess succeeded to all the personalty; amongst them to these same watches. After a few months of weeds—one cannot say of mourning—she married the Rev. Dr. ———, and the watches, of course, came into his possession.

The Countess of Charleville, whose rare qualities have been well described in her 'Diary' by Lady Morgan, was one of her most prized friends. The letters of this lady to Lady Morgan give, indeed, an insight into a character of singular good sense and gentleness. Of a cultivated mind, this venerable lady, with her singular charm of manner and of person, attracted around her most of the eminent men and women of letters of the day; Tom Moore, 'who would not sing until a large audience of pretty women were collected to hear him;' William Spencer, whose verses, airy, polished, graceful like his person, made him the idol of society, whilst the charm of his manner and of his character converted the acquaintance of an evening into the friends of a lifetime; Captain Morris, the lyrist;—these were among the lions of those drawing-rooms in which Lady Charleville, wheeled from one room to another by her handsome son, then Lord Tullamore, formed a picture of no ordinary interest. The good sense and good spirit of this lady's letters to Lady Morgan, her gentle sincerity and excellent criticisms, denote a superiority of intellect very rare, because it was combined with the greatest humility.

This beloved and respected lady had lost the use of her lower limbs before she had passed middle life, yet she survived till the age of ninety, and died, a short time previously to Lady Morgan, in 1858. Their friendship was the friendship of half a century. They were both Irishwomen, Lady Charleville being one of the Cremorne family; both witty; though perhaps Lady Charleville's wit had the greater refinement of the two; both women of society, yet not in the disparaging sense. Had Lady Charleville been a Frenchwoman and lived in France, 'she would have been assigned a place in social history with the Sévignés and Du Deffands.'

One cannot but confess that Lady Charleville shows her *tact* in her avowal that she could not comprehend Sir Charles Morgan's work on the 'Philosophy of Life,' the principles of which were attacked by Reynolds, the Christian Advocate at Cambridge. Lady Cork disapproved of Sir Charles's philosophy, and therefore sheltered herself under the plea of being 'overwhelmed by the detail and quantity of the physical knowledge it contained. Yet the work was praised by Humboldt, and translated into French by Lacroix. It was accused of materialism.

Then at Lady Cork's, Lady Morgan added to her now increasing circle of society. It seems, indeed, like speaking of another age to recall, as she does in her 'Diary,' Lady Ameland, the insulted wife of the late Duke of Sussex, and the mother of the Prince and Princess D'Este. 'Oh, these men, and their laws!' exclaims Lady Morgan; 'so lightly made, so lightly broken, as passion or expediency suggests; from Henry VIII. and his pope—before, and after!' This was on Lady Cork's pink night: the next was her blue evening, when editors and reviewers went to meet people of science.

Lady Morgan, in her selections from her 'host of friends,' showed better taste than to separate classes or to have pink or blue nights. Those who had been much in London during the last five-and-twenty years cannot forget the assemblage of noble if not royal authors; of beauty, and fashion, and science, and musical skill, which rendered her drawing-room so remarkable.

That room was in itself a picture. Ascending a not very wide staircase, you entered a small *salon*, opening with folding doors into another, which terminated in a verandah. The furniture was red: and without any attempt at splendour, the room had a comfortable aspect. The walls were crowded with pictures of great interest, but no value. Lady Morgan's own portraits—the earlier ones, in a scanty, *décolleté* dress—a girdle—a bodice two inches in length—curled locks—a pen in one hand, the other supporting her head—formed a main feature. During the latter years of her life, a small likeness was painted of her in her widow's cap, and in black, which gave her all the kindly expressions of her character. Near her seat Lord Byron's face rivetted those who sat opposite to it. Around the room were portraits of Madame de Pompadour, La Belle Jennings, and one or two likenesses painted by Lady Morgan's beloved niece A variety of small pictures, to each of which '*une histoire*' was attached, filled up every corner; articles of *virtù* of all sorts; memorials of the great and the lettered, dead and living, always elicited some rapid anecdote, so promptly told as scarcely to interrupt the conversation which was passing through the circle. Then you were always invited to walk into the back drawing-room, and take a survey of her 'shrine,' which had a curtain drawn before its precious contents—miniatures, relics, rare books. A large *portière* hanging over the folding doors divided the rooms when Lady Morgan had a large reception. On a little sofa in the corner sat the lady paramount of the *salon*, always in the shade—always with the green fan, either to shade her from the fire or from the light.

Lady Morgan was rarely from home in the afternoons, and that was one secret of her popularity in London and Paris. People like best to knock at a door where they know they shall be let in. London is too large to call on absentees. In Paris no one likes to mount the stairs and to go down again—the sport of the *concierges*, who often choose to be ignorant as to the lady '*au second*' being at home or not. Then Lady Morgan was 'there and then' ready to say something pleasant as soon as you came in. On Sunday afternoons her little rooms were crowded. On Sunday evenings she often collected a few intimates, who walked in *sans façon*. Her round of society was, indeed, transiently interrupted by the death of Sir Charles Morgan in 1847. He was carried off by a fever, to her deep affliction. Yet, in the course of a month, her rooms were again opened to those she best knew and most liked. Though she survived him many years, those who had long remembered Lady Morgan saw that for some time she was a changed person. Her Irish drollery, her cherished vanity, so amusing and so really natural, was quenched. Yet still she paused not, she retired not, and many blamed her for want of feeling. 'I take to company,' she said one day with a deep sigh, 'as others take to drinking—to drown sorrow.' Let it be remembered she had no family, few home cares to console or employ her. Whatever were Sir Charles's religious convictions, he died in them, and died happy, and his widow was not alarmed as to his eternal fate. That latitudinarianism is the only cloud that rests on Lady Morgan's memory.

Before Sir Charles's death she had visited Belgium and written 'The Princess,' by far the ablest of her novels. In it she draws a picture of fashionable life. It is the life, however, of Holland House, rather than of the large class which she portrays in general. Her Princess is an improbable, an impossible being; but so great is the skill with which each incident is dovetailed into the others that one's common sense is beguiled. In her opinions of Belgium, Lady Morgan's judgment has been confirmed by the happy results of a long and liberal rule over that country. As a 'Queen of Society' her reputation was now at its acme. Lord Brougham, the Earl of Carlisle (then Lord Morpeth), Sheil (whose death she deeply lamented), and many other political characters were her visitors. Her heart beat with pleasure when her two favourites, Sir Henry Bulwer and Sir Edward Bulwer Lytton, sat by her sofa. She lived, perhaps, to feel that they had forgotten her, and before her death mentioned that it was several years since she had seen the great author of 'Pelham.' 'He always expresses himself kindly when on any occasion he writes to me, but that is *all* My house is not what it was,' she added, sadly.

A younger tribe of aspirants first found themselves in that salon before the year 1848. Eliot Warburton—gifted, openhearted—the very type of a true Irish gentleman, was her especial favourite. We saw him at one of her latest *dejeûners*, with that bright eye, that gay smile, which won every heart. His brother, too, the accomplished author of 'Hochelaga,' and the 'History of Canada,' the manly, intellectual soldier—as a man beloved, respected, and mourned—he, too, was almost always one of her most cherished guests. Both are gone hence in their prime: their lives sunshine—their deaths tragedies.

Many foreigners of distinction, or of notoriety, crowded near that *portière*, and listened to professional music, which always varied Lady Morgan's *soirées*. Malibran, of whom she hoped much, too much, has been seen in her house. Lady Morgan spoke French with facility, though with accent. Her notes, her conversation, were objectionably interlarded with French idioms.

As age advanced Lady Morgan became more and more rigid in the ladies whom she admitted to her house. A change in her ideas as to the tone of society certainly marked the decline of her life. She was speaking one day of two ladies not without the pale of respectability, but somewhat disposed to overstep it. 'I never see them now,' she said, gravely. 'My house is a dull house for that sort of people.'

Her last literary project was the publication of her own 'Memoirs.' Strange to say, she still writhed under the lash of the departed Croker, and wished to rescue her family and herself from his contemptuous assertions.

In 1854 her brother-in-law, Sir Arthur Clarke, wrote to her, strongly urging her to put this idea into execution, and offering to be her amanuensis. It was still her frequent theme when her decline of health made it appear almost impossible. Croker was dead: she would never have attempted it whilst he held the knout, and held it with a cruel unsparing hand. She made a compromise between wishes, which stimulated her to the task, and time, which said no; for the dark shadows of the tomb were even gathering round her when, on Christmas day, 1858, she wrote the last words in which she ever addressed her 'dear public.' She gave some portion of her autobiography to the world in an 'odd volume, which at some future day may drop into a more important series, where I may yet be able to wind up the confessions of my life and errors, as the old Puri-

Last Years and Death.

tans phrased it, and obtain absolution without going into the confessional.'

This sanguine idea, which was expressed after Lady Morgan had had 'all but a fatal illness,' to use her own words, was not realized.

During the last three years of her existence it hung on a thread. She continued to receive, and rather to urge, the visits of friends whom she liked, in the evening. But she was scarcely equal to the exertion. 'I am so tired,' she said one evening to her niece; 'I feel so low.' What a change from the gay spirits of the wild Irish girl! Yet to the last she was full of life—in its best sense—its affections to some strong, its interests in all undying. She was even eloquent at times; but the flashes that used to irradiate, died away from physical not from mental weakness. Her memory was spared, her hearing remained, and her sight seemed never to have failed much more than at eighty-two all things fail.

She died on the 16th of April, 1859: and with her ends one of those few remaining literary cliques, easy, when once formed, to maintain, but difficult ever to bring together again. She belonged, it has truly been said, to another age, another world—that of Rogers, Byron, Moore; yet she was not out of date in this: her feelings as well as her manners had wonderful youth in them. All the young liked her; none felt that they had, in visiting Lady Morgan, been seeing an old woman—her sympathies were so fresh, her manners so genial. Let not the world speak of her as solely one of themselves. Whilst of the world, whilst, perhaps, judging it not rightly, her heart was benevolent, her affections ever in the right source.

JANE DUCHESS OF GORDON.

Jane Maxwell's Portrait.—A Haughty Beauty.—The Court of George III.—The Beautiful Duchess of Rutland.—The Splendid Duke.—The Duchess as Whipper-in.—Lord George the Rioter.—No-Popery Riots.—Fire and Destruction.—The Agreeable Dinner Party.—Lord George in the House.—From Protestant to Jew.—Beattie's Absurd Adulation.—Anecdote of Hume.—Beattie at Gordon Castle.—Eccentric Lords.—The Duchess's Sons.—A Pit for Pitt.—Pitt Outwitted.—True Nobility.—Paris in 1802.—Waiting for the First Consul.—Enter Bonaparte.—Eugène Beauharnais.—'Had I Known.'—The Father of Lord John Russell.—The Prince of Wales.—A Public Lie.—Death of the Duchess.—The Duke's Second Marriage.

EW women, says Sir Nathaniel Wraxall, have performed a more conspicuous part, or occupied a higher place on the public theatre of fashion, politics, and dissipation, than the Duchess of Gordon.

Jane, afterwards Duchess of Gordon, the rival in beauty and talent to Georgiana Duchess of Devonshire, was born in Wigtonshire, in Scotland. Her father, Sir William Maxwell of Monreith (anciently Mureith), represented one of the numerous families who branched off from the original stock—Herbert of Caerlaverock, first Lord Maxwell, the ancestor of the famous Earl of Nithsdale, whose countess, Winifred, played so noble a part when her husband was in prison during the Jacobite insurrection. From this honourable house descended, in our own time, the gallant Sir Murray Maxwell, whose daughter, Mrs. Carew, became the wife of the too well-known Colonel Waugh: the events which followed are still fresh in the public mind. Until that blemish, loyalty, honour, and prosperity marked out the Maxwells of Monreith for 'their own.' In 1681, William Maxwell was created a baronet of Nova Scotia. Various marriages and intermarriages with old and noble families, kept the blood *pure*, a circumstance as much prized by the Scotch as by the Germans. Sir William, the father of the Duchess of Gordon, married Magdalene, the daughter of William Blair, of Blair, and had by her six children —three sons and three daughters—of whom the youngest but one was Jane, the subject of this memoir.

This celebrated woman was a true Scotchwoman—stanch to her principles, proud of her birth, energetic, and determined. Her energy might have died away like a flash in the pan had it not been for her determination. She carried through everything that she attempted; and great personal charms accelerated her influence in that state of society in which, as in the French capital, women had, at that period, an astonishing though transient degree of ascendancy.

The attractions of Jane Maxwell appeared to have been developed early, for before she entered on the gay world, a song, 'Jenny of Monreith,' was composed in her honour, which her son, the Duke of Gordon, used to sing, long after the charms, which were thus celebrated, had vanished. Her features were regular; the contour of her face was truly noble; her hair was dark, as well as her eyes and eyebrows; her face long and beautifully oval; the chin somewhat too long; the upper lip was short, and the mouth, notwithstanding a certain expression of determination, sweet and well defined. Nothing can be more becoming to features of this stamp, that require softening, than the mode of dressing the hair then general. Sir Joshua Reynolds has painted the Duchess of Gordon with her dark hair drawn back, in front, over a cushion, or some support that gave it waviness; round and round the head, between each rich mass, were two rows of large pearls, until, at the top, they were lost in the folds of a ribbon; a double row of pearls round the fair neck: a ruff, opening low in front, a tight bodice, and sleeves full to an extreme at the top, tighter towards the wrists, seem to indicate that the dress of the period of Charles I. had even been selected for this most lovely portrait. The head is turned aside—with great judgment—probably to mitigate the decided expression of the face when in a front view.

As she grew up, however, the young lady was found to be deficient in one especial grace—she was not feminine; her person, her mind, her manners, all, in this respect, corresponded. 'She might,' says one who knew her, 'have aptly represented Homer's Juno.' Always animated, with features that were constantly in play, one great charm was wanting—that of sensibility. Sometimes her beautiful face was overclouded with anger; more frequently, nevertheless, was it irradiated with smiles. Her conversation, too, annihilated much of the impression made by her commanding beauty. She despised the usages of the world, and, believing herself exempted from them by her rank, after she became a duchess, she dispensed with them, and sacrificed to her venal ambition some of the most loveable qualities of her sex. One of her speeches, when honours became, as she thought, too common at court, betrays her pride and her coarseness. 'Upon my word,' she used to say, 'one cannot look out of one's coach window without spitting on a knight.' Whatever were her defects, her beauty captivated the fancy of Alexander, the fourth Duke of Gordon, a young man of twenty-four years of age, whom she married on the 28th of October, 1767. The family she entered, as well as the family whence she sprang, were devoted adherents of the exiled Stuarts, and carried, to a great extent, the hereditary Toryism of their exalted lineage. The great-grandmother of the duke was that singular Duchess of Gordon, who sent a medal to the Faculty of Advocates in Edinburgh, with the head of James Stuart, the Chevalier, on one side, and on the other the British Isles, with the word *Reddite* inscribed underneath. The Faculty were highly gratified by this present. After a debate, they accepted the medal, and sent two of their body to thank the duchess, and to say they hoped she would soon be enabled to favour the society with a second medal on the *Restoration*. Duke Alexander, the husband of Jane Maxwell, showed in his calm and inert character no evidence of being descended from this courageous partisan. He was a man of no energy, except in his love of country pursuits, and left the advancement of the family interests wholly to his spirited and ambitious wife. They were married only six years after George III. had succeeded to the throne. Never was a court more destitute of amusements, than that of the then youthful sovereign of England. Until his latter days, George II. had enjoyed revelries, though of a slow, formal, German character; but his grandson confined himself, from the age of twenty-two, to his public and private duties. He neither frequented masquerades nor joined in play. The splendours of a court were reserved for birthdays, and for those alone; neither did the king usually sit down to table with the nobility or with his courtiers. Never was he known to be guilty of the slightest excess at table, and his repasts were simple, if not frugal. At a levee, or on the terrace at Windsor, or in the circle of Hyde Park, this model of a worthy English gentleman might be seen, either with his plain-feathered queen on his arm, or driven in his well-known coach, with his old and famous cream-coloured horses. Junius derided the court, 'where,' he said, 'prayers are morality and kneeling is religion.' But although wanting in animation, it was far less reprehensible than that which preceded or that which followed it. The Duchess of Gordon, irreproachable in conduct, with her high Tory principles, was well suited to a court over which Lord Bute exercised a strong influence. She had naturally a calculating turn of mind. Fame, admiration, fashion, were agreeable trifles, but wealth and rank were the solid aims to which every effort was directed. Unlike her future rival, the Duchess of Devonshire, who impoverished herself in her boundless charities, the Duchess of Gordon kept in view the main chance, and resolved from her early youth to aggrandize the family into which she had entered.

Her empire as a wit was undisputed, for the Duchess of Devonshire was then a mere girl, at her mother's knee; but that for beauty was disputed by Mary Duchess of Rutland, well remembered in our own time, as she survived till 1831.

This exquisite specimen of English loveliness, compared by some to Musidora, as described by Thomson, was the most beautiful woman of rank in the kingdom. Every turn of her features, every form of her limbs, was perfect, and grace accompanied every movement. She was tall, of the just height; slender, but not thin; her features were delicate and noble; and her ancestors, the Plantagenets, were in her represented by a faultless sample of personal attributes. She was the daughter of a race which has given to the world many heroes, one philosopher, and several celebrated beauties—that of Somerset; and as the descendant of the defenders of Raglan Castle, she might be expected to combine various noble qualities with personal gifts. But she was cold, although a coquette. In the Duchess of Devonshire it was the *besoin d'aimer*, the cordial nature recoiled into itself from being linked to an expletive, that betrayed her into an encouragement of what offered her the semblance of affection—into the temptation of being beloved. To the Duchess of Gordon her conquests were enhanced by the remembrance of what they might bring; but the Duchess of Rutland viewed her admirers in the light of offering tributes to a goddess. She was destitute of the smiles, the intelligence, and sweetness of the Duchess of Devonshire; and conscious of charms, received adoration as her due. 'In truth,' Sir Nathaniel Wraxall, who knew her well, writes, 'I never contemplated her except as an enchanting statue, formed to excite admiration rather than to awaken love, this superb production of nature not being lighted up by corresponding mental attractions.'

This lady was united to one of the most attractive and popular of men, but one of the most imprudent and convivial. The son of that celebrated Marquis of Granby whom Junius attacked, the young Duke of Rutland was a firm partisan of Pitt, whom he first brought into the House of Commons, and at whose wish he accepted the government of Ireland in 1784. Never was there such splendour at the vice-regal court as in his time. Vessels laden with the expensive luxuries from England were seen in the Bay of Dublin at short intervals, the banquets given were most costly; the evenings at the Castle were divided between playing and drinking; and yet the mornings found the young duke breakfasting on six or seven turkey's eggs. He then, when on his progress, rode forty or fifty miles, returned to dinner at seven, and sat up to a late hour, supping before he retired to rest.

The duchess had little place in his heart, and the syren, Mrs. Billington, held it in temporary thraldom; but constancy was to a man of such a calibre impossible. Nevertheless, when the duke saw his wife surrounded by admirers, whom her levity of manner encouraged, he became jealous, and they parted, for the last time, as it proved, on bad terms. One evening, seeing him engaged in play, the duchess approached the window of the room in which he sat, and tapped at it. He was highly incensed by this interference with his amusements. She returned to England, an invalid, in order to consult Dr. Warren, the father of the late physician of that name. Whilst residing with her mother in Berkeley Square, she heard that the Duke was attacked with fever. She sent off Dr. Warren to see him, and was preparing to follow him when the physician returned.

At Holyhead he had heard that the duke was no more. He died at the early age of thirty-three, his blood having been inflamed by his intemperance, which, however, never affected his reason, and was, therefore, the more destructive to his health. His widow, in spite of their alienation, mourned long and deeply. Never did she appear more beautiful than when, in 1788, she reappeared after her seclusion. Like Diana of Poictiers, she retained her wonderful loveliness to an advanced age. Latterly, she covered her wrinkles with enamel, and when she appeared in public, always quitted a room in which the windows, which might admit the dampness, were opened. She never married again, notwithstanding the various suitors who desired to obtain her hand.

For a long time the Duchess of Gordon continued to reign over the Tory party almost without a rival. When at last the Duchess of Devonshire came forward as the female champion of the Foxites, Pitt and Dundas, afterwards Lord Melville, opposed to her the Duchess of Gordon. At that time she lived in the splendid mansion of the then Marquis of Buckingham, in Pall Mall. Every evening, numerous assemblies of persons attached to the administration gathered in those stately saloons, built upon, or near the terrace whereon Nell Gwynne used to chat with Charles II. on the grass below, as he was going to feed his birds in his gardens. Presuming on her rank, her influence, her beauty, the Duchess of Gordon used to act in the most determined manner as a Government *whipper-in*. When a member on whom she counted was wanting, she did not scruple to send for him, to remonstrate, to persuade, to *fix* him by a thousand arts. Strange must have been the scene—more strange than attractive. Everything was forgotten but the one grand object of the evening, the theme of all talk—the next debate and its supporters.

In the year 1780, events, however, took place which for some time appeared likely to shake the prosperity of the Gordon family almost to its fall.

The duke had two brothers, the elder of whom, Lord William was the Ranger of Windsor Park, and survived to a great age. The younger, Lord George, holds a very conspicuous but not a very creditable place in the annals of his country. No event in our history bears any analogy with that styled the 'Gordon Riots,' excepting the Fire of London in the reign of Charles II.; and even that calamity did not exhibit the mournful spectacle which attended the conflagrations of 1780. In the former instance, the miserable sufferers had to contend only with a devouring element; in the latter, they had to seek protection, and seek it in vain, from a populace of the lowest description, and the vilest purposes, who carried with them destruction wherever they went. Even during the French Revolution, revolting and degrading as it was, the firebrand was not employed in the work of destruction; the public and private buildings of Paris were spared.

The author of all these calamities, Lord George Gordon, was a young man of gentle, agreeable manners, and delicate, high-bred appearance. His features were regular and pleasing; he was thin and pale, but with a cunning, sinister expression in his face that indicated wrong-headedness. He was dependent on his elder brother, the duke, for his maintenance; six hundred pounds a year being allowed him by his Grace. Such was the exterior, such the circumstances of an incendiary, who has been classed with Wat Tyler and Jack Cade, or with Kett, the delinquent in the time of Edward VI.

It was during the administration of Lord North that the Gordon Riots took place, excited by the harangues and speeches of Lord George. On the 2nd of June he harangued the people; on the 7th these memorable disturbances broke out: Bloomsbury Square was the first point of attack. In Pope's time this now neglected square was fashionable:

> 'In Palace Yard, at nine, you'll find me there;
> At ten, for certain, sir, in Bloomsbury Square.'

Baxter, the Nonconformist, and Sir Hans Sloane, once inhabited what was, in their time, called Southampton Square, from Southampton House, which occupied one whole side of Bloomsbury Square, and was long the abode of Lady Rachel Russell, after the execution of her lord. Like every other part of what may be called 'Old London,' it is almost sanctified by the memories of the lettered and the unfortunate. But the glory of Bloomsbury Square was, in those days, the house of Lord Mansfield, at the north end of the east side; in which that judge had collected many valuables, among which his library was the dearest to his heart; it was the finest legal library of his time. As soon as the long summer's day had closed, and darkness permitted the acts of violence to be fully recognized, Hart Street and Great Russell Street were illuminated by large fires, composed of the furniture taken from the houses of certain magistrates. Walking into Bloomsbury, the astounded observer of that night's horrors saw, with consternation, the hall door of Lord Mansfield's house broken open; and instantly all the contents of the various apartments were thrown into the square, and set on fire. In vain did a small body of foot soldiers attempt to intimidate the rioters. The whole of the house was consumed, and vengeance would have fallen on Lord Mansfield and his lady had they not escaped by a back door a few minutes before the hall was broken into: such was that memorable act of destruction—so prompt, so complete. Let us follow the mob, in fancy, and leaving the burning pile in Bloomsbury Square, track the steps of the crowd into Holborn. We remember, as we are hurried along, with a bitter feeling, that Holborn was the appointed road for criminals from Newgate to Tyburn. It is now one blaze of light: in the hollow near Fleet Market, the house and warehouses of Mr. Langdale, a Catholic—a Christian like ourselves, though not one of our own blessed and reformed Church—is blazing: a pinnacle of flame, like a volcano, is sent up into the air. St.

Andrew's Church is almost scorched with the heat; whilst the figures of the clock—that annalist which numbers, as it stands, the hours of guilt—are plain as at noon-day. The gutters beneath, catching here and there gleams of the fiery heavens, run with spirituous liquors from the plundered distilleries; the night is calm, as if no deeds of persecution sullied its beauty; at times it is obscured by volumes of smoke, but they pass away, and the appalled spectators of the street below are plainly visible. Here stands a mother with an infant in her arms looking on; there, a father, leading his boy to the safest point of observation. We wonder at their boldness; but it is the direst sign of affright—in their homes they are insecure—everywhere, anywhere, the ruthless unseen hand may cast the brand, and all may perish. At this early hour there seems to be no ringleader—no pillage; it appears difficult to conceive who could be the wretch who instigates, who directs this awful riot: but, at the windows, men are seen calmly tearing away pictures from the walls; furniture, books, plate, from their places, and throwing them into the flames. As midnight draws near, the ferocious passions of the multitude are heightened by ardent spirits: not a soldier, either horse or foot, is visible. 'Whilst we stood,' says an eye-witness, 'by the wall of St. Andrew's churchyard, a watchman, with his lanthorn in his hand, passed on, calling the hour as if in a time of profound security.'

Meantime the King's Bench Prison was enveloped in flames; the Mansion House and the Bank were attacked. But the troops were killing and dispersing the rioters on Blackfriars Bridge; a desperate conflict between the horse and the mob was going on near the Bank. What a night! The whole city seemed to be abandoned to pillage—to destruction. Shouts, yells, the shrieks of women, the crackling of the burning houses, the firing of platoons towards St. George's Fields, combined to show that no horrors, no foes are equal to those of domestic treachery, domestic persecution, domestic fury and infatuation.

It was not alone the Roman Catholics who were threatened. Sir George Savile's house in Leicester Square—once the peaceful locality in which Dorothy Sydney, Waller's 'Sacharissa' bloomed—was plundered and burned. Then the Duchess of Devonshire took fright, and did not venture to stay at Devonshire House for many nights after dusk, but took refuge at Lord Clermont's in Berkeley Square, sleeping on a sofa in the drawing-room. In Downing Street, Lord North was dining with a party: his brother Colonel North, Mr. Eden, afterwards Lord Auckland, the Honourable John St. John, General Fraser, and Count Malzen, the Prussian minister, formed the company. The little square then surrounding Downing Street was filled with the mob. 'Who commands the upper story?' said Lord North. 'I do,' answered Colonel North; 'and I have twenty or thirty grenadiers well armed, who are ready to fire on the first notice.'

'If your grenadiers fire,' said Mr. Eden, calmly, 'they will probably fire into my house just opposite.'

The mob was now threatening; every moment the peril was increasing. Mr. St. John held a pistol in his hand; and Lord North, who never could forbear cutting a joke, said, 'I am not half so much afraid of the mob as of Jack St. John's pistol.' By degrees, however, the crowd, seeing that the house was well guarded, dispersed, and the gentlemen quietly sat down again to their wine until late in the evening, when they all ascended to the top of the house, and beheld the capital blazing. It was here that the first suggestion of a coalition between Lord North and Fox, to save the country and themselves, was started, and afterwards perfected behind the scenes of the Opera House in the Haymarket. During this memorable night George III. behaved with the courage which, whatever their failings, has ever highly distinguished the Hanoverian family. By the vigorous measures, late indeed, but not too late, which he acceded to at the Council, London was saved. But the popular fury had extended to other towns. Bath was in tumult: a new Roman Catholic chapel there was burned. Mrs. Thrale, hearing that her house at Streatham had been threatened, caused it to be emptied of its furniture. Three times was Mrs. Thrale's town house attacked; her valuables and furniture were removed thence also; and she deemed it prudent to leave Bath, into which coaches, chalked over with

'No Popery,' were hourly driving. The composure with which the rioters did their work seemed to render the scene more fearful, as they performed these acts of violence as if they were carrying out a religious duty rather than deeds of execrable hatred.

It was not until two or three days after tranquillity had been restored that Lord George Gordon was apprehended. Ministers were justly reproached for not having sent him to the Tower on the 2nd of June, when he had assembled and excited a mob to extort compliance with their wishes from the House of Commons. Such a step, when the House was surrounded by multitudes, and when, every moment, it was expected that the door would be broken open, would have been hazardous: had that occurred, Lord George would have suffered instant death. General Murray, afterwards Duke of Atholl, held his sword ready to pass it through Lord George's body the instant the mob rushed in. The Earl of Carnarvon, the grandfather of the present earl, followed him closely with the same intent.

The indignation of the insulted Commons was extreme and the distress and displeasure of Lord George's own family doubtless excessive. The House of Commons have never been thus insulted before. It is difficult to determine what could be Lord George's motives for the conduct which led to these awful results, during the whole of which he preserved a composure that bordered on insensibility: he was a perfect master of himself whilst the city was in flames. Much may be laid to fanaticism, and the mental derangement which it either produced or evinced. When too late he tried in vain to abate the fury he had excited, and offered to take his stand by Lord Rodney's* side when the bank was attacked, to aid that officer, who commanded the Guards, in its defence.

Lord George then lived in Welbeck Street, Cavendish Square, and tradition assigns as his house that now occupied by Mr. Newby the publisher, No. 30, and for many years the house of Count Woronzoff, the Russian ambassador, who died there. Lord George there prepared for his defence, which was in-

* Second Baron Rodney, son of the Admiral, then a Captain in the Guards.

trusted to the great Erskine, then in his prime, or, as he was called in caricatures, with which the shops were full, from his extreme vanity, *Counsellor Ego*. In February, 1781, the trial took place, and Lord George was acquitted. He retired to Birmingham, became a Jew, and lived in that faith, or under the delusion that he did so. The hundreds who perished from his folly or insanity were avenged in his subsequent imprisonment in Newgate for a libel on Marie Antoinette, of which he was convicted. He died a very few years after the riots of 1780, in Newgate, generally condemned, and but little compassionated.

It appears from the letters addressed by Dr. Beattie to the Duchess of Gordon, that she was not in London during the riots of June, 1780. The poet had been introduced to her by Sir William Forbes, and frequently visited Gordon Castle. We find him, whilst London was blazing, sending thither a parcel of 'Mirrors,' the fashionable journal. 'Count Fathom,' 'The Tale of a Tub,' and the fanciful, forgotten romance by Bishop Berkeley, 'Gaudentio di Lucca,' to amuse her solitude. 'Gaudentio,' he writes, 'will amuse you, though there are tedious passages in it. The whole description of passing the deserts of Africa is particularly excellent.' It is singular that this dream of Bishop Berkeley's of a country fertile and delicious in the centre of Africa should have been almost realized in our own time by the discoveries of Dr. Livingstone.

To his present of books, Dr. Beattie added a flask of whisky, which he sealed with his usual seal—' The three graces, whom I take to be your *Grace's near* relations, as they have the honour, not only to bear one of your titles, but also to resemble you exceedingly in form, feature, and manner. If you had lived three thousand years ago, which I am very glad you did not, there would have been four of them, and you the first. May all happiness attend your Grace!'

This graceful piece of adulation was followed by a tender concern for 'her Grace's' health. A sportive benediction was offered whilst the duchess was at Glenfiddick, a hunting seat in the heart of the Grampian Hills—a wild, sequestered spot, of which Dr. Beattie was particularly fond.

'I rejoice in the good weather, in the belief that it extends to Glenfiddick, where I pray that your Grace may enjoy all the health and happiness that good air, goats' whey, romantic solitude, and the society of the loveliest children in the world can bestow. May your days be clear sunshine; and may a gentle rain give balm to your nights, that the flowers and birch-trees may salute you in the morning with all their fragrance! May the kids frisk and play tricks before you with unusual sprightliness; and may the song of birds, the hum of bees, and the distant waterfall, with now and then the shepherd's horn resounding from the mountains, entertain you with a full chorus of Highland music! My imagination had parcelled out the lovely little glen into a thousand little paradises; in the hope of being there, and seeing every day in that solitude, what is

> "Fairer than famed of old, or fabled since,
> Of fairy damsels, met in forests wide
> By errant knights."

But the information you received at Cluny gave a check to my fancy, and was indeed a great disappointment to Mrs. Beattie and me; not on account of the goats' whey, but because it keeps us so long at such a distance from your Grace.'

When at Gordon Castle, the duchess occupied herself with pursuits that elevated whilst they refreshed her mind. She promised Dr. Beattie to send him the history of a *day*. Her day seems to have been partly engaged in the instruction of her five daughters, and in an active correspondence and reading. It is difficult to imagine this busy, flattered woman reading Blair's sermons—which had then been recently published—to her family on Sundays; or the duke, whom Dr. Beattie describes as 'more astronomical than ever,' engrossed from morning to night in making calculations with Mr. Copland, Professor of Astronomy in Marischal College, Aberdeen. Beattie's letters to the duchess, although too adulatory, were those of a man who respects the understanding of the woman to whom he writes. The following anecdotes, the one relating to Hume, the other to Handel, are in his letters to the Duchess of Gordon, and they cannot be read without interest.

'Mr. Hume was boasting to the doctor (Gregory) that among his disciples he had the honour to reckon many of the fair sex.

"Now tell me," said the doctor, "whether, if you had a wife or a daughter, you would *wish* them to be your disciples? Think well before you answer me; for I assure you that whatever your answer is, I will not conceal it." Mr. Hume, with a smile and some hesitation, made this reply: "No; I believe scepticism may be too sturdy a virtue for a woman." Miss Gregory will certainly remember she has heard her father tell this story.'

Again, about Handel—

'I lately heard two anecdotes, which deserve to be put in writing, and which you will be glad to hear. When Handel's Messiah was first performed, the audience were exceedingly struck and affected by the music in general; but when the chorus struck up, "For the Lord God Omnipotent reigneth," they were so transported that they all, together with the king (who happened to be present), started up, and remained standing till the chorus ended: and hence it became the fashion in England for the audience to stand while that part of the music is performing. Some days after the first exhibition of the same divine oratorio, Mr. Handel came to pay his respects to Lord Kinnoul, with whom he was particularly acquainted. His lordship, as was natural, paid him some compliments on the noble entertainment which he had lately given the town. "My Lord," said Handel, "I should be sorry if I only entertained them—I wish to make them better."'

Beattie's happiest hours are said to have been passed at Gordon Castle, with those whose tastes, in some respects differing from his own, he contributed to form; whilst he was charmed with the beauty, the wit, the cultivated intellect of the duchess, and he justly appreciated her talents and virtues. Throughout a friendship of years her kindness was unvaried;

> 'Ne'er ruffled by those cataracts and breaks
> Which humour interposed too often makes.'

The duchess felt sincerely for poor Beattie's domestic sorrows; for the peculiarities of his wife, whom he designated as 'nervous;' for the early death of his son, in whom all the poet's affections were bound up, and to whose welfare every thought of his was directed.

One would gladly take one's impressions of the Duchess of Gordon's character from Beattie, rather than from the pen of political writers, who knew her but as a partisan. The duchess, according to Beattie, was feelingly alive to every fine impulse: demonstrative herself, detesting coldness in others; the life of every party; the consoling friend of every scene of sorrow; a compound of sensibility and vivacity, of strength and softness. This is not the view that the world took of her character. Beattie always quitted Gordon Castle 'with sighs and tears.' It is much to have added to the transient gleams of happiness enjoyed by so good and so afflicted a man. 'I cannot think,' he wrote, when under the pressure of dreaded calamity—that of seeing his wife insane; 'I am too much agitated and *distrait* (as Lord Chesterfield would say) to read anything that is not very desultory; I cannot play at cards; I could never learn to smoke; and my musical days are over: my first excursion, if ever I make any, must be to Gordon Castle.'

There he found what is indispensable to such a man—congeniality. Amusement was not what he required; it was soothing. It was in the duchess's presence that he wrote the following 'Lines to a Pen'—

> 'Go, and be guided by the brightest eyes,
>   And to the softest hand thine aid impart;
> To trace the fair ideas as they arise,
>   Warm from the purest, gentlest, noblest heart;

lines in which the praise is worth more than the poetry. The duchess sent him a copy by Smith of her portrait by Sir Joshua Reynolds, a picture to which reference has been already made.

In 1782 the duchess grieved for the death of Lord Kaimes, for whom she had a sincere friendship, although the religious opinions of that celebrated man differed greatly from those of Beattie. Lord Kaimes was always at variance with the eccentric Lord Monboddo, the author of the theory that men have had tails. Lord Kaimes passed some days at Gordon Castle shortly before his death. Monboddo and he detested each other, and squabbled incessantly. Lord Kaimes understood no Greek: and Monboddo, who was as mad and as tiresome about Greek and Aristotle, and as absurd and peculiar on that score as Don Quixote was about chivalry, told him that without understanding Greek he could not write a page of good English. Their arguments must have been highly diverting. Lord Kaimes, on his death-bed, left a remembrance to the Duchess of Gordon, who had justly appreciated him, and defended him from the charge of scepticism. Lord Monboddo compared the duchess to Helen of Troy, whom he asserted to have been seven feet high; but whether in stature, in beauty, or in the circumstances of her life, does not appear.

The happiness of the duchess was perfected by the blessings granted to her in her family. In 1770 the birth of her eldest son George, long beloved in Scotland whilst Marquis of Huntley, took place. Dr. Beattie describes him as 'the best and most beautiful boy that was ever born;' he proved to be one of the most popular of the young nobility of that period. Dr. Beattie strongly advised the duchess to engage an English tutor, a clergyman, for him, recommended either by the Archbishop of York, or by the Provost of Eton. When it afterwards became a question whether the young heir should go to Oxford or to Cambridge, the doctor, who seems to have been an universal authority, allowed that Cambridge was the best for a man of study, whilst Oxford had more dash and spirit in it: so little are matters altered since that time.

Fifteen years appear to have elapsed before the birth of a second son, Alexander. Both these scions of this ducal house became military men: the young marquis was colonel of the Scots Fusileer Guards, served in the Peninsular war, and became eventually Governor of Edinburgh Castle. Long was he remembered by many a brother officer, many an old soldier, as a gallant, courteous, gay-hearted man; with some of the faults and all the virtues of the military character. He married late in life Elizabeth, daughter of Alexander Brodie, Esq., of Arnhall, N.B., who survived him. Lord Alexander Gordon died unmarried; but five daughters added to the family lustre by noble and wealthy alliances.

Wraxall remarks 'that the conjugal duties of the Duchess of Gordon pressed on her heart with less force than did her maternal solicitudes.' For the elevation of her daughters she thought, indeed, no sacrifice too great, and no efforts too laborious. In the success of her matrimonial speculations she has been compared to Sarah Duchess of Marlborough, who numbered among her sons-in-law two dukes and three earls. But the daughters of the proud Sarah were, it has been observed, the children of John Churchill, and on them were settled, successively, Blenheim and the dukedom. The Ladies Gordon were portionless, and far less beautiful than their mother. To her skilful diplomacy alone were these brilliant fortunes owing.

Lady Charlotte, the eldest, was eighteen years of age when her mother first entertained matrimonial projects for her, and chose for their object no less a personage than Pitt, then prime minister. Her schemes might have proved successful had not Pitt had that sure impediment to maternal management—a friend. This friend was the subtle Henry Dundas, afterwards Lord Melville; one of those men who, under the semblance of unguarded manners and a free open bearing, conceal the deepest designs of personal aggrandisement. Governing India, governing Scotland, the vicegerent in Edinburgh for places and pensions, Dundas was looking forward to a peerage; and kept his eye steadily on Pitt, whom he guided in many matters, adapting his conduct and his conversation to the peculiar tone of the minister's mind. Flattery he never used—dictation he carefully avoided: both would have been detrimental to his influence with the reserved statesman.

Pitt was by no means calculated to win the affection of a blooming girl of eighteen, who, whatever Wraxall may have thought, lived to be one of the most beautiful and graceful women of her time. Many years ago, during the life of Sir Thomas Lawrence, his portrait of the Duchess of Richmond, formerly Lady Charlotte Gordon, was exhibited at Somerset House. So exquisite were the feminine charms of that lovely face, so elegant the form he had portrayed, that all crowded to look upon that delineation of a woman no longer young; whilst beauties in the bloom of youth were passed by as they hung on the walls in all the glowing colours of girlhood.

On most intimate terms with the duchess, Pitt seems to have been touched with the attractions of Lady Charlotte, and to have paid her some attentions. He was one of the stiffest and shyest of men : finely formed in figure, but plain in face ; the last man to be fascinated, the last to fascinate. Drives to Dundas's house at Wimbledon when Pitt was there ; evenings at home, in easy converse with these two politicians ; suppers, at which the premier always finished his bottle, as well as the hardier Scotchman, failed to bring forward the reserved William Pitt. The fact was, that Dundas could not permit any one, far less the Duchess of Gordon, to have the ascendancy over the prime minister that so near a relationship would occasion. He trembled for his own influence. A widower at that time—his wife, a Miss Rennie of Melville, who had been divorced from him, being dead—he affected to lay his *own* person and fortune at Lady Charlotte's feet. Pitt instantly retired, and the sacrifice cost him little ; and Dundas's object being answered, *his* pretensions also dropped through. Two years afterwards, Lady Charlotte became the wife of Colonel Lennox, afterwards Duke of Richmond, and in the course of time the mother of fourteen children : one of whom, Henry Adam, a midshipman, fell overboard from the 'Blake' in 1812, and was drowned. According to Wraxall, the Duke of Richmond had to pay the penalty of what he calls 'this imprudent, if not unfortunate marriage,' in being banished to the snowy banks of St. Lawrence under the name of governor.

In modern times, our young nobility of promise have learned the important truth ably enforced by Thomas Carlyle, that *work* is not only man's appointed lot, but his highest blessing and safeguard. The rising members of various noble families have laid this axiom to heart ; and, when not engaged in public business, have come grandly forward to protect the unhappy, to provide for the young, to solace the old. The name of Shaftesbury carries with it gratitude and comfort in its sound ; whilst that of him who figured of old in the cabal, the Shaftesbury of Charles II.'s time, is, indeed, not forgotten, but remembered with detestation. Ragged schools ; provident schools ; asylums for the aged governess ; homes in which the consumptive may lay their heads in peace and die ; asylums for the penitent ; asylums for the idiot ; homes where the houseless may repose ;

—these are the monuments to our Shaftesbury, to our younger sons. The mere political ascendancy—the garter or the coronet—are distinctions which pale before these, as does the moon when dawn has touched the mountains' tops with floods of light. As lecturers amid their own people, as the best friends and counsellors of the indigent, as man bound to man by community of interest, our noblemen in many instances stand before us—Catholic and Protestant zealous alike. 'Jock of Norfolk' is represented by a descendant of noble impulses. Elgin, Carlisle, Stanley—the Bruce, the Howard, the Stanley of former days—are our true heroes of society, men of great aims and great powers.

The Duchess of Gordon was indefatigable in her ambition, but she could not always entangle dukes. Her second daughter, Madelina, was married first to Sir Robert Sinclair: and secondly, to Charles Fyshe Palmer, Esq., of Luckley Hall, Berkshire. Lady Madelina was not handsome, but extremely agreeable, animated, and intellectual. Among her other conquests was the famous Samuel Parr, of Hatton, who used to delight in sounding her praises, and recording her perfections with much of that eloquence which is now fast dying out of remembrance, but which was a thing *à part* in that celebrated Grecian. Susan, the third daughter of the duke and duchess, married William Duke of Manchester, thus becoming connected with a descendant of John Duke of Marlborough.

Louisa, the fourth daughter, married Charles, second Marquis Cornwallis, and son of the justly celebrated Governor of India; and Georgiana, the fifth and youngest, became the wife of John the late Duke of Bedford.

Such alliances might have satisfied the ambition of most mothers; but for her youngest and most beautiful daughter the Duchess of Bedford, the Duchess of Gordon had even entertained what she thought higher views. In 1802, whilst Bonaparte was first Consul, and anticipating an imperial crown, the Duchess of Gordon visited Paris, and received there such distinctions from Napoleon Bonaparte, then First Consul, as excited hopes in her mind of an alliance with that man whom, but a few years previously, she would probably have termed an adventurer!

Paris was then, during the short peace, engrossed with fêtes, reviews, and dramatic amusements, the account of which makes one almost fancy oneself in the year 1852, that of the *coup d'état*, instead of the period of 1802. The whirlwinds of revolution seemed then, as now, to have left all unchanged: the character of the people, who were still devoted to pleasure, and sanguine, was, on the surface, gay and buoyant as ever. Bonaparte holding his levees at the Tuileries, with all the splendour of majesty, reminds one of his nephew performing similar ceremonies at the Elysée, previously to his assuming the purple. All republican simplicity was abandoned, and the richest taste displayed on public occasions in both eras.

Let us picture to ourselves the old, quaint palace of the Tuileries on a reception day *then;* and the impression made on the senses will serve for the modern drama; be it comedy, or be it tragedy, which is to be played out in those stately rooms wherein so many actors have passed and repassed to their doom.

It is noon, and the First Consul is receiving a host of ambassadors within the consular apartment, answering probably to the '*Salle des Maréchaux*' of Napoleon III. Therein the envoys from every European state are attempting to comprehend, what none could ever fathom, the consul's mind. Let us not intermeddle with their conference, but look around us, and view the gallery in which we are waiting until he, who was yesterday so small, and who is to-day so great, should come forth amongst us.

How gorgeous is the old gallery, with its many windows, its rich roof, and gilded panels! The footmen of the First Consul, in splendid liveries, are bringing chairs for the ladies who are awaiting the approach of that schoolmaster's son: they are waiting until the weighty conference within is terminated. Peace-officers, superbly bedizened, are walking up and down to keep ladies to their seats and gentlemen to the ranks, so as to form a passage for the First Consul to pass down. Pages of the back stairs, dressed in black, and with gold chains hanging round their necks, are standing by the door to guard it, or to open it when *he* on whom all thoughts are fixed should come forth.

But what is beyond everything striking is the array of Bonaparte's aides-de-camp—fine fellows—war-worn—men such as he, and he alone, would chose: and so gorgeous, so radiant are their uniforms, that all else seem as if in shadow in comparison.

The gardens of the Tuileries meantime are filling with troops whom the First Consul is going to review. There are no Zouaves there; but these are men whom the suns of the tropics have embrowned; little fellows, many of them, of all heights, such as we might make drummers of in our stalwart ranks: but see how muscular, active, and full of fire they are; fierce as hawks, relentless as tigers. See the horse-soldiers on their scraggy steeds; watch their evolutions, and you will own, with a young guardsman who stood gazing fifty years afterwards on the troops which followed Napoleon III. into Paris, that 'they are worth looking at.'

The long hour is past; the pages in black are evidently on the watch; the double door which leads into the *Salle des Maréchaux* is opened from within; a stricter line is instantly kept by the officers in the gallery. Fair faces, many an English one among them, are flushed. Anon he appears, whilst an officer at the door, with one hand raised above his head and the other extended, exclaims, '*Le Premier Consul.*'

Forth he walks, a firm, short, stolid form, with falling shoulders beneath his tight, deep-blue frock. His tread is heavy rather than majestic—that of a man who has a purpose in walking, not merely to show himself as a parade. His head is large, and formed with a perfection which we call classic: his features are noble, modelled by that hand of Nature which framed this man 'fearfully,' indeed, and 'wonderfully.' Nothing was ever finer than his mouth—nothing more disappointing than his eye: it is heavy, almost mournful. His face is pale, almost sallow, while—let one speak who beheld him—'not only in the eye, but in every feature, care, thought, melancholy and meditation are strongly marked with so much of character, nay, genius, and so penetrating a seriousness, or rather sadness, as powerfully to sink into an observer's mind.'

It is the countenance of a student, not of a warrior; of one deep in unpractical meditation, not of one whose every act and plan had then been but a tissue of successes. It is the face of a man wedded to deep thought, not of the hero of the battle-field, the ruler of assemblies; and, as if to perfect the contrast, whilst all around is gorgeous and blazing, he passes along without a single decoration on his plain dress, not even a star to mark out the First Consul. It is well: there can but be one Napoleon in the world, and he wants no distinction.

He is followed by diplomatists of every European power, vassals, all, more or less, save England; and to England, and to her sons and daughters, are the most cherished courtesies directed. Does not *that* recall the present policy?

By his side walks a handsome youth whom he has just been presenting to the Bavarian minister—that envoy from a strange, wild country, little known save by the dogged valour of its mountaineers. The ruler of that land, until now an Elector, has been saluted King by Napoleon the powerful.

On the youth who addresses him as *mon père*, a slight glance is allowed even from those downcast eyes which none may ever look into completely. Eugène Beauharnais, his step-son, the son of his ever-loved Josephine, has a place in that remorseless heart. 'All are not evil.' Is it some inkling of the paternal love, is it ambition, that causes the First Consul to be always accompanied by that handsome youth, fascinating as his mother, libertine as his step-father, but destitute at once of the sensibilities of the former and of the powerful intelligence of the latter?

It is on him—on *Eugène Beauharnais*—that the hopes of the proud Duchess of Gordon rest. Happily for her whom she would willingly have given to him as a bride, her scheme was frustrated. Such a sacrifice was incomplete.

Look now from the windows of that gallery; let your gaze rest on the parade below, in the Rue de Rivoli, through which Bonaparte is riding at the head of his staff to the review. He has mounted a beautiful white horse; his aides-de-camp are by his side, followed by his generals. He rides on so carelessly that an ordinary judge would call him an indifferent equestrian. He holds his bridle first in one hand, then in another, yet he has the animal in perfect control : he can master it by a single movement. As he presents some swords of honour, the whole bearing and aspect of the man change. He is no longer the melancholy student : stretching out his arm, the severe, scholastic mien assumes instantly a military and commanding air.

Then the consular band strike up a march, and the troops follow in grand succession towards the Champs Elysées. The crowds within the gallery disappear : I look around me : the hedges of human beings, who had been standing back to let the hero pass are broken, and all are hurrying away. The pages are lounging ; the aides-de-camp are gone ; already is silence creeping over that vast gallery of old historic remembrances. Do not our hearts sink? Here, in this centre window, Marie Antoinette showed her little son to the infuriated mob below. She stood before unpitying eyes. Happier had it been for him, for her, had they died then. Will those scenes, we thought, ever recur? They have—they *have!* mercifully mitigated, it is true : yet ruthless hands have torn from those walls their rich hangings. By yon door did the son of Egalite escape. Twice has that venerable pile been desecrated. Even in 1852, when crowds hastened to the first ball given by Napoleon III., the traces of the *last* Revolution were pointed out to the dancers. They have darkened the floors ; all is, it is true, not only renovated, but embellished, so as to constitute the most gorgeous of modern palaces ; yet for how long?

It is, indeed, in mercy that many of our wishes are denied us. Eugène Beauharnais was, even then, destined to a bride whom he had never seen, the eldest daughter of that Elector of Bavaria to whom Bonaparte had given royalty ; and the sister of Ludwig, the ex-King of Bavaria, was the destined fair one. They were married ; and she, at all events, was fond, faithful, nay, even devoted. He was created Duke of Leuchtenberg, and Marie of Leuchtenberg was beautiful, majestic, pious, graceful ; but she could not keep his heart. So fair was she, with those sweet blue eyes, that pearl-like skin, that fine form, made to show off the *parures* of jewels which poor Josephine bequeathed to her—so fair was she, that when Bonaparte saw her before her bridal, he uttered these few words: 'Had I *known*, I would have married her myself.' Still she was but *second*, perhaps third, perhaps fourth ('tis a way they have in France) in Eugène's affections; nevertheless, when he died, and it was in his youth, and Thorwaldsen has executed a noble monument of him in the Dom Kirche at Munich—when that last separation came, preceded by many a one that had been voluntary on his part—his widow mourned, and no second bridal ever tempted her to cancel the remembrance of Eugène Beauharnais.

For Lady Georgiana Gordon a happier fate was reserved. She married, in 1803, John, the sixth Duke of Bedford, a nobleman whose character would have appeared in a more resplendent light had he not succeeded a brother singularly endowed, and whose death was considered to be a public calamity. Of Francis Duke of Bedford, who was summoned away in his thirty-seventh year, Fox said: 'In his friendships, not only was he disinterested and sincere, but in him were to be found united all the characteristic excellencies that have ever distinguished the men most renowned for that virtue. Some are warm, but volatile and inconstant: he was warm too, but steady and unchangeable. Where his attachment was placed, there it remained, or rather there it grew.' * * * 'If he loved you at the beginning of the year, and you did nothing to lose his esteem, he would love you more at the end of it; such was the uniformly progressive state of his affections, no less than of his virtue and friendship.'

John Duke of Bedford was a widower of thirty-seven when he married Georgiana, remembered as the most graceful, accomplished, and charming of women. The duke had then five sons, the youngest of whom was Lord John Russell, and the eldest Francis, the late duke. By his second duchess, Georgiana, the duke had also a numerous family. She survived until 1853. The designs formed by the duchess to marry Lady Georgiana to Pitt first, and then to Eugène Beauharnais, rest on the authority of Wraxall, who knew the family of the Duke of Gordon personally; but he does not state them as coming from his own knowledge. 'I have good reason,' he says, 'for believing them to be founded in truth. They come from very high authority.'

Notwithstanding the preference evinced by the Prince of Wales for the Duchess of Devonshire, he was at this time on very intimate terms with her rival in the sphere of fashion, and passed a part of almost every evening in the society of the Duchess of Gordon. She treated him with the utmost familiarity, and even on points of great delicacy expressed herself very freely. The attention of the public had been for some time directed towards the complicated difficulties of the Prince of Wales's situation. His debts had now become an intolerable burden: and all applications to his royal father being unavailing, it was determined by his friends to throw his Royal Highness on the generosity of the House of Commons. At the head of those who hoped to relieve the prince of his embarrassments were Lord Loughborough, Fox, and Sheridan. The ministerial party were under the guidance of Pitt, who avowed his determination to let the subject come to a strict investigation.

This investigation referred chiefly to the prince's marriage with Mrs. Fitzherbert, who, being a Roman Catholic, was peculiarly obnoxious both to the court and to the country, notwithstanding her virtues, her salutary influence over the prince, and her injuries.

During this conjuncture the Duchess of Gordon acted as mediator between the two conflicting parties, alternately advising, consoling, and even reproving the prince, who threw himself on her kindness. Nothing could be more hopeless than the prince's affairs if an investigation into the source of his difficulties took place; nothing could be less desired by his royal parents than a public exposure of his life and habits. The world already knew enough and too much, and were satisfied that he was actually married to Mrs. Fitzherbert. At this crisis, the base falsehood which denied that union was authorised by the prince, connived at by Sheridan, who partly gave it out in the house, and consummated by Fox. A memorable, a melancholy scene was enacted in the House of Commons on the 8th of April, 1787—a day that the admirers of the Whig leaders would gladly blot out from the annals of the country. Rolle, afterwards Lord Rolle, having referred to the marriage, Fox adverted to his allusion, stating it to be a low, malicious calumny. Rolle, in reply, admitted the *legal* impossibility of the marriage, but maintained 'that there were modes in which it might have taken place.' Fox replied that he denied it in point of *fact*, as well as of *law*, the thing never having been done in *any* way. Rolle then asked if he spoke from authority. Fox answered in the affirmative, and here the dialogue ended, a profound silence reigning throughout the house and the galleries, which were crowded to excess. This body of English gentlemen expressed their contempt more fully by that ominous stillness, so unusual in that assembly, than any eloquence could have done. Pitt stood aloof: dignified, contemptuous, and silent. Sheridan challenged from Rolle some token of satisfaction at the information; but Rolle merely returned that he had indeed received an answer, but that the house must form their own opinion on it. In the discussions which ensued a channel was nevertheless opened for mutual concessions—which ended eventually in the relief of the prince from pecuniary embarrassments, part of which were ascribed to the king's having appropriated to his own use the revenues of the Duchy of Cornwall, and refusing to render any account of them on the prince's coming of age. It was the mediation of the Duchess of Gordon that brought the matter promptly to a conclusion; and through her representations, Dundas was sent to Carlton House, to ascertain from the prince the extent of his liabilities; an assurance was given that immediate steps would be taken to relieve his Royal Highness. The interview was enlivened by a considerable quantity of wine; and after a pretty long flow of the generous bowl, Dundas's promises were energetically ratified. Never was there a man more 'malleable,' to use Wraxall's expression, than Harry Dundas. Pitt soon afterwards had an audience equally amicable with the prince.

From this period until after the death of Pitt, in 1805, the Duchess of Gordon's influence remained in the ascendant. The last years of the man whom she had destined for her son-in-law, and who had ever been on terms of the greatest intimacy with her, were clouded. Pitt had the misfortune not only of being a public man—for to say that is to imply a sacrifice of happiness—but to be a public man solely. He would turn neither to marriage, nor to books, nor to agriculture, nor even to friendship, for the repose of a mind that could not, from insatiable ambition, find rest. He died involved in debt—in terror and grief for his country. He is said never to have been in love. At twenty-four he had the sagacity, the prudence, the reserve of a man of fifty. His excess in wine undermined his constitution, but was a source of few comments when his companions drank more freely than men in office had ever been known to do since the time of Charles II. Unloved he lived; and alone, uncared for, unwept, he died. That he was nobly indifferent to money, that he had a contempt for everything mean, or venal, or false, was in those days no ordinary merit.

During the whirl of gaiety, politics, and match-making, the Duchess of Gordon continued to read, and to correspond with Beattie upon topics of less perishable interest than the factions of the hour. Beattie sent her his 'Essay on Beauty' to read in manuscript; he wrote to her about Petrarch, about Lord Monboddo's works, and Burke's book on the French Revolution; works which the duchess found time to read and wished to analyze. Their friendship, so honoured to *her*, continued until his death in 1803.

The years of life that remained to the Duchess of Gordon must have been gladdened by the birth of her grandchildren, and by the promise of her sons George, afterwards Duke of Gordon, and Alexander. The illness of George III., the trials of Hastings and of Lord Melville, the general war, were the events that most varied the political world, in which she ever took a keen interest. She died in 1812, and the duke married soon afterwards Mrs. Christie, by whom he had no children.

The dukedom of Gordon became extinct at his death; and the present representative of this great family is the Marquis of Huntly.

www.ingramcontent.com/pod-product-compliance
Lightning Source LLC
Chambersburg PA
CBHW021209230426
43667CB00006B/630